TRAGIC DILEMMAS IN CHRISTIAN ETHICS

TRAGIC DILEMMAS IN CHRISTIAN ETHICS

KATE JACKSON-MEYER

GEORGETOWN UNIVERSITY PRESS / WASHINGTON, DC

The publisher is not responsible for third-party websites or their content. URL links were active at time of publication.

Library of Congress Cataloging-in-Publication Data
Names: Jackson-Meyer, Kate, author.
Title: Tragic Dilemmas in Christian Ethics / Kate Jackson-Meyer.
Other titles: Moral traditions series.
Description: Washington, DC: Georgetown University Press, 2022. | Series: Moral traditions | Includes bibliographical references and index.
Identifiers: LCCN 2021049820 (print) | LCCN 2021049821 (ebook) | ISBN 9781647122669 (hardback) | ISBN 9781647122676 (paperback) | ISBN 9781647122683 (ebook)
Subjects: LCSH: Christian ethics. | Augustine, of Hippo, Saint, 354–430—Ethics. | Thomas, Aquinas, Saint, 1225?–1274—Ethics. | Ethics.
Classification: LCC BJ1251.J33 2022 (print) | LCC BJ1251 (ebook) | DDC 241—dc23/eng/20211115
LC record available at https://lccn.loc.gov/2021049820
LC ebook record available at https://lccn.loc.gov/2021049821

♾ This paper meets the requirements of ANSI/NISO Z39.48-1992 (Permanence of Paper).

23 22   9 8 7 6 5 4 3 2   First printing

Printed in the United States of America

Cover design by Nathan Putens.
Cover image: Vincas Kisarauskas, Pačias brangiausias godas […] ČDM G 128204, © M. K. Čiurlionis National Museum of Art, https://www.limis.lt/greita-paieska /perziura/-/exhibit/preview/363261059.
Interior design by Bookcomp, Inc.

To Hans

CONTENTS

ACKNOWLEDGMENTS

I owe many thanks to all those who have supported me in the pursuit of publishing this book. As this is a book about dilemmas, albeit tragic ones, I am acutely aware that good things require choices and trade-offs. To all those involved in choices that made this project a reality, thank you. Those choices (hopefully!) were not dilemmatic in the way I define dilemmas here, but they were likely trade-offs of some kind. I pray they were happy ones. They certainly were for me.

This book evolved from my dissertation at Boston College, so I am indebted to my dissertation committee: Lisa Sowle Cahill, Andrea Vicini, SJ, and Stephen Pope. Their encouragement gave me the push to further this research and for that I am eternally grateful. Lisa Cahill was my dissertation director, and she is a model scholar and mentor. Our conversations over the years have informed my thinking and my concern for the messiness of ethics. A mere mortal might find that Lisa's many commitments to her scholarly work, students, and family would produce impossibly conflicting obligations, yet Lisa manages to impeccably fulfill them all. I hope this book meaningfully engages with her work. Thank you to Andrea Vicini, SJ, who has become an invaluable mentor and confidant. He is so generous with his time and he embodies a commitment to building up the community of Christian ethicists. His attention to both global issues and individual pastoral needs is so vital for the field. It is an honor to learn from and with him. My arguments in this book are undoubtably improved because of rigorous discussions with Stephen Pope. I am grateful for his time and attention to my work. I am a better thinker and scholar because of him. And his sense of humor is unrivaled. My doctoral studies were supported financially by the John J. and Margaret O'Brien Flatley Fellowship in Theological Ethics and the Boston College Graduate School of Arts and Sciences Sixth Year Dissertation Fellowship, for which I am grateful.

I finished this manuscript while teaching part-time in the Theology Department at Boston College, an edifying opportunity for which I am incredibly grateful. Thank you to Joshua Snyder, who brought me on to teach for the Faith, Peace, and Justice minor, where I have taught and learned from spectacular students willing to tackle hard issues about war, peace, and justice. I am grateful for the support of Jim Keenan, SJ, who is committed to helping junior scholars and contingent faculty not only in word but also in deed. His vision for Christian ethics inspires so many of us. I am thankful to Kristin Heyer for her encouragement over the years. I am grateful to have learned from M. Shawn Copeland, who, among other things, introduced me to imagery of the "pensive Christ," a version of which adorns this book's cover. Her compassion and commitment to justice continue to inform my thought.

I have undoubtably been influenced by the scholarship and mentorship of many in the Boston College Theology Department, including Kenneth Himes, OFM, Elizabeth Antus, Catherine Cornille, John Darr, Richard Gaillardetz, Mary Ann Hinsdale, IHM, M. Cathleen Kaveny, Erik Owens, and Brian Robinette. And thanks to Patti Donnellan and (in the past) Cara Burke, who keep the department running. I am thankful for the support of the ethics community, especially my doctoral cohort who were critical in my formation, David Chiwon Kwon, Cristina Richie, and Aaron Taylor. I am grateful for my fellow students who have become colleagues and friends over the years: Grégoire Catta, Jon Cahill, John Carter, Chris Jones, Autumn Ridenour, Marcus Mescher, Kevin Brown, Jessica Coblentz, Mia Cruz, Dan DiLeo, Pete Fay, Nichole Flores, Craig Ford, Dan Horan, Conor Kelly, Jen Lamson-Scribner, Andrew Massena, Megan McCabe, Xavier Montecel, Katie Mahowski Mylroie, James O'Sullivan, Jen Sanders, Annie Selak, Katie Wrisley Shelby, Sarah Thomas, and Kate Ward.

This book is informed by my time at Yale Divinity School. Working with Gene Outka on my master's thesis made me a more compassionate ethicist (and one who is dissuaded from using split infinitives). Thank you, also, to Fred Simmons, who has been a source of encouragement since my Yale days and who saw the potential in this book project.

The ideas in this book took form over many transformative experiences prior to writing it. My work as a hospital ethics intern with MC Sullivan was crucial to learning about hard cases of bioethics. Her ethical and cultural competencies are unparalleled, and I am indebted to her for all she taught me. I am also grateful for my year as a Jesuit Volunteer, an experience from which I am "ruined for life" after becoming more attentive to various structures of injustice. And my time as an undergraduate student in Michael Blackie's Thematic Option writing course at the University of Southern California taught me that hard conversations are both possible and necessary.

Thank you to Amber Herrle, who not only provided proofreading and fact checking support for this book but whose enthusiastic comments also energized me. Thank you, also, to Christine Cacic for help with proofreading. I am thankful for June Sawyer's attention to detail when crafting a thorough index for this book.

I am grateful to Glenn Saltzman and Elizabeth Crowley Webber of Georgetown University Press for their commitments to expediency, consistency, and clarity. I am also grateful for the Press's care in producing the cover art for the book. Thank you to Patricia Bower of Diligent Editorial for very fine and swift copyediting.

Many thanks to Al Bertrand, director of Georgetown University Press, who has made publishing with Georgetown University Press a smooth and enjoyable process. Thank you to the editors of the Moral Traditions series, David Cloutier, Andrea Vicini, SJ, and Darlene Weaver, for their continued support of this work from its early stages until it became a finished text. I am especially grateful for David Cloutier's advice throughout this process. His clear and precise editorial comments ensured that my arguments were focused and cogent. Thank you, also, to the two anonymous peer reviewers whose insights made this book better and whose encouraging assessment of this work added momentum to my project.

I am thankful for the many friends and colleagues with whom I was connected during the writing of this book, even when those connections were virtual due to the restrictions of the coronavirus pandemic. A special thank you to the supportive band of women who bless my life.

Thank you to my parents who raised me in a loving home that encouraged curiosity and learning. My father taught me the value of striving for the good life, and my mother taught me the joy of writing a well-crafted sentence. My brother's friendship is one of my greatest blessings in this life. As an adult, his lifegiving Sunday evening phone calls have provided fuel for each week ahead.

I am grateful for the energetic love of my daughters, Anna and Lea, who have such an enthusiasm for life that they literally run everywhere. Parenthood has produced many obligations that have not always been aligned with my personal and professional goals in obvious ways. I hope that while writing this book I did right by both of them when determining how to navigate my duties.

Finally, this book is dedicated to my husband, Hans, who graciously and lovingly forwent his negotiable obligations in order to support me so I could complete this book. I aspire daily to care and compromise like he does. I am blessed by our partnership and by our love.

INTRODUCTION

This book argues for a category of tragic dilemmas within Christian ethics. A tragic dilemma is a particular kind of moral dilemma. In a moral dilemma, a moral agent cannot fulfill all of her obligations. A tragic dilemma is a moral dilemma that involves tragedy of some sort. According to classical philosophical and theological ethical theories, unmet moral obligations that are impossible to fulfill are no longer binding if the moral agent acts in the best way possible, thus eliminating any truly dilemmatic situations. However, according to theorists who accept moral or tragic dilemmas, the unmet obligations remain. But how, why, and which obligations endure are matters of debate.

This book develops an understanding of tragic dilemmas that builds on insights and debates from theology and philosophy. The Augustinian and Thomistic traditions do not make space for the possibility of moral or tragic dilemmas, but they do acknowledge hard cases. I identify both the limits of these approaches and the theological resources they offer for thinking about dilemmas. While Augustine decries the "misery of these necessities" of life and Paul Ramsey offers the paradigm of love transforming justice, I show that these approaches do not adequately solve all difficult cases.[1] Nevertheless, the Augustinian view highlights the importance of lament. Recognizing the limits of both the Thomistic hierarchy of goods and the principle of double effect, I lift up Thomas Aquinas's notion of "repugnance of the will."[2]

Building my case, I turn to insights from philosophy. I apply to a Christian context Lisa Tessman's distinction between "negotiable" and "nonnegotiable" moral obligations, and I take seriously Rosalind Hursthouse's contention that "a virtuous agent cannot emerge [from a tragic dilemma] with her life unmarred."[3]

My central claim is this: In a tragic dilemma, a moral agent chooses between—with sufficient knowledge—conflicting nonnegotiable moral obligations rooted in Christian commitments to protect human life and the

vulnerable and recognized by Augustinian lament. Transgressing a nonnegotiable obligation involves wrongdoing that causes great harm and may mar
an agent's life, but personal culpability is mitigated so long as the agent acts
with repugnance of the will, and societal culpability is operative when the
tragic dilemma is a result of structural sin. In response, Christian communities should offer individual and communal healing after tragic dilemmas.

In this view, the only kind of event that presents a true moral dilemma
is a situation that is inherently tragic because, by definition, it involves the
inability to protect sacred goods (human life or the vulnerable) and involves
wrongdoing. So then, according to this Christian view that I am proposing,
the only kind of situation that can be conceptually understood as a moral
dilemma is by definition a tragic dilemma. This conceptualization of a tragic
dilemma relies on a broad view of moral responsibility that calls for recognizing and indicting unjust social structures that cause dilemmatic situations.
This should spur action to transform the unjust structures that often cause
tragic dilemmas.

This book considers cases where classic approaches to hard situations leave
moral agents feeling uncertain about ethical decisions, even when they seem
to have made the best choices possible. For instance, hospitals and health
care professionals were forced to make difficult decisions about resource
allocation amid the coronavirus pandemic. Especially excruciating were
decisions early in the pandemic regarding who would receive a ventilator.
Common secular ethical guidelines, exemplified by Ezekiel Emanuel and
colleagues, follows utilitarianism, arguing that hospitals ought to follow a
maximizing approach to ensure that the most people and the most years of
life are saved.[4] The Roman Catholic approach, articulated by Daniel Daly in a
publication for the Catholic Health Association, is not primarily consequentialist and so considers consequences only after prioritizing intention, the
inherent dignity of each human person, the demands of the common good,
and the preferential option for the poor.[5] Although based on different frame-
works, these approaches often lead to similar conclusions. For instance, both
Daly and Emanuel and colleagues advocate to prioritize a younger patient
with no comorbidities over an older patient with no comorbidities, but they
also explicitly warn against using "quality of life" as a decision factor given
that it is prejudicial, especially against people with disabilities. Importantly,
both approaches assume that a best decision is possible. Both views propose
that ethics committees or other groups make rationing decisions in order to
prevent health care professionals from taking on that burden alone.[6] This is

very important in light of the likelihood that health care professionals may experience moral distress amid these circumstances.[7]

However, narratives from the front lines of the coronavirus pandemic indicate that health care professionals are troubled by these decisions, no matter what decision-making rubric they use and no matter who makes the decisions. For instance, Dr. Sadath A. Sayeed, reflecting on his work in Massachusetts, worries about the burden of resource allocation decisions during the pandemic: "Nevertheless, I also cannot help feel that a crucial part of our humanity will be chipped away each and every time such decisions are actually made."[8] But the decision-making guidelines put forward by Emanuel and colleagues and Daly make no space for such concerns. It seems possible that cases of resource allocation are situations of tragic dilemmas, but this category is absent from traditional Christian ethics. What, then, are we to make of Dr. Sayeed's fears, and how can the Christian community support him and other health care professionals who share his concerns?

The existence of true moral and tragic dilemmas is highly debated within philosophical literature, and definitions are often vague and imprecise. Theories about moral and tragic dilemmas share a concern for the problem of competing obligations where right action is ambiguous, even if one acts in the best way possible. But the literature leaves open many questions that I address throughout this book—issues around logic, autonomy, the nature of moral requirements, blame, and healing. Not all theorists distinguish between moral and tragic dilemmas. Of those who do, not all systemically examine each category. For those who hold the distinction, major transgressions or sad repercussions are usually what characterize moral dilemmas as specifically tragic. But how this relates to Christian ethics has been unclear. This book sets out to fill that lacuna.

The foundational arguments for and against moral dilemmas have unfolded primarily within the field of moral philosophy, and they raise important questions for theology. The discourse in philosophy has tended to focus on moral dilemmas generally, with fewer scholars taking up the issue of tragic dilemmas specifically or comprehensively. When considering the current literature on moral and tragic dilemmas, it is accurate to say that all tragic dilemmas are moral dilemmas, but not all moral dilemmas are tragic dilemmas. I think much more should be made of these two categories and the kinds of distinctions they assume. I argue that the only plausible kind of moral dilemma, from a Christian perspective, is a tragic dilemma. To make this claim, I attend to the expansive literature on moral dilemmas as well the more pointed discussions on tragic dilemmas.

Those who deny the existence of moral dilemmas usually do so following Aquinas, Immanuel Kant, or John Stuart Mill.[9] With these thinkers, they affirm that obligations cannot conflict and that an ethical system must always guide agents in deliberation. For these scholars, ethics must follow reason, and because dilemmas are illogical, they must be rejected.

However, this position was thrust into the contemporary philosophical spotlight when it was questioned by philosopher Bernard Williams in an influential essay in 1965, "Ethical Consistency."[10] The matter has not yet been settled. Williams worries that a focus on reason to the exclusion of feelings has prevented philosophers from recognizing important aspects of the moral life, including the existence of moral dilemmas. This omission renders ethics unable to capture moral experience, and what good is ethics if it doesn't speak to the moral life as we experience it? This raises issues for theology as well—issues that theologians have tended to ignore.

At times the philosophical debates around moral dilemmas seem intractable.[11] Christopher Gowans explains that part of the issue is that a good deal of the moral dilemma debate is a dispute between *rationalism* and *experientialism*, where rationalists think dilemmas are illogical and experientialists think experience shows otherwise.[12] It is also the case that some will conclude that guilt or something similar is a valid reaction to a dilemmatic situation, while others may regard guilt as an ethically unfounded response.[13] If arguments fail to convert the dilemma skeptic, many theorists who assert the existence of moral dilemmas seem to admit that one either intuitively accepts the premise that dilemmas exist or one does not.

Even when the existence of dilemmas has been granted, the category itself remains nebulous. As I will show, some philosophers remain elusive or ambivalent on what constitutes a dilemma and the role of blame after a dilemma. Many philosophers seem, essentially, to hold the position that even though they cannot precisely define a moral dilemma, they are willing to accept a mentality of "I know it when I see it."[14] Many of the arguments for moral dilemmas rely on human experience, but this is difficult to weigh because experience is not self-validating. This raises questions for how theology and philosophy ought to handle insights from experience.

Despite these shortcomings, theorists who posit the existence of moral dilemmas believe there is an urgent need to incorporate them into our ethical systems. They question why our ethics ought to be beholden only to logic, and they aim to imbue ethical thought with authentic positions that acknowledge the messiness of life. These are matters that Christian ethics ought to consider as well.

But theologians have tended to deny the existence of dilemmas. Augustine famously laments the "miseries" of this life but (seemingly) does not go so far as to admit the possibility of inevitable wrongdoing in hard cases.[15] A highly influential conceptual rejection comes from Aquinas, whose ethical system affirms that there is always a "right" choice.[16] God's demand that Abraham sacrifice Isaac seems to be a dilemma, but influential interpretations of this by Aquinas and Søren Kierkegaard imagine the scenario in a way that the obligation to not kill one's son is lifted.[17] These dismissals of moral dilemmas are understandable insofar as religion posits God as good, and what kind of good God would put humans in situations where wrongdoing is inevitable? However, even secular philosophers contend that dilemmas are often the result of structural injustices.[18] To see dilemmas as the result of societal sin is certainly a plausible theological position.

The few theologians who have gestured toward the existence of moral dilemmas offer little in the way of a sustained theory, which might explain why their work is rarely referenced in the literature on moral dilemmas. For instance, Reinhold Niebuhr offers a relatively overt treatment of moral dilemmas insofar as he recognizes "the whole moral ambiguity of warfare" and that it is necessary to accept "guilt" for the seemingly justified action of killing civilians in World War II bombings of German cities.[19] This is, arguably, a deeply disturbing conclusion. Despite his commitment to pacifism, Dietrich Bonhoeffer supported Abwehr conspirators who attempted to assassinate Adolf Hitler.[20] In doing so, he lived out the challenge of discerning God's call and taking on suffering and guilt in the face of hard realities. In response, Bonhoeffer focuses his theology on the suffering Jesus.[21] But his work is incomplete because he was killed in a concentration camp when he was only thirty-nine years old.[22] Philip Quinn develops a notion of tragic dilemmas through analyses of both God's command for Abraham to sacrifice Isaac and Shūsaku Endō's character Sebastian Rodrigues in the novel *Silence*.[23] While Quinn's work is helpful, I find both of these stories to be questionable sources for unfurling the complexity of moral or tragic dilemmas. In the case of Abraham, God spares him from sacrificing Isaac. In the case of the novel, Endō's main point seems to be that loving God can take various forms, and these might be hard to accept, especially when God seems absent or "silent." Most recently, Lisa Sowle Cahill has argued for the category of "irreducible moral dilemmas" within the context of war.[24] She argues that both Christian just war theorists and Christian pacifists offer incomplete analyses because they do not acknowledge the moral transgressions inherent in their positions—that is, killing in the case of just war theory and abstaining from violence while others die in the case of pacifism.

When other theologians have entered the debates on dilemmas, they have tended to deny the existence of dilemmas without, in my view, solving the issues that drive the concern for dilemmas, such as how to weigh experience, the role of feelings in ethics, the relationship between constrained agency and guilt, the relationship between intention and foreseeable consequences, the role of discernment, the limits of the principle of double effect, the existence of tragedy, and the inadequacy of current ethical systems.[25]

To study moral dilemmas is to take seriously experiences of workers on the front lines of the coronavirus pandemic while also acknowledging the messiness of dilemmas, the ambiguity of feelings, the difficulty of accounting for human experience, and the implications of all this for theology and ethics. I assert that the questions that Dr. Sayeed's concerns raise and the questions moral dilemma theorists ask are fundamental to theology and what it means to be human. To the extent that theologians avoid these questions, they neither contribute to nor learn from the insights arising from the real world and from the debates around dilemmas.

Sequentially, this book begins with cases and then discusses dilemmas primarily within the context of philosophy before moving into theology. This might seem as if I am overemphasizing the role of experience or that I am starting from philosophy and moving to theology, but those would be mischaracterizations because Christian ethics is at the heart of this book. I begin with human experience—a major source of theology—and then move to reason as argued from the point of view of philosophy, another major source of theology.[26] I believe the moral experiences described in the cases call theologians to reexamine some ethical categories. These moral experiences do not justify or ground new categories in and of themselves because moral experience is not self-validating, but these moral experiences ought to prompt an investigation of our current ethical categories. Furthermore, theology can benefit from engagement with philosophical thought; in turn, philosophical thought can learn from theology. This does not mean it is necessary for Christian ethics to adopt philosophical positions wholesale, but it is important for theologians to acknowledge and to engage thoughtfully with this conversation about moral dilemmas.

I draw on narratives, cases, and stories to produce a work that is relevant beyond my positioning as a Roman Catholic, American, white, upper-middle-class, and educated woman. As I will discuss, I use of the method of "portraiture" as a way to responsibly investigate and reflect on other people's stories.[27]

In chapter 1 I lay out the major philosophical debates surrounding moral dilemmas, and I highlight touchstones, questions, ambiguities, and problems these debates bring to theology. Moral philosophy's treatment of dilemmas is incomplete, in part because moral philosophy lacks the theological tools of Christian ethics: an acute awareness of the reality of sin and tragedy, a robust view of the moral agent that recognizes moral development in light of a relationship with God, a well-developed understanding of forgiveness, and an emphasis on the role of the community. Accounting for what these resources offer, I argue that it is incumbent on Christian ethicists to take up the questions raised by moral philosophy on the issue of dilemmas.

In chapter 2 I argue that Augustine and the Augustinian tradition create the groundwork for an approximation of the categories of moral and tragic dilemmas. I draw out how their attention to the reality of hard cases and the prevalence of sin attunes them to the tragedy of life. Augustine is at once both optimistic about the reign of God's providence and acutely aware of the reality of sin, lamenting the miseries that beset Christians, especially those tasked with the responsibility for political order in the earthly city, such as his infamous judge. Furthermore, without an explicit category of dilemmas, I argue that Augustine presents an inconsistent ethical system in an attempt to justify killing evidenced by the dueling theological anthropologies buttressing his ethics. Protestant ethicists who take up Augustine's legacy as it relates to dilemmas—namely, Ramsey—have shied away from developing a robust and systematic account of dilemmas. However, even Ramsey seems to admit limits in his ethical system, hinting at times when love's transforming power cannot fully solve hard cases and noting the difficulties for the Christian politician who tries to act well.

In chapter 3 I assess Aquinas and the Thomistic tradition's treatment of moral and tragic dilemmas. Although Aquinas explicitly denies the possibility for moral dilemmas that are not the agent's fault, I find new points of contact between Aquinas and moral dilemma theorists. I argue that Thomists' primary strategies for solving apparent dilemmas—the hierarchy of goods and the principle of double effect—are essentially ineffective. Although Aquinas does not acknowledge the categories of moral dilemmas and tragic dilemmas, I argue that analogs and resonant themes are found in his discussion on repugnance of the will and mixed actions.

In chapter 4 I use Christian thought to develop a definition and understanding of tragic dilemmas. In doing so I hope to provide a theological answer to some of the major unresolved philosophical issues within the moral dilemmas debate: What features of moral and tragic dilemmas can be defended, how can an agent's life be marred, and when does an agent become morally responsible for a tragic dilemma? I affirm the distinction, raised in philosophy by Tessman, between negotiable and nonnegotiable moral requirements, and I argue that in the Christian tradition nonnegotiable requirements are supported by the Christian duties to honor others' humanity and to respond to the vulnerability of others. This forms the basis of a Christian understanding of tragic dilemmas. Tragic dilemmas are marked by lament for the great harm that is caused by moral transgressions. Agents are morally responsible for any lingering nonnegotiable moral obligations and the resultant harm caused. However, moral responsibility is mitigated in these constrained situations so long as agents act with repugnance of the will. The concept of tragic dilemma also demands that we acknowledge and address the structural issues that cause dilemmas. And as real-life cases of moral injury from war show, tragic dilemmas can cause distress, thus potentially marring agents' lives.

In chapter 5 I offer Christian strategies for healing from tragic dilemmas. I argue that the healing process is a practice that ushers in God's grace. The process must allow the agent to atone for the wrong committed, to restore emotional health, and to reconnect to the community. Because we are social beings and because society often bears some blame for the occurrence of tragic dilemmas, healing must also happen in, with, and among the community members.

CASES OF MORAL AND TRAGIC DILEMMAS

Moral and tragic dilemmas are conceptually untidy at first glance because they posit that certain ethical issues can remain open in various ways. I begin this book by sketching a somewhat fuzzy picture of dilemmas by way of examples with the hope that the picture will become clearer as I add layers of analysis throughout the book, returning to these cases to develop and to defend a cogent Christian understanding of tragic dilemmas. At first pass, these examples will showcase important features of the broader category of moral dilemmas. After deep analysis and by the end of the book, these examples will serve to illustrate and support the most salient features of tragic dilemmas in the Christian view.

Portraiture Method

Some of the cases presented here are described by the agents themselves while other cases describe hard situations found in real life. Characterizing the cases as moral or tragic dilemmas is often a work of interpretation on my part or on the part of others. This is appropriate because it is necessary to interpret experience. I do this following the method of portraiture.

Emmanuel Katongole employs the method of "portraiture" in theological reflection.[28] This approach relies on the theory developed by Sara Lawrence-Lightfoot and Jessica Hoffmann Davis. In this method of storytelling, Lawrence-Lightfoot and Davis explain that the writer makes an effort not only to tell someone's story but to tell it in a way that produces "new understandings and insights" even for the subjects themselves.[29] Lawrence-Lightfoot and Davis explain that through portraiture, subjects can see themselves in "a perspective that they had not considered before."[30] The result of portraiture, in their view, is a sketch that sheds new light on a situation.

Following this method, I interpret cases using portraiture and a theo-ethical lens. With this perspective, I may characterize some cases as dilemmas even when the subjects or others do not. The cases are important because they offer a fresh perspective to theology by highlighting experiences that theological ethics ought to take seriously, and analysis from a theological perspective enhances understanding of these complex moral cases. Thus, the portraits and theology have a dialectical relationship, mutually informing each other.

Case Studies

When possible, I reproduce the agents' descriptions of the situations, and when that is not practical, I describe the cases. The examples presented here are derived from a variety of sources: some are personal testimonies, others are fictional scenarios made popular in film or books, and the rest are meant to represent other ways moral dilemmas may occur in real life. The goal is to give a sense of what I and others are thinking about when we refer to moral and tragic dilemmas. If the case has been used in a way germane to this study, I have included some short commentary in order to convey how the case has been included in some of the dilemma literature. Throughout the book, and especially in the conclusion, I return to these cases and assess them according to the Christian understanding of tragic dilemmas that this book develops.

COVID-19 and Resource Allocation

During the coronavirus pandemic, with hospitals operating at overcapacity and lacking enough ventilators to serve everyone, hospitals and doctors were forced to make excruciating decisions about who received a ventilator—and thus a chance to live—and who did not.[31] This was an especially acute problem early on in the pandemic, when ventilators were scarce and thought to be the most optimal intervention.[32]

Survival and Hiding from Nazis

Holocaust survivor Celia K. describes the following situation that occurred after escaping from a camp:

> We were all little groups of Jews in the woods. I ran into a group of Jews, maybe twelve, fifteen. And there was a cousin of mine with her children, a little girl of four or five and a little boy of maybe eight, ten, eleven months. And he had a voice. It was such a raspy voice. It was impossible. And in the woods, when a child cries it really rings out, and the Germans would really come very fast. So the group of Jews said to her, "Look Teitle. You can't be in the woods with this child. Either get away or kill him." She became wild. Anyway, she had to do it. There was no choice. She had the little girl and herself to think of. I saw her put the child in the swamp. With her foot on his neck, she drowned him. I saw it with my own eyes. And that wasn't the only isolated incident. There were a lot of incidents like this.[33]

Tessman interprets this case and others like it, usually called "Crying Baby" cases, as moral dilemmas. She says, "I take such cases to be clear cases of dilemmatic morality: there is no option that does not involve violating a non-negotiable moral requirement."[34] The mother is forced to decide between her duties to her daughter, her son, and the other hiding Jews.

Mothers' Hard Decisions in a Concentration Camp

Holocaust survivor Clara L. describes the following situation at Auschwitz/Birkenau:

> The young and able were sent to one side, and the old and young women with children on their arms were sent to the other side. There, also these Polish people, both Jews and non-Jews, helped because they would say to these young women who carried their babies on their arms, "Give it to your mother, give it to your mother-in-law. Don't be a fool! You can save your life." And many, many women did that. They handed their babies to the older women and they went to the working side and they were saved. Their children perished.[35]

Tessman regards this as a moral dilemma because a nonnegotiable require-ment must be violated.[36] In these cases the lives of the children jeopardize the lives of the mothers. The children will die no matter what, but the mothers can be saved.

A Mother Who Can Only Save One Child

A mother in Ethiopia is physically unable to carry both of her children to a food source.[37] She leaves one child behind and in doing so, we presume, the child will die. Walter Sinnott-Armstrong offers this as an example of "symmetrical moral dilemmas" where goods of the same value are at stake.[38] How does the mother decide which child to take with her?

Sophie's Choice

Sophie, a character from William Styron's novel *Sophie's Choice*, is forced by the Nazis to choose which one of her two children can live.[39] No action seems "right," and inaction is not an option. Sinnott-Armstrong explains that this is also an example of "a symmetrical moral dilemma."[40] According to Tessman, the novel portrays not only Sophie's difficult choice but also how this choice devastated the rest of her life. From Tessman's point of view, the thrust of the novel is the question, "'How was Sophie destroyed by the choice(s) that confronted her?'"[41] But, according to Tessman, that perspective is missed when the focus is only on what Sophie ought to do, or whether Sophie acted rightly, leading to "an optimistically skewed picture of moral life," according to Tessman.[42]

End-of-Life Decision-Making and the Case of Mr. C.

In a text analyzing bioethics outside of a Western perspective, physician Josephine M. Lumitao describes the case of "Mr. C.," a seventeen-year-old living in the Philippines.[43] He is the eldest of seven children and contributes to his family's income by selling newspapers. He becomes paralyzed from the neck and below after suffering massive injuries from a car accident when going to Christmas mass. His mother diligently takes care of him at the hospital while he is on a ventilator, even at the expense of caring for her other children. The hospital bills accumulate and are unaffordable for the family. After finding out that he would need to be on life support for the rest of his life, Mr. C. asks to be removed from the costly ventilator because he knows his family cannot afford it.[44] According to Lumitao, "His mother is indecisive" about how to proceed.[45] Presumably, the mother wonders whose good—Mr. C.'s good or the family's good—to prioritize. Lumitao explains that the mother "should be reassured, however, that although the withdrawal of treatment is a painful decision, it is the best for Mr. C. and the family."[46]

Drone Warfare and the Likely Loss of Innocent Life

The 2015 film *Eye in the Sky* depicts a situation in which armed forces are planning to bomb a compound via drone in order to prevent suicide bombers from preparing and initiating an attack.[47] However, outside the compound is a little girl selling bread who will likely die in the blast. Some people in the chain of command try to pass on the decision to someone else because they are reluctant to kill the little girl. The drone pilot tasked to pull the trigger on the attack is especially hesitant.

As ethicist Deane-Peter Baker explains, this is a moral dilemma because protecting the life of the innocent girl is at odds with the many innocent lives that would be saved by preventing the terror attack.[48] As such, it is a case that fits into traditional applications of the principle of double effect, which is taken up later in this book. Those involved in the situation know that an innocent girl will likely die in the pursuit of saving many and that this can be justified according to various ethical understandings, yet some of those involved are hesitant to make the call to initiate the attack. This reveals the hardship of moral decision-making despite a decision-making rubric.

Combat in War and the Case of Camilo

Camilo Mejía was raised Catholic and is a veteran of the Iraq War. While in combat, Camilo is faced with a dilemma of what to do when confronted with a man holding a grenade. The man and his grenade pose a threat to the soldiers and civilians around him; lives are in danger. But Camilo is distressed about how to proceed because eliminating the threat requires ending a life. Ultimately, he kills the man. Camilo has difficulty living with himself in light of this transgression. He seeks professional help from a therapist but finds it ineffective because the therapist insists Camilo's action was justified. Camilo is left feeling ignored and unheard.[49]

Self-Defense in War and the Case of Nick

Nick Rudolph is a Marine who fought in Afghanistan. While in battle, he and his comrades are shot at by a young Afghan boy around thirteen years old. Nick shoots and kills the boy. He is troubled by the event, especially because of the boy's young age. He later turns to alcohol to cope and is charged with driving under the influence. After three deployments he is honorably discharged from the Marine Corps. A year later he is living and working in Philadelphia as a bodyguard but cannot escape the memories and pain of combat.[50]

NOTES

1. Augustine, *City of God*, 19.6; and Ramsey, *War and the Christian Conscience*.
2. Aquinas, *Summa Theologiae* (hereafter *ST*), I-II q.6 a.6; See also *ST* I-II q.6 a.8; See also *ST* I-II q.6 a.7 ad.2 where he says, "repugnance of the will."
3. Tessman, *Moral Failure*, 1; and Hursthouse, *On Virtue Ethics*, 79.
4. Emanuel et al., "Fair Allocation."
5. Daly, "Guidelines for Rationing Treatment."
6. Daly, 54; Emanuel et al., "Fair Allocation," 2051–52, 2054.
7. A full discussion of moral distress is beyond the scope of this book. For more on this, see Jackson-Meyer, "Moral Distress."
8. Sayeed, "The Psychological Toll."
9. For an influential interpretation of Aquinas on this issue, see Donagan, "Consistency in Rationalist Moral Systems"; see also Donagan, *The Theory of Morality*, 144–46. For other influential arguments, see Kant, "Moral Duties," 34–51; Kant, *The Metaphysics of Morals*; Mill, *Utilitarianism*; and Mill, "Utilitarianism and Moral Conflicts," 52–61.
10. Williams, "Ethical Consistency."
11. Lisa Tessman refers to the "'moral dilemmas debate'" as involving a number of important philosophers, including Christopher Gowans, and centered on the possibility of the existence of a "genuine moral dilemma" or "unavoidable wrongdoing," (Tessman, *Moral Failure*, 11–12, esp fns 1 and 2). When I reference the "debates around moral dilemmas" I am referring to a similar body of literature, as well as more recent discussions coming out both theology and philosophy (including Tessman).
12. Gowans, "Moral Theory, Moral Dilemmas," 199.
13. Gowans, 203.
14. This is a reference to the phrase used by Supreme Court Justice Potter Stewart in his opinion statement when he describes the difficulty of defining obscenity. See *Jacobellis v. Ohio*, No. 378 U.S. 184 (1964).
15. Augustine, *City of God*, 19.6.
16. *ST* I-II q.19 a.6 ad.3; *ST* II-II q.62 a.2 obj.2; *ST* III q.64 a.6 ad.3; and Aquinas, *Questiones Disputatae de Veritate* (henceforth *de Veritate*), q.17 a.4 ad.8. This interpretation was made famous by Alan Donagan; see Donagan, *The Theory of Morality*, 144–46. See also Dougherty, *Moral Dilemmas in Medieval Thought*, 112–67.
17. Genesis 22; *ST* I-II q.100 a.8 ad.3; See also Kierkegaard, *Fear and Trembling*. For a good discussion on this, see Quinn, "Agamemnon and Abraham."
18. Tessman, "Against the Whiteness of Ethics," 200–205.
19. Niebuhr, "The Bombing of Germany," 222. Later Niebuhr is skeptical of using nuclear weapons, suggesting that his view may have evolved in some (somewhat unclear) ways. On this and Niebuhr's relationship to dilemmas, see Cahill, *Blessed Are the Peacemakers*, 287–97.
20. Dramm, *Dietrich Bonhoeffer and the Resistance*; Green, "Peace Ethic or 'Pacifism'?" For an analysis of the relationship between Bonhoeffer and dilemmas, see Cahill, *Blessed Are the Peacemakers*, 297–305.
21. Bonhoeffer, *Ethics*; and Bonhoeffer, *The Cost of Discipleship*.
22. Metaxas, forward to *The Cost of Discipleship*, 6.
23. Quinn, "Agamemnon and Abraham"; and Quinn, "Tragic Dilemmas." A similar theme on Endō's novel is taken up in Głąb, "Tragic and God's Hiddenness." For Endō's novel, see Endō, *Silence*.

24. Cahill, *Blessed Are the Peacemakers*, viii; see also 91–172; 297–312. For my view of Cahill's positions, see Jackson-Meyer, "Just War, Peace, and Peacemaking."

25. For an earlier theological take on the topic, see a work from 1987, Santurri, *Perplexity in the Moral Life*. For more recent theological works, see Bowlin, *Contingency and Fortune*; Dougherty, *Moral Dilemmas in Medieval Thought*; and McInerny, *The Difficult Good*. These authors offer some fine and formidable theological arguments against dilemmas, especially for how and why Aquinas and the Thomistic tradition preclude the need for a category of moral dilemmas. I take up the later texts and some of their insights in chapter 3, where I discuss Bowlin, Dougherty, and McInerny.

26. On these as sources of theology, see Leonard, "Experience as a Source for Theology"; and Lawler and Salzman, "Human Experience and Catholic Moral Theology."

27. Lawrence-Lightfoot and Davis, *The Art and Science of Portraiture*. Emmanuel Katongle's use of this in theology was influential to me. See Katongole, *Born from Lament*, 33–37.

28. Katongole, *Born from Lament*, 33–37.

29. Lawrence-Lightfoot and Davis, *The Art and Science of Portraiture*, 5.

30. Lawrence-Lightfoot and Davis, 5.

31. Sayeed, "The Psychological Toll."

32. Patel, Kress, and Hall, "Alternatives."

33. Greene and Kumar, *Witness*, 85–87.

34. Tessman, *Moral Failure*, 164–65.

35. Greene and Kumar, *Witness*, 118.

36. Tessman, *Moral Failure*, 164.

37. Sinnott-Armstrong, *Moral Dilemmas*, 57. Presumably, both children must be carried due to their age or the circumstances. I rely on this text for the description of case, unless otherwise noted.

38. Sinnott-Armstrong, 57.

39. Styron, *Sophie's Choice*. I rely on this text for the description of case, unless otherwise noted. This is a frequently used case for dilemma theorists. See also McConnell, "Moral Dilemmas."

40. Sinnott-Armstrong, *Moral Dilemmas*, 57.

41. Tessman, *Moral Failure*, 161.

42. Tessman, 161–62.

43. Lumitao, "Death and Dying," 98–99. I rely on this text for the description of case, unless otherwise noted.

44. The case presented by Lumitao states that Mr. C. was first placed on a "ventilator" (a costly life support system) and then later refers only to a "respirator" (a type of mask). Lumitao's text states that Mr. C. asks to be removed from the respirator. In my adaption of this case, I presume and state that the boy asks to be removed from a ventilator (rather than a respirator). I do this to stress the tragedy of not being able to afford a costly medical intervention, which seems to be at the heart of Lumitao's case. This is in line with Lumitao's main points: removing the apparatus will lead to Mr. C.'s death, the family cannot afford the apparatus, Mr. C. wants the apparatus removed, and the mother has to make a decision.

45. Lumitao, "Death and Dying," 99.

46. Lumitao, 99.

47. Hood, *Eye in the Sky*, film. I rely on this film for the description of case, unless otherwise noted.

48. Baker, "*Eye in the Sky* and Moral Dilemmas."
49. Brock and Lettini, *Soul Repair*, 86–89. I rely on this text for the description of case, unless otherwise noted. See also Mejía, *Road from Ar Ramadi*.
50. Wood, "Moral Injury." I rely on this text for the description of case, unless otherwise noted.

1

PHILOSOPHICAL AND THEOLOGICAL PROBLEMS WITH MORAL AND TRAGIC DILEMMAS

A moral dilemma is an ethical situation that cannot be fully resolved because an agent is unable to fulfill all her moral obligations. A tragic dilemma is a special kind of moral dilemma that involves great harm. The existence of moral and tragic dilemmas is contested within moral philosophy and denied by many scholars of Christian ethics. At first glance, a moral dilemma seems nonsensical: How can a moral agent be obligated to satisfy a duty that is impossible to fulfill? Added confusion comes from the fact that there are various definitions of moral and tragic dilemmas. Yet real-life experience often contradicts philosophy and theology's insistence that moral and tragic dilemmas are untenable concepts and thus nonexistent.

The foundational arguments for and against moral and tragic dilemmas have unfolded primarily within the field of moral philosophy where many issues about dilemmas remain unresolved. As such, philosophy brings many questions to Christian ethics. The philosophical literature on moral and tragic dilemmas raises two major problems for Christian ethics: (1) ambiguity about the definitions of moral and tragic dilemmas from the point of philosophical thought, and (2) difficulty with appeals to experience and emotions upon which much of the philosophical support for dilemmas relies. The first issue requires additional precision that can be found using the resources of Christian ethics, while the second is a methodological issue that Christian ethics must contend with when grappling with dilemmas. The goal of this chapter is to lay out these challenges that are then taken up in a Christian context throughout the rest of the book.

Christian ethics can and must provide clarity to the concepts of moral and tragic dilemmas. Much of the philosophical debate centers on the existence of moral dilemmas, of which tragic dilemmas can be considered a subset, if a distinction is noted at all. As such, this investigation follows the debate on dilemmas and starts with the literature on moral dilemmas in general before moving to treat tragic dilemmas specifically.

WHAT IS A MORAL DILEMMA?

Philosophy, dating back to the Greeks, explores hard cases where important principles conflict.[1] In Book I of Plato's *Republic*, Cephalus defines justice as repaying debts and being honest.[2] But Socrates points out that these are not absolute principles because in certain circumstances a just act might require one to override honesty or debt repayments. To make this point he gives the example of someone who promises to hold a friend's weapons. It would not be just to return the weapons to the friend if he asks for them while "out of his mind."[3] In that case, protecting life trumps keeping promises.[4] However, there could be other cases where it is more vital to keep a promise than to prevent a small amount of harm to a person or to oneself.[5] Dilemmatic situations appear in Greek mythology as well. For instance, Agamemnon has to choose between either appeasing the god Artemis by sacrificing his daughter or having his expedition fail.[6] In Sophocles's *Antigone*, Antigone must decide between following the rules of the city to not bury her brother—a traitor— or following the religious rules to bury him.[7]

Later, Immanuel Kant and then John Stuart Mill, in the eighteenth and nineteenth centuries, respectively, are clear that there are no genuine dilemmas because an agent satisfies her obligations when determining the best course of action.[8] These ideas will be addressed in more detail later in the chapter.

In the early 1800s Georg Wilhelm Friedrich Hegel's work opens the possibility for moral conflict.[9] According to Hegel, two people can be justified in pursuing conflicting goals, but the conflict is only solved at the end of time.

F. H. Bradley makes way for the plausibility of moral dilemmas in the late nineteenth century by building on Hegel and arguing, against Kant, that particular duties often conflict.[10] He writes, "It has been remarked truly that *every* act can be taken to involve such collision."[11] Bradley does not take a clear stance on moral dilemmas per se. He recognizes that the realms of "self-realization" may conflict, but he also acknowledges that duties can be hierarchical.[12] According to Bradley, our intuition determines right action. Even though he does not offer much content on this matter, he makes way for the notion that ethics is not always reducible to reason.

British intuitionists from the eighteenth century until the early twentieth century challenge traditional approaches to ethics, proposing that moral claims are "self-evident."[13] In this view, one uses intuition, and not rules, to determine what to override in cases of conflict because, when weighing moral claims, intuition assigns the moral weights.[14]

Jean-Paul Sartre famously gives the dilemmatic example of a student who faces a hard choice after the student's older brother is killed when Germans invaded France in 1940.[15] The young man wants to seek retribution for his brother's death by joining the Free French Forces to fight Hitler, but he also wants to stay with his mother, who needs her son. On the one hand, the young man knows that staying with his mother will give her a reason to live, and it will ensure that his life is spared. On the other hand, the effects of fighting are unknown—Will he be effective? Will he die? As Sartre shows, the student is caught between acting on behalf of his mother's welfare with relatively certain results or taking on the cause of fighting Hitler with less certain results.

In the 1960s Bernard Williams begins to challenge standard ideas about dilemmas and the priority of reason by investigating emotions.[16] I address his argument in more detail later in this chapter, but the thrust of his contribution is that feelings of "regret" after a moral conflict indicate that there is something unresolved about moral conflicts, and this takes on a special quality in tragic cases.[17] This is a challenge to Kant's notion that obligations are satisfied after adjudicating an apparent moral conflict. Another of Williams's contributions that I address later is that he argues, contra others such as Kant, that moral conflicts are not logical inconsistencies. Williams focuses on "moral conflict," which he defines as follows:

> By "moral conflict" I mean only cases in which there is a conflict between two moral judgements that a man is disposed to make relevant to deciding what to do; that is to say, I shall be considering what has traditionally, though misleadingly, been called "conflict of obligations," and not, for instance conflicts between a moral judgment and a non-moral desire, though these, too, could naturally enough be called "moral conflicts."[18]

According to Williams, in moral conflicts "neither of the *ought's* [*sic*] is eliminable" and so these cases are not "soluble without remainder."[19] Williams limits his analysis to cases where the moral conflicts result from contingency. As such, Williams explains that moral conflicts usually appear in two ways: (1) cases when two obligations cannot both be fulfilled or (2) cases when one ought to and ought not to fulfill the same obligation.[20] Williams's work is influential to those who support the notion of moral dilemmas.

Some theorists make much of the distinction between resolvable and irresolvable dilemmas, while others do not.[21] Irresolvable dilemmas are those situations when there are no clear courses of action. For some, these are the only kinds of situations that constitute moral dilemmas. Resolvable dilemmas, on the other hand, are often characterized by the quality that a moral agent can determine what is a better course of action but still considers the situation dilemmatic for various possible reasons.

For many scholars, this distinction does little work. Lisa Tessman, for instance, does not focus on this distinction because in her view both irresolvable and resolvable cases can be counted as moral dilemmas when they involve "moral failure."[22]

Rosalind Hursthouse emphasizes the idea of a "remainder," noting that irresolvable and resolvable dilemmas can both involve a "remainder" of some sort and can both be considered moral dilemmas.[23] She explains that in a resolvable dilemma, one is able to discern what to do because option "x is worse than y."[24] Even though Hursthouse calls these resolvable dilemmas, they are apparently never fully resolved, evidenced by an enduring "remainder."[25]

Turning to the alternative kind of dilemma, Hursthouse explains that an irresolvable dilemma is "a situation in which the agent's moral choice lies between x and y and there are no moral grounds for favouring doing x over doing y."[26] Following Philippa Foot, who suggests this can happen in a positive way, Hursthouse offers the example of an irresolvable dilemma when choosing a birthday present for her daughter. After narrowing down the presents to a list of good possibilities, there is no clear rationale for choosing one present over another.[27] Hursthouse explains that in grim and unfortunate cases of irresolvable dilemmas, there are equal reasons *not* to perform any of the available options.[28]

As it relates to virtue ethics, irresolvable dilemmas are cases when two virtuous agents in identical situations act differently, yet both are considered virtuous.[29] In the case of the birthday present, Hursthouse explains that two virtuous parents may decide between present *a* and present *b*, but "there are no moral grounds for favouring one over the other."[30] Both virtuous parents "act generously and hence *well*," even when they choose different presents.[31] In a grave example of this, Hursthouse offers the case of deciding whether to extend extraordinary care for an unconscious, elderly sick mother. Two virtuous agents might proceed differently, yet both have "acted *well*."[32]

But if there are "no moral grounds" for any action, then many would argue that it is not a moral decision. However, Hursthouse frames this in such a way that these are still moral situations. As she points out in the case of the ill mother, the agents thoughtfully evaluate the situation.[33] This is why, Hursthouse explains, they act as virtuous agents should. So these are moral situations and thus moral dilemmas.

Hursthouse asserts that virtue ethics may tend to not only affirm the possibility of irresolvable dilemmas but also to admit that such cases are frequent because virtue theory does not offer a strict "decision procedure" for moral decision-making.[34] In her view, virtue ethics still upholds rules but not stringent guidance for how to encounter each situation. She calls these the "v-rules."[35]

When defining moral dilemmas, some theorists emphasize the obligations that cannot be fulfilled. Ruth Barcan Marcus explains, "In the one-person case there are principles in accordance with which one ought to do x and one ought to do y, where doing y requires that one refrain from doing x."[36] Earl Conee, who denies the possibility of dilemmas, defines them as times "when the agent cannot do everything that is morally obligatory for him to do in the situation, though he can carry out each obligation."[37]

Walter Sinnott-Armstrong argues that the classic cases of Agamemnon and Sartre show that the most basic feature of a moral dilemma is that "an agent ought to adopt each of two alternatives separately but cannot adopt both together."[38] Although, as he points out, sometimes the issue is that the agent must not act, such as when Agamemnon ought not kill his daughter (but ought to lead his troops). Sinnott-Armstrong admits that this definition of moral dilemmas is limited and somewhat vague since *ought* can take on different senses of responsibility in different cases. He gives the example that *ought* conveys a different meaning when saying "you ought to keep your promises" versus "the train ought to be here soon," among other examples.[39] He explains that these are distinct because "there is a moral reason to keep your promise," and this is different from expecting the train to arrive.[40] As he shows, a definition alone does not help one sort out what kind of ought is in play.

In an attempt to offer a more thorough definition, Sinnott-Armstrong puts together four features of a moral dilemma:

1. There is a moral requirement for an agent to adopt each of two alternatives,
2. neither moral requirement is overridden in any morally relevant way,

3. the agent cannot adopt both alternatives together, and
4. the agent can adopt each alternative separately.[41]

Yet he admits that ambiguity remains because his definition is best applied to more obvious moral dilemmas. Naming a perennial issue when trying to define moral dilemmas, he writes, "This definition is only supposed to capture the clear cases that most philosophers on both sides have in mind when they discuss moral dilemmas. It is not intended to include every situation that is interesting or that could legitimately be called a moral dilemma."[42] And he admits that some "borderline cases" would be tricky to defend as moral dilemmas.[43]

Sinnott-Armstrong also explains that an important feature of moral dilemmas is that they involve conflicting moral requirements, as opposed to conflicting moral ideals.[44] In this view, requirements are things we must do, while ideal actions are not necessary. He points out that which charity to donate to is a conflict of ideals, not of requirements. However, Sinnott-Armstrong's distinction is only of limited helpfulness because what counts as an ideal versus a requirement seems open to interpretation. For instance, the demands of Christianity make charity a requirement.

Crucial to Sinnott-Armstrong's definition, and like Williams's view, is his second feature that "neither moral requirement is overridden."[45] This means that even if an agent is justified in choosing one moral requirement over another, the moral requirement left unfulfilled remains obligatory. The requirement is not eliminated even though it was decided against and cannot be fulfilled. There is a strong consensus that this is a major feature of dilemmas. However, as I show later in the chapter, there are various views on what constitutes a requirement that cannot be eliminated and what this means for culpability.

According to Sinnott-Armstrong, "stronger" moral claims "overrid[e]" weaker ones.[46] He explains that moral dilemmas occur when overriding is impossible, such as when moral obligations are of equal or incomparable strengths. Furthermore, he argues that no wrongdoing is committed in a moral dilemma when an agent can be justified in making some decision.[47] But as I will show, this is not an unequivocally accepted position.

Thomas Nagel sheds some light on why a moral requirement may remain when he defines a moral dilemma as a "practical conflict" or a "conflict between values which are incomparable for reasons apart from uncertainty about the facts."[48] According to him, in "genuine dilemmas . . . there is decisive support for two or more incompatible courses of action or inaction."[49] The problem lies in the incomparability of values, for if values cannot be compared, then how can any demand be lifted? He offers five basic values that can be the source of conflict: "Obligations, rights, utility, perfectionist ends, and private commitments."[50] This makes way for the possibility that more than two values can conflict, although not all theorists agree that in a dilemma there are more than two conflicts.[51]

Foot, who denies the possibility of true moral dilemmas, can see that what theorists call moral dilemmas are times when precious goods are at stake.[52] She writes: "And indeed most moral dilemmas concern what might intelligibly be called 'human goods' such as health, life, liberty, and knowledge."[53] This points to the idea that somehow the obligations at play are obligations involving goods of great value.

Tessman argues that others' vulnerabilities often put moral demands on us that we do not necessarily consent to yet are beholden to, thus creating moral dilemmas.[54] For her, this explains why some moral requirements cannot be overridden. Later in the chapter I address in more detail Tessman's contribution to the issue of overriding moral requirements. Tessman offers her definition of a moral dilemma:

> I define a *moral dilemma* as a situation of conflict in which there is a moral requirement to do A and a moral requirement to do B, where one cannot do both A and B, and where neither moral requirement ceases to be a moral requirement just because it conflicts with another moral requirement, even if for the purpose of action-guidance it is overridden. In a dilemma, whichever action one chooses to perform, one violates what has become, through one's choice, the impossible moral requirement to do the other action. I take such a violation as a moral failure. Thus, dilemmas are situations in which moral failure is unavoidable.[55]

For Tessman, even if one can discern an action plan, when the remaining requirement is unable to be eliminated, the situation is a moral dilemma and a case of moral failure or wrongdoing. Tessman is attuned to how oppressive social structures force dilemmas, and her ideas on this are taken up in chapter 4.[56]

M. V. Dougherty also emphasizes wrongdoing.[57] He states, "A moral dilemma is any situation in which an agent cannot fulfill all genuine impending moral obligations," the implication being that "whatever one does, one will commit a moral wrong."[58] Dougherty points out that medieval discussions about moral dilemmas are about sin, but sin is no longer primary in the contemporary philosophical literature on dilemmas.[59]

Coming out of political philosophy, Michael Walzer postulates a similar emphasis on wrongdoing using Niccolò Machiavelli's paradox of the politician with "dirty hands."[60] Dirty hands is essentially a framework for moral dilemmas but focused on the political sphere where Walzer contends that moral dilemmas occur more frequently as a result of the nature of politics.[61] Walzer contends that, to govern well, sometimes a politician will have to do something that is wrong but justified. In addition to affirming that the best or justified action will be a transgression, Walzer adds the importance of guilt. He argues that the politician's sense of guilt is a sign of his goodness when his hands are unclean.[62]

Lisa Sowle Cahill also highlights wrongdoing, arguing for the possibility of moral dilemmas within a theological framework against the backdrop of what she regards as the shortcomings of Christian pacifist and Christian just war theories that do not appreciate the inherent moral dilemmas of their positions.[63] Cahill limits her discussion to "irreducible moral dilemmas," defined as "situations in which there is no available course of action that does not somehow involve the agent in wrongdoing, *even though* the action on the whole may be justified."[64] According to Cahill, in an irreducible moral dilemma, an agent is involved in a moral transgression even when performing the best action because the situation is such that it is impossible to avoid wrongdoing. To make her case, Cahill appeals to the futility of holding to strict Christian pacifist and just war positions. She highlights activists such as Dietrich Bonhoeffer and Dorothy Day, who were willing to betray their pacifist ideals when the concrete situations demanded decisive, aggressive action.[65] Furthermore, Cahill argues that Augustine and Thomas Aquinas put forward theories with ambivalences, when trying to defend killing in light of Jesus's commands to love the enemy and to turn the other cheek.[66]

In summary, while different theorists stress various aspects of a moral dilemma, they also share some ideas. A basic definition of a moral dilemma, then, is that a moral dilemma occurs when an agent cannot meet competing obligations and the unmet obligation is not satisfied even if the agent can determine the best possible course of action. For some thinkers, the action required may also be a transgression, or not fulfilling an obligation may be a transgression, but the extent to which this applies to all moral dilemmas is unclear. I take this up in more detail in the next section. In sum, Marcus offers a compelling description of a moral dilemma when she says that in a dilemma, "you are damned if you do and you are damned if you don't."[67]

WHAT IS A TRAGIC DILEMMA?

Not all theorists who argue for moral dilemmas make a distinction between moral and tragic dilemmas, and those who do, do not always provide a systematic account of the two categories. Sometimes the distinction between moral and tragic dilemmas is overlooked or not acknowledged, leading to confusion amid the inconsistencies between various thinkers' definitions of the categories. To the extent that both kinds of dilemmas are acknowledged, wrongdoing leading to tragedy is what tends to separate tragic dilemmas from moral dilemmas.

For Williams, moral and tragic conflicts are related yet different. When discussing moral conflicts generally, Williams emphasizes the remainder; when discussing tragic cases specifically, Williams emphasizes the transgressive action. Williams writes, "Conflicts of obligation are peculiar in presenting a conflict between determinately specified actions, while the tragic ones among them are further peculiar in lying beyond the ordinary routes of moral thought."[68] Williams describes "tragic cases" as "the most extreme cases of moral conflict," which possess the "peculiarity" that "'acting for the best' may very well lose its content."[69] And Williams clarifies that in tragic cases "an agent can justifiably think that whatever he does will be wrong."[70] So in a tragic case, no matter what an agent does, she commits a wrongdoing, a moral transgression. Thus, Williams offers a broad framework to defend the possibility of moral conflict—at least one lingering, unmet obligation identified by the remainder—and then specifies that moral conflicts involving a transgression are tragic.

Foot questions what Williams means in suggesting that tragic cases may involve what she describes as "the possibility of inescapable wrongness."[71] She points out that it is unclear what exactly Williams means by "wrong," as it seems that he is thinking about something not usually associated with wrongdoing.[72] This indicates not only that Foot recognizes that wrongdoing is critical to Williams's understanding of tragic conflicts but also that Williams may be stretching previous understandings of what constitutes right and wrong action.

Philip Quinn uses wrongdoing to differentiate moral dilemmas from tragic dilemmas. He starts with Sinnott-Armstrong's definition of a moral dilemma, which specifically denies wrongdoing, and then argues that "in a tragic dilemma violating either requirement is wrong."[73] Quinn offers the following definition of a tragic dilemma: "(1) There are requirements for an agent to adopt two alternatives, (2) it is wrong to violate either requirement, (3) the agent cannot adopt both alternatives together, and (4) the agent can adopt each alternative separately."[74] As he points out, this view relies on his presumption that some moral requirements are unable to be nullified.

Martha Nussbaum also links transgression and tragic dilemmas when she says that "tragic cases" involve "serious wrongdoing" that may include a "neglect of some important obligation."[75] She discusses this wrongdoing through various cases, and her thought is taken up in more detail later in the chapter. Relating to her own life, she relays her experience of preventable "minitragedies" as a junior professor at Harvard University arising from trying to balance childcare with a regular evening philosophy colloquium.[76]

Christopher Gowans takes up the transgressive nature of moral dilemmas and offers ways to think about how and when the transgression is related to tragedy or harm.[77] He is acutely sensitive to tragedies and sees dilemmas occurring in a world where there exists great loss and sadness. Gowans focuses on "moral tragedy," which involves a "tragic choice" between "conflicting moral responsibilities."[78] Gowans says in moral tragedy there is "inescapable moral wrongdoing" because some moral responsibility will go unfulfilled.[79] Gowans admits that a thorough definition of this is impossible because while some situations are obviously tragic, others are less obviously so, and therefore "it would be pointless to insist on a definitive answer to the question whether or not they are really tragic."[80] Instead he offers "tragic-making characteristics" that moral tragedies tend to possess.[81] And when many of these characteristics are present in situations of wrongdoing, there exists, essentially, a tragic dilemma. According to Gowans, moral tragedy occurs when one hurts "a person or social entity to whom the agent is morally responsible."[82] And harm is tragic to Gowans if it involves death or torture, if it "is either irreversible or extremely difficult to repair," if it is "far-reaching," if it "undoes that which a responsibility requires to be done," if it involves someone "the agent especially values," if the harmed is a "person who is especially undeserving of this harm or neglect," or if the harm contributes to another's sinister plans.[83] In sum, for Gowans, moral tragedy involves wrongdoing and some amount of harm.

Other theorists do not emphasize, or necessarily argue for, wrongdoing when defining tragic dilemmas. For instance, Hursthouse argues that tragic dilemmas involve only gruesome options that are difficult to characterize as "right" even when the best decision is made. But Hursthouse also adds another characteristic of tragic dilemmas: serious personal repercussions. As such, Hursthouse offers this understanding of tragic dilemmas:

> An action is right iff it is what a virtuous agent would, characteristically, do in the circumstances, except for tragic dilemmas, in which a decision is right iff it is what such an agent would decide, but the action decided upon may be too terrible to be called "right" or "good." (And a tragic dilemma is one from which a virtuous agent cannot emerge with her life unmarred).[84]

Hursthouse explains that the virtuous agent does not act "badly" but can't act "well."[85] That the situation is such that the virtuous agent cannot "emerge with her life unmarred" is crucial to her understanding of a tragic dilemma, but what Hursthouse means by "marred" is unclear, and she does not explain how or why this works. In chapter 4, I unpack what it might mean to mar an agent's life. For now, I use the term *mar* as a placeholder that points to a profound repercussion an agent experiences after being involved in a tragic dilemma; in my view, this is both a description of a tragic dilemma and an important property of a tragic dilemma.

Tessman discusses tragic dilemmas within the context of an Aristotelian virtue framework in her earlier work.[86] She argues that "tragic dilemmas can cause *action* guidance and *action* assessment to come apart because although one can decide which action to take, none of the available actions, given such a dilemma, can be linked to a good life, and an action must be linked to a good life to be assessed as good."[87] This position is controversial because it challenges the fundamental definition of virtuous action as connected to flourishing, so I do not take it up at length here. Tessman's most relevant points to my project are that (1) tragic dilemmas may involve situations where one can determine the best action, and (2) the action is, presumably, something that a moral agent would not choose in better circumstances.

Interestingly, in later work Tessman seems to interchange moral dilemmas and tragic dilemmas. When she argues for "impossible demands of morality," she doesn't home in on a distinction between moral and tragic dilemmas, and she uses the phrase "tragic dilemma" at one point to describe a case where a parent is forced to choose between saving only one of her children, but in other places she describes similar cases as moral dilemmas.[88]

Recognizing a distinction between moral and tragic dilemmas helps to clarify some confusion around these categories. As I have demonstrated, scholars such as Dougherty, Cahill, and Tessman use definitions of moral dilemmas that emphasize wrongdoing, but this is closer to what Williams describes when discussing tragic conflicts and what Quinn and others regard as tragic dilemmas. Without the added specificity of separate categories, it is easy for scholars to talk past each other. I argue that distinguishing moral dilemmas from tragic dilemmas adds precision to the dilemmas debate and avoids confusion.

After reviewing the literature, a basic and general philosophical definition of a tragic dilemma emerges: a tragic dilemma involves a moral transgression that causes great harm or mars an agent's life even when one acts in the best way possible. Much of the tragedy of a tragic dilemma is the great harm that Gowans describes, and Hursthouse is onto something profound when she recognizes that a tragic dilemma mars an agent's life. I contend that tragic dilemmas can occur in both resolvable and irresolvable cases, so it can be true for situations where the moral agent can determine a "best" option or when all options are equally bad, respectively. In chapter 4 I further assess these ideas and apply them to a theological context.

ARE THE PRIMARY PHILOSOPHICAL STRATEGIES PUT FORWARD TO SOLVE MORAL CONFLICTS PERSUASIVE?

There are various philosophical strategies that those who deny the possibility of dilemmas employ in order to solve cases of moral conflicts.[89] For proponents of moral dilemmas, these are not comprehensive enough to eliminate the possibility of true moral dilemmas. A deontological solution is to distinguish between different types of duties and to affirm the priority of a certain duty. Many consequentialists use the maximizing principle to determine right action according to consequences, and a cost-benefit analysis calculates how to achieve the "best" results.

A Deontological Approach

To solve an apparent conflict between duties, deontologist and British intuitionist W. D. Ross makes the distinction between an "actual duty" and a "conditional duty."[90] This means that duties are conditional, and it is only a particular situation that determines actual duties. For example, Ross explains that when faced with breaking a promise to meet a friend in order to help someone in need, meeting the friend is a "prima facie duty"—it remains potential or "conditional" because after examining the situation, one determines it is not an actual duty at that time, while helping someone is the actual duty.[91] Ross offers provisional prima facie duties, which Gowans summarily lists as "fidelity, reparation, gratitude, justice, beneficence, self-improvement, and nonmaleficence."[92] For Ross, it is only when faced with an actual situation that these duties may legislate demands.

The problem with this approach is that, while it is clear that a duty to protect life generally trumps the duty to break promises, discerning actual duties or principles becomes more difficult when seemingly equal and urgent duties are at stake. For instance, in the case of Mr. C. from the introduction, Mr. C.'s mother is dealing with duties to her son's health, his wishes, and her family's well-being. All of these obligations are demanding and important, and the mother wants to honor all of them.

Aquinas believes the hierarchy of goods solves all hard cases, which I take up in more detail in chapter 3. However, as I show, like discerning duties, the hierarchy is not always clear.

Sinnott-Armstrong explains that many moral dilemmas involve "limited incomparability."[93] Sinnott-Armstrong argues that while we can compare some moral requirements, we can't compare all of them every time for various reasons including the problem of "inexactness," problems in ranking the requirements ("ordinality"), and the trouble that, when each good is weighed on its own scale, goods are hard to compare.[94]

Particularly troubling are cases of "symmetry," where the goods are of equal value. For instance, Marcus asks how one would determine who to save if two siblings, specifically twins, are drowning.[95] This raises the same issues that the cases of the mother in Ethiopia and Sophie's predicament highlight in this book's introduction. Recall the mother in Ethiopia who cannot carry both of her children to find food, and whomever she leaves behind will presumably die. How could the mother favor one child over the other? And so it is impossible for the mother to determine what to do. The same goes for Sophie, who is put in a situation by Nazis to decide which of her two children will live.

In response specifically to Marcus, but it could be applied to the other cases mentioned above as well, Alan Donagan asserts that if a situation is totally symmetrical, then there is no moral question since there are no moral reasons for choosing one person over the other; this is only a "practical conflict."[96] For Donagan, these are not essentially moral issues. However, as William Styron's novel showcases, Sophie experiences her decision as having enormous moral weight, as would most parents in such a scenario.

A Consequentialist Approach

From a consequentialist standpoint, right action is determined according to the consequences.[97] For classical utilitarians, this means producing the most utility measured by pleasure.[98] With a maximizing benefit approach, when faced with any choice, one chooses the action that leads to the greatest amount of good for the greatest number of people. If the happiness maxim leads me to perform action A over action B, then the moral requirement of A has been satisfied and the requirement of B has been eliminated.[99] If all things are equal, a random choice is permitted.

Since this approach has no reference to inherent goods, it must be rigorously assessed, reassessed, and qualified to be applied responsibly; otherwise, consequentialism can lead to morally troubling conclusions, such as justifying torture in an attempt to protect the lives of many. The maximizing principle is the main approach used to allocate scarce resources in the coronavirus pandemic discussed in this book's introduction. Some iterations of this rationing approach were critiqued by disability rights activists who argued that the maximizing principle was being used to disqualify persons with disabilities from receiving ventilators because their quality of life was judged as less desirable than those without disabilities.[100] Thoughtful consequentialists, such as Emmanuel and colleagues, avoid this by specifically warning against using "future quality of life" when applying the maximizing principle.[101] However, the existence of different interpretations shows that without added qualifications and rigorous discussions, such protections are not obvious within consequentialism.

Furthermore, as Hursthouse points out, utilitarianism is critiqued for the way it "misrepresents the texture of our moral experience" because it often seems that there is more going on than only utility or benefit.[102] This is exemplified in part by health care workers on the front lines of the coronavirus pandemic who were incredibly distraught when implementing the rationing policies.[103]

A Cost-Benefit Analysis Approach

Nussbaum addresses the limits of a cost-benefit analysis.[104] She defines a cost-benefit analysis "as a strategy for choice in which weightings are allocated to the available alternatives, arriving at some kind of aggregate figure for each major option."[105] But she argues that a cost-benefit analysis itself does not prescribe how to weigh each cost and benefit, and so for this she suggests using her "capabilities approach."[106]

According to Nussbaum, hard cases call for both the "obvious question" of what ought to be done and the less obvious "tragic question" of whether an action plan is free from "moral wrongdoing."[107] While a cost-benefit analysis is a way to answer the obvious question, Nussbaum contends that it can conceal the tragic question. The benefits of asking the tragic question are numerous for Nussbaum: to clarify the values and issues at stake, to admit the existence of a tragic dilemma and in doing so "reinforc[e] commitments to important moral values" in light of circumstances where any action is wrong, to admit our complicity (what she describes as our "dirty hands") and so encourage "reparations," and to ask how society can change in order to avoid tragic situations in the future.[108] Nussbaum shows that without sensitivity to tragedy, a cost-benefit analysis is incomplete.

The theorists who ascribe to these strategies assume that the obligations not acted upon are eliminated and the issue is solved. Proponents of dilemmas tend to disagree, asserting that even if one can figure out how to act, the obligation not acted upon remains.

ARE MORAL DILEMMAS ILLOGICAL?

Within philosophical literature, Kant offers the seminal argument against moral dilemmas, stating that they are a logical impossibility. Kant presents a duty-based ethic where agents act for duty's sake following the universal moral law.[109] Kant's ethical system and his denial of dilemmas relies on an enormous amount of confidence that the world can be organized according to the rules of logic.[110] Kant and his followers are convinced that logic reigns supreme.

Because Kant's argument is highly influential in the dilemmas debate, I reproduce a long portion from his "Introduction to the Metaphysics of Morals":

> A *conflict of duties* (*collisio officiorum s. obligationum*) would be a relation between them in which one of them would cancel the other (wholly or in part).—But since duty and obligation are concepts that express the objective practical *necessity* of certain actions and two rules opposed to each other cannot be necessary at the same time, if it is a duty to act in accordance with one rule, to act in accordance with the opposite rules is not a duty but even contrary to duty; so a *collision of duties* and obligations is inconceivable (*obligationes non colliduntur*). However, a subject may have, in a rule he prescribes to himself, two *grounds* of obligation (*rationes obligandi*), one or the other of which is not sufficient to put him under obligation (*rationes obligandi non obligantes*), so that one of them is not a duty.—When two such grounds conflict with each other, practical philosophy says, not that the stronger obligation takes precedence (*fortior obligatio vincit*), but that the stronger *ground of obligation* prevails (*fortior obligandi ratio vincit*).[111]

As this passage shows, Kant asserts that duties cannot conflict. When grounds of obligations seem to conflict, the way forward for Kant is to prioritize the ground of obligation that has the most strength. Kant asserts that there are two kinds of duties: perfect and imperfect.[112] There are perfect duties to oneself and to others and imperfect duties to oneself and others. Kant explains that perfect duties prescribe action and must always be fulfilled, while imperfect duties prescribe no particular action for concrete cases and are not always obligatory. In Kant's view, there is no actual conflict when imperfect duties seem to clash because imperfect duties do not prescribe discrete actions. This is how the Kantian view denies dilemmas because what often seems to be a moral dilemma may really be a conflict between an imperfect and a perfect duty. In these cases, Kant asserts that perfect duty always prevails.

Gowans clearly describes Kant's thinking when he explains that, for Kant, dilemmas are illogical in part because Kant posits there are three types of actions: "the necessary, the impossible, and the permissible."[113] As Gowans explains, dilemmas confuse these categories in ways that are unintelligible to Kant because necessary actions cannot also be impossible. This is illogical and thus not a possibility for Kant.

Kant establishes positions that become the basis of deontic logic. He provides the fundamental ideals that are at stake in the debate on whether dilemmas are illogical. Here I focus on the following: the principle of deontic consistency, "ought implies can," and the principle of agglomeration.[114]

The "principle of deontic consistency" is a deontic logic premise, which states that an obligation cannot also be forbidden.[115] But this is violated in a moral dilemma when one ought to and ought not do some action.[116] In order to accept the possibility of moral dilemmas, this principle could be relinquished. However, this seems to be a lot to give up.

"Ought implies can" is a standard rule of deontology that states that agents are only morally obligated to perform actions that are possible.[117] According to this rule, if one ought to do A and one ought to do B, but one cannot do both A and B, then one is not obligated to do both A and B. If one determines that A is the best course of action, and this makes it impossible to do B, then B is no longer an obligation. The benefit of this way of thinking is that it seems unjust to judge people harshly for not doing the impossible.

However, many theorists who affirm moral dilemmas believe that ought does not necessarily imply can.[118] For these theorists, obligation B remains even though it is impossible. As Marcus explains, "'Ought' *does* imply 'can' for *each* of the conflicting obligations, *before* either one is met. And after an agent has chosen one of the alternatives, there is still something which he ought to have done and could have done and which he did not do. 'Can,' like 'possible,' designates a modality that cannot always be factored out of conjunction."[119] This means that one is still obligated to do things that are considered by some as logically impossible insofar that each action is possible before a course of action is decided upon.

Another principle at stake is the agglomeration principle, which applies the addition principle to deontic logic.[120] For people who deny dilemmas, applying the agglomeration principle is meant to show that dilemmas are illogical. Their argument is usually expressed along the following lines. Imagine a situation where the starting premises are these: one has an obligation to A, one has an obligation to B, and one cannot do both A and B. After applying the agglomeration principle, then one ought to do A and B. But this is contrary to the premise that one cannot do both A and B, so then it is illogical that one has obligations to both A and B. The agent must reassess the situation to determine whether she ought to do A or she ought to do B. After reexamining her obligations, she will find that she is not in a dilemma.

But Williams denies the agglomeration principle. For Williams, if you ought to do A, and you ought to do B, that does not mean it is necessary to add oughts to conclude that one ought to do A *and* B.[121] He calls the agglomeration principle into question via an analog to a man who wants to marry Susan and who wants to marry Joan but who does not want to be married to both Susan and Joan.[122] Williams contends that a similar thing happens with obligations: both "apply" even though both cannot be done.[123] Thus, one has an obligation to do each action, and we can leave it at that. In his view, an agent is obligated to do each action because each applies to the situation, and since each apply, fulfilling one obligation does not eliminate the other, so the obligation remains.

Williams explains that competing obligations are not necessarily inconsistent because moral obligations function like desires, which can conflict, and not like beliefs, which cannot conflict.[124] According to Williams, two beliefs that cannot both be true are inherently contradictory, but two desires that cannot both be fulfilled are not necessarily contradictory.[125] For instance, if I believe all cockapoo dogs are cuddly and friendly and I believe that the aggressive, standoffish, furry, barking creature I encountered at the dog park this morning is a cockapoo, then I am forced to forfeit one belief for the sake of consistency: either not all cockapoos are friendly or I did not have a run-in with a cockapoo earlier today. But desires are different according to Williams. He explains that it is often the case "that the clash between the desires arises from some contingent matter of fact. This is a matter of fact that makes it impossible for both the desires to be satisfied; but we can consistently imagine a state of affairs in which they could both be satisfied."[126] So desires are at odds in a particular situation, but there could just as well be a situation where those desires are not at odds. Williams uses an example of a lazy man wanting a drink to show that conflicts of desires can arise from situational contingency.[127] The man cannot fulfill both his desire to recline on the sofa and to have the cold lemonade on the counter fifteen feet away.[128] But once the man's roommate enters the room, let's say, there is someone who can help him to achieve both desires. So the desires are not inherently inconsistent; it is that they are at odds in that particular situation.[129]

Marcus, like Williams, supports the view that dilemmas do not present a logical inconsistency as the demands only conflict in a particular situation. She asserts that "a set of rules is inconsistent if there are *no* circumstances, no possible world, in which all the rules are satisfiable."[130] She gives the example of a game of cards that follows two rules: black cards beat red cards, and high-numbered cards beat low-numbered cards, with ace being a high card; when two players have the same cards, it's a draw and the play continues.[131] As Marcus explains, it is possible to play the whole game and never face the dilemma of a high red card versus a low black card. Marcus's point is that the rules are not logically inconsistent insofar as it is possible to play the game without facing an issue. This is how moral dilemmas are not necessarily inconsistent.

The value of Marcus's view is limited, however. As Terrance McConnell points out, knowing that a moral dilemma is not technically inconsistent because there is another universe where such a conflict could not occur does very little for agents facing the moral dilemma in this universe.[132] The arguments presented here show how philosophers have defended the logical possibility for moral dilemmas.

HOW ABOUT THE CASE FOR REMAINDERS FROM MORAL SENTIMENTS?

Those who deny the existence of moral dilemmas assert that when two (or more) moral demands are in conflict, the demand not acted upon is no longer an obligation (assuming the best course of action is taken). This is seen in the strategies discussed above, and it is especially forceful in the claim that it is illogical for two obligations to remain as requirements if it is impossible to fulfill both demands. But arguing from the point of view of moral sentiments, Williams stresses that feelings of "regret" indicate that, in a moral conflict, the ought not acted upon remains even when the best course of action is determined, and so there exists a "remainder."[133] Yet the content of these "remainders" is vague, but Hursthouse attempts to clarify it.[134] The idea of a remainder is rooted in moral sentiments. This is contentious and must first be justified in order to defend moral dilemmas within moral philosophy or Christian ethics.

The Validity of Arguments Based on Moral Sentiments

Emotions have been a dubious source for some thinkers in Christian ethics and philosophy who worry that emotions are untrustworthy.[135] For instance, when emotions arise from an ill-formed conscience or idiosyncrasy, they do not necessarily point to a truth. But others disagree. Proponents of moral sentiments in theology and philosophy argue that emotions offer salient insights into the moral life.[136]

Moral sentiments stem from a variety of sources, and depending on the theory, any of these sources may be emphasized: "emotions, feelings, affects, desires, besires, plans, and dispositions."[137] These can offer insights on a variety of moral issues expressed by the various types of sentimentalists: explanatory, judgment, expressivist, epistemological, and metaphysical.[138]

In various forms of virtue ethics, feelings have a moral aspect in that right action is accompanied by right feeling.[139] And from philosopher David Hume's point of view in the eighteenth century, morality cannot be captured by reason alone, so we need sentiments in order to properly understand morality.[140] For instance, Hume argues that reasons don't motivate us; feelings do.[141] For many theorists, emotions are moral evaluations.[142] For instance, if I am angry about the separation of a seven-year-old Congolese girl from her mother as they await an asylum hearing in the United States, that anger is alerting me to an injustice.[143]

Hailing from contemporary moral psychology, Jonathan Haidt argues that feelings of moral judgments are primarily types of intuitions, which we might reason about after the fact in order to defend our intuitions.[144] But others argue that intuitions can be shaped by reason.[145] The implication of this alternative view is that feelings are more trustworthy than they initially appear if they are the result of reason or tutored by reason.

Others argue that feelings are problematic because they can be malformed due to a variety of personal and cultural influences. To correct for this, there are theories to evaluate feelings. For example, John Rawls's reflective equilibrium is a process to reflect on beliefs and judgments.[146]

Perhaps the strongest case for the importance of feelings for ethics comes from troubling conclusions grounded in reason alone. As Jesse Prinz points out, disturbing principles can be universalized according to Kant's reason-based deontological formulation, proving that reason alone is insufficient to drive our ethics. For instance, Prinz explains that kicking children could become a universal maxim because there is not a logical contradiction that prevents it from becoming universalized.[147]

Deontology can also lead to other startling conclusions. Kant explains that we have a duty to never lie, and this duty remains primary even in surprising cases. He famously declares that if a murderer asks where a person is hiding and one knows the location, the duty of truth-telling means one cannot lie about the hider's location, even if this leads to the person's death.[148]

Utilitarian philosopher Peter Singer argues that our moral sentiments are untrustworthy. For instance, Singer has provocatively argued that infanticide is morally permissible.[149] To the extent that such a conclusion goes against most of our moral our sensibilities, he says that is a problem with our sentiments and not a problem with the conclusion.[150]

But for moral sentimentalists, emotional aversions to Singer's and Kant's conclusions are signs that the conclusions are questionable or "off." From my point of view, an ethical system is not doing much good if it renders permissible such abhorrent behaviors. Feelings, then, are crucial to ensure that reason does not lead us astray.

Feelings of regret do not offer absolute proof that obligations linger, but they are pieces of evidence that prompt an investigation. Williams offers a reasoned justification for what feelings may point to in ethics, which I take up in the next section.

Williams on Remainders

Williams argues that by ignoring emotions, ethicists have missed the "regret" that persists after moral conflicts, and this regret points to the reality of lingering oughts.[151] For Williams, "a neglect of moral psychology and in particular of the role of emotion in morality has distorted and made unrealistic a good deal of recent discussion."[152] Williams admits that feelings are tricky and that his discussion is incomplete, as his treatment of emotion and regret "is certainly less clear than I should like."[153] But despite the difficulty of pinning them down, Williams contends that emotions illuminate something important about ethics.

Williams makes the case for how emotions of regret are justified, arguing that feelings of regret are warranted sources of insight about ethics because they arise from moral situations and are telling of moral situations. According to Williams, it is reasonable that feelings of regret point to "ineliminable" oughts because moral conflicts operate like conflicts of desires in crucial ways.[154] He argues that, like desires, oughts can linger. As addressed in a previous section, Williams explains that when beliefs compete, one belief is canceled. However, he argues that this is not the case with conflicts of desires, where desires remain even after the event. In moral conflicts, there perdures a "remainder" of the ethical event, and this is evidence that the unmet ought has not been eliminated.[155] So one feels regret after adjudicating a moral conflict, even if one "acted for the best."[156]

But Williams is vague about the content of this regret. He says one feels regret "for what I did not do."[157] This regret may take the form of trying to "'make up' to people involved for the claim that was neglected."[158] The unfulfilled ought lingers because even though the event is over, the ought endures.

For many, regret will seem illogical or poorly founded. But Williams argues that regret is not an irrational response or emotion. Recall that Williams argues that regret takes on a strong quality in the case of tragic conflicts. He argues that it is fitting and rational for Agamemnon to have these emotions about his action: "It would seem a glib moralist who said, as some sort of criticism, that he [Agamemnon] must be irrational to lie awake at night, having killed his daughter."[159] Thus, after tragic conflicts, regret lingers, and understandably so. As Williams writes in a later paper, in tragic cases "the agent will have reason to feel regret at the deepest level" for having done something wrong while acting in the best way possible.[160]

Foot argues that feelings of regret after moral conflicts are inappropriate. But this disagreement might be caused by imprecise definitions as she thinks "sorrow" or "horror" might be appropriate but not regret.[161] This is because she believes regret means the agent thinks she should have acted in a different way. But regret described by Williams focuses on the idea that some obligations cannot be dismissed. In Williams's notion of tragic conflicts, the problem is that whatever the agent does is wrong, not that the agent does one action and later wishes she did something else.

To those who concede that an "admirable moral agent" would experience regret but who do not think that such feelings reveal anything about the nature of the conflict, Williams says that this position depends on a questionable or difficult to determine distinction between "*natural* motivations" and "*moral* motivations."[162] Again, Williams is vague on definitions. He defines *moral motivations* as "motivations that spring from thinking that a certain course of action is one that one ought to take."[163] Natural motivations seem to be all motivations that are not moral motivations. Despite these imprecise definitions, the force of his point is that, in order to assume that feelings after a moral conflict are not revelatory of the moral conflict itself, there must be some kind of meaningful, identifiable distinction between moral motivations and other motivations. And while this might be true sometimes, it seems unlikely to Williams that such a distinction is operating in all instances of regret because the feelings come out of moral situations, and they are feelings about the moral situation. To explain this he writes: "If a man in general thinks that he ought not to do a certain thing, and is distressed by the thought of doing that thing; then if he does it, and is distressed at what he has done, this distress will probably have the shape of his thinking that in doing that thing, he has done something that he ought not to have done."[164]

In response, one might argue that Agamemnon was rightly upset at night when thinking over his ordeal, but this does not reveal anything about moral conflict; it only shows that a virtuous agent is rightly upset when he kills his daughter, even when the reasons are justified (if they are). To which Williams would probably reply something along the lines of, "How could his feelings not tell us something about the conflict itself? The feelings are directly related to the conflict, and they cannot be separated from it!" Furthermore, if we agree that many virtuous agents would appropriately feel some kind of regret, then there is an even stronger case for looking into what these feelings reveal about moral conflicts.

This is also seen when someone feels regret for having reneged on a promise, and in that case the regret very clearly "arise[s] *via* a moral thought," according to Williams.[165] Williams thinks this regret is positive because it shows "an agent took his promises seriously."[166] Donagan offers a rebuttal to this line of thinking when taking up a similar point in Marcus's work. Donagan writes, "You show that giving your word is a serious matter by your scrupulousness in ensuring that those to whom you give it understand the conditions on which you do so and in keeping it when those conditions are fulfilled."[167] So, then, for Donagan it is one's actions around a promise that are critical, not one's feelings about a promise.

But Williams maintains that feelings of regret are perfectly reasonable because there is no reason why the ought not acted upon is eliminated. To eliminate the ought implies that "it did not actually apply."[168] In his view both obligations do apply and continue to apply even after choosing a course of action because that is why there were two obligations in the first place. The two demands are not dependent on one another, so it is not the case that one demand no longer "applies" just because the other is fulfilled.

To those who think regret is irrational in these cases, Williams is open to conceding that maybe sometimes moral agents are irrational.[169] While this may seem to undermine Williams's argument, it does not because it speaks to the notion that, on some level, acceptance of moral dilemmas is intuitive and to those who cannot be convinced, so be it! Perhaps agents *are* sometimes irrational because moral obligation and responsibility are not always "rational." Reality is not always "rational," and in response, neither are moral agents.

Hursthouse on Remainders

Hursthouse worries that when practical ethicists deny the remainder of a dilemma, a hard case appears to be deceptively straightforward; this obscures salient ethical features of the issue.[170] Hursthouse expounds on how remainders function. Admitting the existence of both remainders and tragic dilemmas, Hursthouse builds on Williams's work, making the case that tragic dilemmas have the power to harm the agent.

Hursthouse claims virtuous agents are permanently affected by having acted amid a tragic dilemma:

> However, if a genuinely tragic dilemma is what a virtuous agent emerges from, it will be the case that she emerges having done a terrible thing, the very sort of thing that the callous, dishonest, unjust, or in general vicious agent would characteristically do—killed someone, or let them die, betrayed a trust, violated someone's serious rights. And hence it will not be possible to say that she has acted *well*. What follows from this is not the impossibility of virtue but the possibility of some situations from which even a virtuous agent cannot emerge with her life unmarred.[171]

Later she says, "'It follows that a compassionate, just, courageous agent who has done what she has done will never rest content again: her life will be forever marred.'"[172]

The content of the remainder after a tragic dilemma is difficult for Hursthouse to pin down as either remorse or regret. Remorse does not quite fit, in Hursthouse's view. She explains, "For *guilt* and *remorse* are, going strictly by their dictionary definitions, directed to a *wrong* or *sin* committed."[173] Unlike regret, remorse indicates blame and a sense that the agent must live with the pain of having done a certain action. In Hursthouse's understanding of a tragic dilemma, the agent seems to be blameless, which does not constitute remorse. So then Hursthouse wonders whether regret seems fitting. Hursthouse explains that regret points to the notion that one would act differently if given the chance. But that doesn't work either for Hursthouse, who believes the agent acts in the best way possible, and so regret does not capture the despair at having performed the action. Hursthouse explains, "The difficulty here is to find a suitable sense of 'feeling regret' which is sufficiently powerful to be a suitable reaction to having done *x*, this terrible thing."[174] Hursthouse finds it difficult to describe the remainder in a way that captures both the alleged innocence of the agent and the intensity of the agent's grief. Instead of solving the matter, she suggests that rather than focus on the distinction between regret and remorse, one should focus on how "sorrow" accompanying a tragic dilemma has the power to mar the agent's life.[175] But avoiding the question is unsatisfying because the relationship between a tragic dilemma and moral responsibility is still unclear. In chapter 4 I offer my own theological account of the remainder in an attempt to answer what Hursthouse has not.

And what exactly Hursthouse means by "mar" is also unclear. In her view, marring seems to result from the fact that the agent is unable to act "*well*" because she is forced to transgress an inviolable prohibition, such as when one has "killed someone, or let them die, betrayed a trust, violated someone's serious rights."[176] Marring also has something to do with being "haunted by sorrow that she had done *x*."[177] And being marred, according to Hursthouse, does not mean the agent will necessarily develop a vice.[178] Chapter 4 takes up this issue that Hursthouse leaves open—how a moral remainder mars an agent.

WHY DO SOME OUGHTS REMAIN?

If Williams and others are correct about remainders, then the next question is why do some oughts remain? Williams himself offers little in this regard.[179] However, Hursthouse, Nussbaum, Gowans, Tessman, and Cahill all hold that some oughts remain because, essentially, they are inviolable. Foot accuses pro-dilemma theorists of demonstrating the erratic "tendency among moral philosophers who cannot bring themselves to say that there is any kind of action that is wrong in any circumstances whatsoever, and who yet feel that certain actions—say torture—cannot ever be justified."[180] But this does not characterize the scholars I discuss, for as I show in this section, Hursthouse believes in some absolute prohibitions, Nussbaum thinks there are certain "burden[s] that no citizen should have to bear," Gowans believes that "responsibilities to persons" render some obligations indissoluble, Tessman asserts that some "sacred values" are too dear to abandon, and Cahill identifies "moral imperatives" in light of Christianity.[181]

Hursthouse believes some oughts remain because she holds certain "absolute prohibitions."[182] For her, virtue ethics assumes some basic rules, the "v-rules."[183] These absolute prohibitions do not permit an agent to have "killed someone, or let them die, betrayed a trust, violated someone's serious rights."[184] According to her, this is in line with Aristotle, who asserts that actions of "'depravity'" clearly include "'adultery,' theft, and murder."[185]

To those who claim that moral obligations are eliminated when one course of action is chosen over another, Nussbaum replies, "It makes morality the handmaiden of fortune. . . . And it allows agents to wriggle out of commitments that should be regarded as binding over a complete life."[186] She believes that firm moral requirements allow the agent to act consistently throughout life.

According to Nussbaum, certain values should not be transgressed. Such transgressions would cause "burden[s] that no citizen should have to bear."[187] This is because she believes all people deserve "a package of fundamental entitlements."[188] She recognizes that the shape and content of these will vary depending on the society but suggests that a cost no one should have to bear is a cost that transgresses one of her "capabilities."[189]

Building on Nussbaum, Tessman admits that sometimes it will be difficult to determine what can and what cannot be borne. Nevertheless, when using Nussbaum's concept in her own work, Tessman asserts that "conceptually there *is* a distinction to be made" even if the criteria are at times difficult to articulate.[190] And in practice, this approach works. For instance, Nussbaum offers the example of education in India where some families lose a valuable worker when sending a child to school.[191] Nussbaum explains that eventually, in response to this predicament, India changed its laws to make a provision for a school lunch requirement. This relieves some of the economic burden for struggling families, making it economically reasonable or even advantageous for children to attend school.

As already stated, Gowans argues that "moral tragedies" are times when moral dilemmas have tragic repercussions, so "moral wrongdoing is inescapable" according to his "responsibility to persons account."[192] He gives an example using George Bernard Shaw's play *Major Barbara* where a Salvation Army facility is faced with the decision of whether to accept money from an arms dealer or to shut down.[193] As Gowans explains the problem, the shelter has moral responsibilities both to the people they serve and to the innocent people who will die from the weapons. No matter what route they choose, they will let someone down. Gowans stresses that even if the Salvation Army determines that one choice is better, the other responsibility remains. This is because "we have moral responsibilities to particular persons in virtue of our appreciation of the intrinsic and unique value of each of these persons, and of our connections with them."[194] This is why Gowans asserts that obligations are not eliminated even when the best choice is pursued. The Salvation Army, as Gowans demonstrates, cannot undo its responsibilities to either group of people. Gowans explains that his "responsibility to persons account" asks the question, "'How can I properly respond to *each* of these persons and institutions to which I am responsible?'"[195] This questions arises from Gowan's belief that responsibilities to individuals do not easily dissolve because our relationships engender certain commitments to others. Others need something from us, and those needs don't expire, even when Kant or others dismiss them.

Tessman offers a helpful framework with her distinction between two types of moral requirements—"negotiable" and "non-negotiable" moral requirements.[196] According to Tessman, we experience nonnegotiable moral requirements as an "I *must*."[197] These requirements, working from Gowans's thought, "concern significant values for which there can be neither substitutions nor compensations," and, following Nussbaum, losing them involves "costs that no one should have to bear."[198] In Tessman's view, not every unique value constitutes a nonnegotiable moral obligation, but values that are unique and whose losses are unbearable and cannot be made up are nonnegotiable. She argues that nonnegotiable moral requirements do not follow "ought implies can." When two nonnegotiable requirements conflict, Tessman contends that "moral failure" is inevitable because neither nonnegotiable requirement falls away. Tessman explains that she "substitute[s] 'moral failure' for 'moral wrongdoing'" so that it includes many kinds of requirements that are violated, including but not limited to duties.[199] Negotiable moral requirements, however, do not persist when rightly chosen against in a conflict because their value is not "unique" or their value is unique but their loss produces a cost that can be reasonably borne; unlike nonnegotiable requirements, they follow "ought implies can."[200]

Tessman defends this point of view using moral experience and neuroscience. Using data from moral psychology, Tessman argues that we process various moral requirements differently—some through controlled reasoning and others through intuitive reasoning.[201] She argues that nonnegotiable requirements are a special class of moral requirements that are identified by our intuitions and often involve values that have been "sacralized" and so must be protected.[202]

Love often creates situations involving nonnegotiable moral requirements, in Tessman's view.[203] For instance, if a parent needs superhuman strength to save her child lodged under the weight of a heavy car, she would still feel as if she left a moral requirement unmet if she did not have the superhuman ability to bring her child to safety.[204] This is because, according to Tessman, the loved one has value because they are loved.[205]

Other people's vulnerabilities are also a source of nonnegotiable moral requirements for Tessman. She writes, "Vulnerability can be an *inexhaustible* source of moral requirements, which are, thereby, endless and thus impossible to fulfill."[206] Vulnerability makes demands because "one person's need is a call for a response."[207] This is the case, according to Tessman, even when we do not consent to the demands. Gowans worries that the thought of infinite demands will dilute the pull of moral requirements because there are so many.[208] But I believe Tessman is interested in offering an account of morality that speaks to reality, regardless of whether this might overwhelm some people.

Following work by Philip Tetlock and colleagues, Tessman explains the notion of "sacred values."[209] She explains that these are values that are considered to be extraordinarily important and as a result cannot be eliminated or trumped by a competing value. These values must be safeguarded. Tessman offers "protect my child" as an example of a sacred value.[210]

According to Tessman, we evaluate (or do not evaluate) different requirements in different ways so that it is almost impossible to assess a sacred value.[211] She supports scrutinizing negotiable requirements through reason via Rawls's process of reflective equilibrium. In this method, requirements are assessed through public dialogue and compared against the demands of reason and general normative judgments. But, according to Tessman, this is not appropriate for sacred values. This is because Tessman believes that thinking through the value using the process of reflective equilibrium could cause one to transgress the dearly held value. For instance, she explains that in reasoning through the sacred value of protecting one's child, one has already transgressed this deeply held value.[212] This is evidenced by the way I shudder to even write such a sentence.

Tessman is aware that many values can be societally constructed in problematic ways or erroneously cherished, which is why she is a proponent of reflective equilibrium for negotiable values.[213] But she believes that the values we intuitively hold dear are special and thus should not be subjected to the demands of reason or have to be defended. In Tessman's view, our moral intuitions alert us to sacred values, and these do not have to be interrogated or revised. This is because, as Tessman explains, "Sometimes it is best to allow a moral judgment's authority to be constituted by the fact that one's confidence in it is such that it *resists* scrutiny."[214] For instance, in her view there is no reason to rethink the notion that one's child ought to be protected. Sacred values, for Tessman, have authority because we are very sure about them and because we hold them dear.[215]

Tessman differs from someone like Judith Jarvis Thomson, who asserts that consent is crucial to moral obligation.[216] This position is also very different from that of someone like Frances Kamm, who believes that personal needs do not assert a special demand insofar as we are not obligated to persons whom only we can save.[217]

Tessman holds these positions in part because she is a moral constructivist, meaning she believes that our moral values, judgments, and exercises are constructed.[218] However, I think it is plausible to hold her distinction between negotiable and nonnegotiable moral requirements without being a constructivist.

Cahill points to this possibility in her theological notion of irreducible moral dilemmas, which claims that dilemmas are irreducible because "coming to the aid of the vulnerable neighbor" and "respecting the lives of all human beings" are "moral imperative[s]."[219] In this view, the demands remain even when one justifiably acts against one of the moral imperatives. But Cahill does not expound much on why that is, what that means, or what protecting the vulnerable entails. I develop this further in chapter 4, where I make my own case for nonnegotiable moral requirements in a Christian context.

DO AGENTS IN MORAL OR TRAGIC DILEMMAS POSSESS AGENCY?

The issue of agency receives little attention in the moral dilemma literature, which is surprising considering that many moral dilemmas are the result of constrained situations. Tessman addresses this issue, and her biggest contribution is her attention to the complexity of various situations.[220] She distinguishes between "absent morality" and "dilemmatic morality": If an individual cannot exert any agency, then the situation is of "absent morality" wherein morality fails, and this is different from "dilemmatic morality," where moral agents still possess some "control" and a sense of predictability in what will happen in the situation.[221]

Tessman uses Lawrence Langer's work on the Holocaust to unfurl the reality of "absent morality" where extraordinary circumstances can destroy agency.[222] Using Langer, Tessman gives the example of desperation in the Holocaust forcing people to perform actions they otherwise would not do, such as eating human flesh out of pure hunger. She explains that moral agency is lost amid such horror.

Tessman also contends that it can be a very human response to see agency and power where none actually exists, such as in the case of Holocaust survivor Abraham P.[223] During the Holocaust Abraham P. and his brothers were put in a different selection line from their parents, so Abraham P. told his youngest brother to join their parents. As it turned out, Abraham P.'s line was sent to a work camp while all those in the parents' line were killed. Many years later Abraham P. feels responsible for his brother's death. Tessman gives Langer's perspective that Abraham P.'s guilt is inappropriate because he had no real choices—telling his brother where to go was not a moral decision because Abraham had no real information. Tessman affirms that this is a case of absent morality because "he [Abraham P.] had *no* control over his brother's fate."[224]

This depiction of Abraham P.'s lack of agency highlights a problem within theories of agency, for Tessman admits that it is difficult to identify with clarity that Abraham P. has no agency, but Sophie (of *Sophie's Choice* and referenced in a case study in the introduction), for instance, has some agency.[225] This distinction is important because without any agency, Abraham P. was not involved in a moral or tragic dilemma; but with some agency, Sophie was involved in a dilemma.

While Tessman focuses on agency and control to think about agents acting in constrained situations, I show in chapter 3 how Aquinas uses the category of voluntariness. And in chapter 4, I investigate Aquinas's notion of knowledge and the feminist idea of a relational autonomy to shed light on the complex issue of agency amid moral and tragic dilemmas.

ARE AGENTS IN MORAL OR TRAGIC DILEMMAS BLAMEWORTHY?

Theorists who agree with the possibility of moral dilemmas are undecided about whether participation in a moral or tragic dilemma renders one morally culpable. As I show, Williams is silent on the issue, Tessman wants to avoid talking about it, Marcus ascribes guilt to agents acting in moral and tragic dilemmas, Nussbaum and Quinn attribute guilt in cases of tragic dilemmas, Cahill recognizes some guilt in moral dilemmas, and Hursthouse asserts agents are free from blame.

Some theorists avoid discussing the issue of guilt. Williams does not discuss guilt in his influential article on regret where he discusses moral and tragic conflicts.[226] He specifically uses the term *regret* rather than using another term that indicates guilt, such as *remorse*.[227]

Tessman, who does not always operate with a sharp distinction between moral and tragic dilemmas, says she is not interested in "blameworthiness" and, for the most part, attempts to avoid the issue.[228]

Other theorists take a stance. Some presume blame. For Marcus, actors in moral dilemmas and tragic dilemmas are guilty. In her view, feelings of guilt that arise from dilemmas should not be dismissed or ignored as illogical or irrelevant.[229]

Nussbaum believes the tragic question illuminates blame in conjunction with her focus on transgressive action. She writes: "It [the tragic question] keeps the mind of the chooser firmly on the fact that his action is an immoral action, which it is always wrong to choose.... When the recognition is public, it constitutes an acknowledgment of moral culpability."[230] According to Nussbaum, a benefit of admitting a wrong and taking moral responsibility is that it initiates a movement that, hopefully, prevents tragic cases in the future.[231]

Recall that Quinn uses wrongdoing to distinguish between moral and tragic dilemmas. Following this, he asserts that guilt follows from the wrongdoing inherent to tragic dilemmas, and this guilt "is why they are tragic."[232] Along similar lines, Cahill proposes that there is "remorse" and "guilt" involved in irreducible moral dilemmas due to the "wrong done."[233]

Departing from these thinkers, Hursthouse asserts that the agent acting in a tragic dilemma bears no moral culpability yet suffers. In Hursthouse's view, the agent is not guilty because she does not contribute to creating the bad situation. Hursthouse explains that "in making a forced choice, the agent is blameless."[234] In her view, the agent suffers for having acted in the best way possible amid constrained options, which is why the situation is tragic. Despite this position, Hursthouse is rather ambivalent on whether the moral agent experiences remorse or regret after a tragic dilemma, as discussed earlier. This reveals that the issue of blame is not as straightforward as it seems.

It is notable that none of these theorists treats the issue systematically or at great length. In response to these various positions, in chapter 4, I develop a notion of moral responsibility in tragic dilemmas in light of Christian commitments and ideas.

DO THE CATEGORIES OF MORAL OR TRAGIC DILEMMAS ENCOURAGE RESTITUTION?

Most theorists who support the possibility of moral dilemmas cite some kind of restitution as a benefit of a theory that allows for moral dilemmas. Yet these theories are generally rather bare. Although Foot disagrees with Williams's conclusion about moral dilemmas, she appreciates his sensitivity to "'moral cost' and 'moral loss.'"[235] Williams makes various references to the notion of "compensation" that accompanies moral conflicts and that characterizes regret.[236]

This is evidenced by other theorists as well. For instance, Hursthouse mentions that the idea of a "remainder" suggests that some irresolvable moral dilemmas may be accompanied with a kind of "apology or restitution or compensation" and that some resolvable dilemmas may prompt "the recognition of a new requirement."[237] And Tessman suggests "unavoidable wrongdoing" can be "mitigated through forgiveness."[238] Nussbaum believes that a major benefit of the tragic question is that it prompts institutional change that prevents future tragedy.[239] And Cahill discusses the importance of "collective responsibility" for injuries caused by institutional and political bodies, and especially "the need for compensatory and restorative social practices" in response to the harms of war.[240]

Of course, someone can recognize the need to respond to a hard or sad situation without admitting wrongdoing or a moral or tragic dilemma. But as I show, moral dilemma theorists are particularly apt to see the need to respond to the harm of these trying events.

This is a promising but underdeveloped strand in moral dilemma literature. These theorists make gestures toward some additional healing work but without addressing the content of that work. This book fills that lacuna in a specifically Christian way by developing a theory of Christian healing after tragic dilemmas in chapter 5.

WHAT DO MORAL OR TRAGIC DILEMMAS ASSUME ABOUT HUMAN GOODNESS?

Gowans insightfully observes that at the heart of concerns about inevitable wrongdoing is disagreement about the possibility for moral goodness.[241] In my view, his summary is a most fitting description of the debate around tragic dilemmas. He writes: "In brief, those who reject the idea of inescapable moral wrongdoing suppose that moral innocence is possible, while those who accept this idea think that moral tragedy is possible."[242] This sentiment is echoed by Foot, who argues that in order for inescapable wrong to be a plausible possibility, we have to be open to the possibility that "goodness [is] vulnerable to the 'taint' of involvement in a horrifying, humiliating, or tragic situation, or to the hatred of the gods; and then we say that a choice that involves such *badness* is 'wrong.'"[243] Gowans is ready to make that concession in part because he has a strong sensitivity to tragedy. Foot, who does not accept dilemmas, is not willing to make such a concession.

The prospect of moral innocence assumes that it is possible, albeit challenging, to live a life that is morally pure. According to this view, moral agents can choose to be good even when up against the harshest and hardest of circumstances. This coheres with the idea of a good God who would not put people in morally troubling situations. I believe moral innocence is appealing in part because if it is true, then individuals do not have to take responsibility for societal injustices that put others in impossible moral situations. But while one may trust that God does not put people in impossible situations, it is clear that structural sin often does. I take up the issue of structural sin in chapter 4.

As this chapter shows, while moral philosophy's treatment of moral and tragic dilemmas leaves some questions open, the dilemmas debate is rich and thoughtful. The literature on moral and tragic dilemmas raises important questions about the role of feelings in ethics, lingering obligations, nonviolable prohibitions, constrained choices, guilt, regret, remorse, human goodness, and what experience teaches. Because of this, I believe that moral and tragic dilemmas are a worthy topic for theological engagement.

Many features of moral and tragic dilemmas are highlighted in this chapter. Some philosophers offer a humble take on dilemmas, admitting that they are unable to develop a definition that is exhaustive enough to cover all dilemmas or persuasive enough to convince skeptics. Nevertheless, they tend to believe that even though they cannot articulate an all-encompassing definition, this does not mean dilemmas do not exist. Contra Kant, pro-dilemma theorists make a strong case for the fact that moral dilemmas are not logical inconsistencies insofar as dilemmas rely on contingency. And to the extent that concrete, contingent dilemmas may still be considered illogical by some, perhaps we ought to welcome some paradox into our ethics.

Most philosophers who accept the possibility of moral dilemmas argue that dilemmas occur because an ought is unable to be eliminated. This chapter also shows that tragic dilemmas involve wrongdoing, causing great harm or marring the agent. Chapter 4 assesses these fundamental criteria for moral and tragic dilemmas in a Christian context.

The debates around moral and tragic dilemmas pose many questions for Christian ethics. This is in part because moral philosophy lacks the theological tools of Christian ethics. Philosophers are undecided about which oughts remain and why, about how moral remainders function, and about whether agents who act in moral dilemmas are blameworthy. In chapters 2 and 3, I use the Augustinian and Thomistic traditions, respectively, to think through moral and tragic dilemmas in light of theological commitments. I then go on to develop a Christian understanding of tragic dilemmas in chapter 4.

NOTES

1. Bernard Williams and Martha Nussbaum have turned to Greek tragedies to call attention to scenarios where some situations require an agent to choose one very valuable

good over another. See Williams, "Ethical Consistency"; and Nussbaum, *The Fragility of Goodness*.

2. Plato, *Republic*, 330d–331c. Special thanks to Lydia Winn, a Boston College philosophy graduate student, who verified the Stephanus numbers and the Bekker numbers for lines from Plato's *Republic* and Aristotle's *Nicomachean Ethics*, respectively.

3. Plato, *Republic*, 331c.

4. W. D. Ross famously takes up this notion using the example of breaking a promise to meet someone in order to help someone else instead. See Ross, *The Right and the Good*, 18.

5. A relevant and contemporary example of this is when an athlete competes through pain in order to follow through on a commitment to the team to achieve team goals. But there are limits to such sacrifices, further illustrating the notion that these principles are not absolute.

6. Aeschylus, *Agamemnon*. It is debatable whether Agamemnon faces a true dilemma, but it is frequently held up by scholars as an example of a dilemma. For instance, see Williams, "Ethical Consistency," 173–74, 181.

7. Sophocles, *Antigone*.

8. Kant, "Moral Duties"; and Mill, "Utilitarianism and Moral Conflicts."

9. Gowans, "The Debate on Moral Dilemmas," 10–12. See also Hegel, *Aesthetics*.

10. Bradley, "Collision of Duties"; and Gowans, "The Debate on Moral Dilemmas," 10–12.

11. Bradley, "Collision of Duties," 63.

12. Bradley, 73–79.

13. Stratton-Lake, "Intuitionism in Ethics."

14. Gowans, "The Debate on Moral Dilemmas," 12–14. For a description of this view and an argument against it, see Donagan, "Consistency in Rationalist Moral Systems," 291–93.

15. Sartre, *Existentialism Is a Humanism*, 30–34.

16. Williams, "Ethical Consistency."

17. Williams.

18. Williams, 170–71.

19. Williams, 179.

20. Williams, 171.

21. Daniel Statman takes this up at length and his use of the terms informs my understanding as I articulate it in this paragraph. See Statman, "Reality of Moral Dilemmas."

22. Tessman, *Moral Failure*, 15.

23. Hursthouse, *On Virtue Ethics*, 43–87.

24. Hursthouse, 46.

25. Hursthouse, 44–48.

26. Hursthouse, 63.

27. Hursthouse's example to illustrate Foot's point. Hursthouse, 66–68.

28. Hursthouse, 67.

29. Hursthouse, 68–77.

30. Hursthouse, 68.

31. Hursthouse, 69.

32. Hursthouse, 69–71.

33. Hursthouse, 71.

34. Hursthouse, 68.

35. Hursthouse, 36–39.

36. Marcus, "Moral Dilemmas and Consistency," 122.

37. Conee, "Against Moral Dilemmas," 87.
38. Sinnott-Armstrong, *Moral Dilemmas*, 5.
39. Sinnott-Armstrong, 6.
40. Sinnott-Armstrong, 6.
41. Sinnott-Armstrong, 29.
42. Sinnott-Armstrong, 29.
43. Sinnott-Armstrong, 30.
44. Sinnott-Armstrong, 11–15.
45. Sinnott-Armstrong, 29.
46. Sinnott-Armstrong, 15–22.
47. Sinnott-Armstrong, 20.
48. Nagel, "The Fragmentation of Value," 174.
49. Nagel, 175.
50. Nagel, 177. See also 175–77.
51. For a good summary of various philosophical views on how many obligations can conflict, see Dougherty, *Moral Dilemmas in Medieval Thought*, 4n5.
52. Foot, "Moral Dilemmas Revisited."
53. Foot, 184.
54. Tessman, *Moral Failure*, 223–28, 237–52.
55. Tessman, 15.
56. Tessman, "Against the Whiteness of Ethics"; and Tessman, *Burdened Virtues*.
57. Dougherty, *Moral Dilemmas in Medieval Thought*.
58. Dougherty, 3.
59. Dougherty, 6.
60. Walzer, "Political Action: The Problem of Dirty Hands."
61. Walzer, 162–64.
62. Walzer, 164–68, 178–80. In *Just and Unjust Wars*, Walzer gives the example from World War II of bombing German cities and killing many noncombatants as a case of "supreme emergency." In his later work "Emergency Ethics," Walzer suggests that only supreme emergency justifies dirty hands. In-depth discussions on "supreme emergency" and Walzer's evolution are beyond the scope of this book. See Walzer, "Emergency Ethics." See also Walzer, *Just and Unjust Wars*. And for a discussion on Walzer's evolution, see Coady, "The Problem of Dirty Hands." For Williams's view of dirty hands, see Williams, "Politics and Moral Character."
63. Cahill, *Blessed Are the Peacemakers*.
64. Cahill, viii.
65. Cahill, 297–312.
66. Cahill, 91–172. For more on my view of Cahill's take on this, see Jackson-Meyer, "Just War, Peace, and Peacemaking."
67. Marcus, "Moral Dilemmas and Consistency," 127.
68. Williams, "Conflicts of Values," 75.
69. Williams, "Ethical Consistency," 173. Note that Gowans implies that Williams's emphasis indicates an irresolvable dilemma, but I do not think that need be the case. See Gowans, "The Debate on Moral Dilemmas," 28–29.
70. Williams, "Conflicts of Values," 74.
71. Foot, "Moral Dilemmas Revisited," 186.
72. Foot, 187.

73. Quinn, "Agamemnon and Abraham," 183.
74. Quinn, 183.
75. Nussbaum, "Costs of Tragedy," 1014.
76. Nussbaum, 1015.
77. Gowans, *Innocence Lost*.
78. Gowans, 226.
79. Gowans, 226.
80. Gowans, 226.
81. Gowans, 226–28.
82. Gowans, 226.
83. Gowans, 227.
84. Hursthouse, *On Virtue Ethics*, 79. At one point, Hursthouse discusses tragic dilemmas in terms of irresolvable dilemmas but then modifies her position, stating, "And there seems to be no reason to suppose that these [tragic dilemmas] are always irresolvable dilemmas." Hursthouse, 78.
85. Hursthouse, 72–74.
86. Tessman, *Burdened Virtues*.
87. Tessman, 162.
88. Tessman, *Moral Failure*, 53, where Tessman uses the phrase "tragic dilemma" to describe the tragedy of a parent deciding the fate of her child. But when Tessman describes Sophie's case, 161–62, and the "Crying Baby" cases, 164–65—that are both essentially about parents deciding the fate of their children—she focuses on how they are moral dilemmas. I also take up Tessman's characterization of those events in the cases Celia K. and Clara L. describe in the introduction to this book.
89. Theological strategies for solving hard cases are taken up in chapters 2 and 3.
90. Ross, *The Right and the Good*, 20; 19. See also 18–36, 61–64.
91. Ross, 18.
92. Gowans, "The Debate on Moral Dilemmas," 12. See also Ross, "Prima Facie Duties," where Gowans has put together the most pertinent parts of Ross's work in one place.
93. Sinnott-Armstrong, *Moral Dilemmas*, 58–71.
94. Sinnott-Armstrong, 66–71 at 70.
95. Marcus, "Moral Dilemmas and Consistency," 125.
96. Donagan, "Consistency in Rationalist Moral Systems," 307.
97. McConnell, "Moral Dilemmas"; Tessman, *Moral Failure*, 16–24; and Sinnott-Armstrong, *Moral Dilemmas*, 74–81.
98. Bentham, *Collected Works*. See also Mill, *Utilitarianism*. Note that Mill amends Bentham's theory to account for some rights that should not be violated no matter what. A further discussion of this point is beyond the scope of this book.
99. Mill, "Utilitarianism and Moral Conflicts."
100. Stramondo, "Covid-19 Triage and Disability."
101. Emanuel et al., "Fair Allocation," 2052.
102. Hursthouse, *On Virtue Ethics*, 55.
103. Sayeed, "The Psychological Toll."
104. Nussbaum, "Costs of Tragedy." Nussbaum explains that a cost-benefit analysis is not necessarily a type of utilitarianism insofar as costs and benefits are not necessarily defined in terms of utility. She also explains that a cost-benefit analysis can include looking at inherent value or at something else as a cost or a benefit. When that is the case, it

is not a type of consequentialism when consequentialism is defined as only looking at consequences. Because of those reasons, I have given the approach its own subsection. See Nussbaum, 1028–30.

105. Nussbaum, 1028.
106. Nussbaum, 1032, 1021–22. There are many places to read more about Nussbaum's capabilities. For a good start, see Nussbaum, *Creating Capabilities.*
107. Nussbaum, "Costs of Tragedy," 1006–7.
108. Nussbaum, 1016–17.
109. Kant was a prolific writer. Key texts on this topic include but are not limited to Kant, *Critique of Practical Reason*; Kant, *The Metaphysics of Morals*; and Kant, *Groundwork for the Metaphysics of Morals.*
110. Hursthouse offers an alternative view. She believes that deontology denies irresolvable dilemmas due to its religious roots and "an inadequately explored view about what God's Providence would guarantee." Hursthouse, *On Virtue Ethics*, 66.
111. Kant, *The Metaphysics of Morals*, 16–17.
112. Kant, *The Groundwork for the Metaphysics of Morals*, 38; and Kant, *The Metaphysics of Morals*, 32. The content of these categories have been debated, and an in-depth discussion is beyond the scope of this book. For a brief review of how this relates to dilemmas see Gowans, "The Debate on Moral Dilemmas," 7. See also Hill, "Kant on Imperfect Duty and Supererogation" for an important article on this debate.
113. Gowans, "The Debate on Moral Dilemmas," 6.
114. There is more at stake than these principles, but an in-depth discussion of deontic logic is beyond my scope. For more on this, see McConnell, "Moral Dilemmas." See also Gowans, "The Debate on Moral Dilemmas," 20–27; and Tessman, *Moral Failure*, 18–24.
115. McConnell, "Moral Dilemmas."
116. McConnell.
117. McConnell. For a theological discussion on "ought implies can," see Couenhoven, "Indicative in the Imperative." Couenhoven's argument is taken up in more detail in the next chapter.
118. Notably, Williams does not focus his argument on denying "ought implies can"; rather, he denies the agglomeration principle, as I discuss in this chapter. For Williams on "ought implies can," see Williams, "Ethical Consistency," 180–81.
119. Marcus, "Moral Dilemmas and Consistency," 134.
120. Gowans, "The Debate on Moral Dilemmas," 20–22. See also Williams, "Ethical Consistency," 179–86. Both explain the agglomeration principle using the rules of logic, which informs how I describe it in this paragraph.
121. Williams, "Ethical Consistency," 179–86.
122. Williams acknowledges that some people will argue that obligations function differently than what is going on in this example. Williams explains that his main goal is to call into question the agglomeration principle by analogy to show that "it is not a self-evident datum of the logic of *ought*." Williams, 182.
123. Williams, 184.
124. Williams, 166–79.
125. Williams, 169. Although we all know some people (even ourselves) who happily hold contradictory beliefs, and while Williams acknowledges these cases, he regards them as outliers and not part of what constitutes belief. He also acknowledges that sometimes people possess "a desire for the belief to be true" and so "regret" giving up the belief.

Williams, 170. Desiring to hold a belief also seems to me to be an explanation for why logic does not always prevail when confronting a false belief. See Williams, 170.

126. Williams, 167.

127. Williams, 167.

128. My details, expanding on Williams's example of a lazy man who wants a drink.

129. Williams, "Ethical Consistency," 167.

130. Marcus, "Moral Dilemmas and Consistency," 129.

131. Marcus, 128–29.

132. McConnell, "Moral Dilemmas."

133. Williams, "Ethical Consistency," 179.

134. Hursthouse, On Virtue Ethics, 63–87.

135. Goldie, The Oxford Handbook of Philosophy of Emotion.

136. To read an introduction into the debate around the term emotions, see de Sousa, "Emotion." For examples of scholars in theology and philosophy who hold positive views of the relationship between emotions and ethics, see Cates, Aquinas on the Emotions; Jaycox, "Civic Virtues of Social Anger"; and Nussbaum, Upheavals of Thought.

137. Kauppinen, "Moral Sentimentalism." A full discussion of moral sentimentalism is the beyond my scope, but I hope here to introduce some main points.

138. Kauppinen.

139. Kotva, The Christian Case for Virtue Ethics.

140. Hume, A Treatise on Human Nature. See also Kauppinen, "Moral Sentimentalism."

141. Smith, "The Humean Theory of Motivation."

142. Nussbaum, Upheavals of Thought.

143. For the incident I am referring to, see "Opinion: Gratuitous Cruelty by Homeland Security." For an excellent discussion on the righteous anger of those who are oppressed, see Jaycox, "Civic Virtues of Social Anger."

144. Haidt, The Righteous Mind. See also Greene and Haidt, "How (and Where) Does Moral Judgment Work?"

145. Kauppinen, "Moral Sentimentalism."

146. Rawls, A Theory of Justice, 48–51. Tessman takes this up in Tessman, Moral Failure, 100–122.

147. Prinz, The Emotional Construction of Morals, 130–31. Prinz uses the child-kicking example in an illustrative and persuasive way.

148. Kant, "On a Supposed Right to Tell Lies from Benevolent Motives."

149. Singer, Practical Ethics, 151–45, 159–67.

150. Singer, "Ethics and Intuitions."

151. Williams, "Ethical Consistency."

152. Williams, 166.

153. Williams, 166.

154. Williams, 179.

155. Williams, 179.

156. Williams, 172.

157. Williams, 172.

158. Williams, 172.

159. Williams, 173.

160. Williams, "Conflicts of Values," 74.

161. Foot, "Moral Dilemmas Revisited," 185.

162. Williams, "Ethical Consistency," 174.

163. Williams, 174.

164. Williams, 174–75.

165. Williams, 175.

166. Williams, 175.

167. Donagan, "Consistency in Rationalist Moral Systems," 304. Donagan specifically disagrees with Marcus's conception of guilt in these cases, which is different from Williams's focus on regret. Nevertheless, Donagan's point is relevant here to the extent that he raises the idea that it is not one's feelings about promises that demonstrates seriousness about promises; rather, it is attention to the promises and "scrupulousness" that indicates seriousness about promises.

168. Williams, "Ethical Consistency," 184.

169. Williams, 175. Williams writes: "At this point, the objector might say that he still thinks the regrets [sic] irrational, but that he does not intend 'irrational' pejoratively: we must rather admit that an admirable moral agent is one who on occasion is irrational. This, of course, is a new position: it may well be correct."

170. Hursthouse, On Virtue Ethics, 44–48.

171. Hursthouse, 74.

172. Hursthouse, 75.

173. Hursthouse, 76.

174. Hursthouse, 76.

175. Hursthouse, 77.

176. Hursthouse, 74.

177. Hursthouse, 77.

178. Hursthouse says, "Doing what is, say, dishonest solely in the context of a tragic dilemma does not entail being dishonest, possessing that vice; it does not even provide any evidence for it." She discusses this in terms of the unity of the virtues. Note that in moral theology, this is also often seen as a distinction between the sin and the sinner. Further discussion of this point is beyond my scope. Hursthouse, 73n8.

179. In Moral Failure Tessman also points this out: "He [Williams] does not explain why a moral requirement would (or would not) survive even when overridden." Tessman, 30.

180. Foot, "Moral Dilemmas Revisited," 187.

181. Hursthouse, On Virtue Ethics, 83–87; Nussbaum, "Costs of Tragedy," 1019; Gowans, Innocence Lost, 121–27; Tessman, Moral Failure, 91–96; and Cahill, Blessed Are the Peacemakers, 161–62 at 62.

182. Hursthouse, On Virtue Ethics, 83. For her section on absolutism, see 83–87.

183. Hursthouse, 36–42, 60–61.

184. Hursthouse, 74.

185. Aristotle, The Nicomachean Ethics, 1107a10–11; quoted in Hursthouse, On Virtue Ethics, 58.

186. Nussbaum, "Costs of Tragedy," 1010.

187. Nussbaum, 1019.

188. Nussbaum, 1034.

189. Nussbaum, 1020–22. For more on Nussbaum's capabilities, see Nussbaum, Creating Capabilities.

190. Tessman, Moral Failure, 43. Later, I discuss Tessman's attempt to delineate these distinctions.

191. Nussbaum, *Creating Capabilities*, 6. Tessman also discusses this; see Tessman, *Moral Failure*, 41n47.
192. Gowans, *Innocence Lost*, viii. For Gowans on "responsibilities to persons," see 117–54.
193. Gowans, vii–viii.
194. Gowans, ix.
195. Gowans, 223.
196. Tessman, *Moral Failure*, 1. See also 27–28 and her section on these categories, 31–44.
197. Tessman, 1.
198. Tessman, 4, 42; see also 39–49. Tessman does a lot with Gowan's idea of "inconvertibility" that centers on conceptualizing when values do not have a "replace[ment]" or "substitute," Tessman, 33–39 at 33. Tessman differs from Gowans because she adds that "it is not always morally problematic to cause irreplaceable loss, for some losses, even if they are losses of something irreplaceable, are such an acceptable (and sometimes ultimately beneficial) part of human life that they can be treated as trade-offs," Tessman, 38.
199. Tessman, 14.
200. Tessman, 44, where Tessman helpfully uses a chart to summarize these two kinds of requirements. See also 31–55.
201. Tessman, 57–98.
202. Tessman, 94.
203. Tessman, 49–55.
204. My example building off of Tessman's point about requirements and "inhuman physical strength" in Tessman, 54.
205. Tessman, 54.
206. Tessman, 251.
207. Tessman, 247.
208. Gowans, "Review of *Moral Failure*," 1127.
209. Tessman, *Moral Failure*, 94–96 at 94; 120–22.
210. Tessman, 121.
211. Tessman, 100–122.
212. Tessman, 121. Having said that, Tessman does recognize that since values exist in community, others in the community can reflect on another's sacred value without the value-holder having to transgress the value. She gives the example of pro-choicers holding signs and debates making a case for abortion. This public or communal reflection allows pro-lifers to see others reflect on their sacred value (the fetus) without having to transgress the value themselves (imagine when abortion might be permitted). This kind of evaluation is permissible in Tessman's view. On this point, see Tessman, 136–38.
213. Tessman, 100–102, 127–28.
214. Tessman, 101.
215. Tessman, 121.
216. Thomson, "A Defense of Abortion." See also Tessman, *Moral Failure*, 243n28, where Tessman takes up Thomson's view in relation to Eva Feder Kittay.
217. Kamm, *Creation and Abortion*, 20–41.
218. Tessman, *Moral Failure*, 103–49.
219. Cahill, *Blessed Are the Peacemakers*, 162.
220. Tessman, *Moral Failure*, 167–72.
221. Tessman, 168.
222. Tessman 161–74. See also Langer, *Holocaust Testimonies*, 168–71.

223. Tessman, *Moral Failure*, 169–70. My account of Abraham P. relies on Tessman's description and analysis of Abraham P., and Tessman states that her account of Abraham P. derives from Langer's work in *Holocaust Testimonies*.

224. Tessman, 170.

225. Tessman, 170n20.

226. Williams, "Ethical Consistency."

227. Williams. For more on the distinction between remorse and regret, see McConnell, "Moral Dilemmas." In later work, Williams develops the concept of "agent-regret" as the kind of regret one feels because one is the actor in a situation. As it relates here, even when the agent is not blameworthy, the agent feels she should make up for the event in some way. Williams gives the example of the responsible truck driver who unintentionally runs over a child through no fault of the driver. The driver is not blameworthy but experiences "agent-regret" and so makes amends in some way. Expanding beyond the case exemplified by the driver, Williams explains that "agent-regret" shares with conflict cases the reality that one does not necessarily wish one had performed a different action. On this see Williams, "Moral Luck," 27–31.

228. Tessman, *Moral Failure*, 16.

229. Marcus, "Moral Dilemmas and Consistency," 130–33.

230. Nussbaum, "Costs of Tragedy," 1009.

231. Nussbaum, 1009n8.

232. Quinn, "Agamemnon and Abraham," 183.

233. Cahill, *Blessed Are the Peacemakers*, 127.

234. Hursthouse, *On Virtue Ethics*, 74. The full quote: "So to say that there are some dilemmas from which even a virtuous agent cannot emerge having acted well is just to say that there are some from which even a virtuous agent cannot emerge with her life unmarred—not in virtue of wronging (for *ex hypothesi*, in making a forced choice, the agent is blameless), and not in virtue of having done what is right or justifiable or permissible (which would sound very odd), but simply in virtue of the fact that her life presented her with *this* choice, and was thereby marred, or perhaps even ruined," Hursthouse, 74–75. She also notes that, according to Aristotle's discussion of Priam, Aristotle would probably agree that life can be marred but not ruined. On this, see Hursthouse, 75n11.

235. Foot, "Moral Dilemmas Revisited," 183.

236. Williams, "Conflicts of Values," 74. See also Williams, "Ethical Consistency," 172.

237. Hursthouse, *On Virtue Ethics*, 44.

238. Tessman, *Moral Failure*, 252.

239. Nussbaum, "Costs of Tragedy," 1011–17.

240. Cahill, *Blessed Are the Peacemakers*, 129, 131.

241. Gowans, *Innocence Lost*, 218–24.

242. Gowans, 219.

243. Foot, "Moral Dilemmas Revisited," 188.

2

PROBLEMS WITH AUGUSTINIAN
APPROACHES TO MORAL
AND TRAGIC DILEMMAS

Augustine and those who follow his approach, particularly Paul Ramsey, demonstrate an acute awareness of the difficulties of life in our fallen world, and they tend to pay special attention to the various decisions and trade-offs this involves. Augustine is known for his musings on the challenges of life and his struggles to do what he perceived to be right. Augustine does not explicitly address the topic of moral or tragic dilemmas, but his thinking interacts and overlaps with many of the themes invoked by those categories. Augustine addresses the expectation for the Christian to embody the example of Christ while living in a sinful world as well as the moral challenges that occur when navigating professional duties and other responsibilities inherent to living in a society. Ramsey, a twentieth-century Protestant theologian and ethicist, continues Augustine's legacy by using Augustine's thought to delve into debates on challenging and contentious questions in war and bioethics.

While both Augustine and Ramsey would likely deny the possibility that God's providence would lead a moral agent into a situation where any action involves some wrongdoing, close analysis of their theologies reveals areas of their thought that affirm the messiness of real life. Augustine's "wise judge" invites an analysis of Augustine's view of competing obligations, and his inability to put forward a cohesive anthropology that connects his ethics of both war and sex makes way for the possibility that killing in war is a problem that cannot be dealt with adequately without a concept of moral or tragic dilemmas. Ramsey's view of how love transforms justice is meant to create a blueprint for dealing with hard cases in ethics. However, when applying the tenets of love and justice, Ramsey seems to admit that some ethical events are not always fully resolved. Additionally, Ramsey's description of the

Christian politician reveals the complexities of shrewd decision-making in politics. While these are not moral or tragic dilemmas, per se, they are areas that reveal the need for a Christian notion of dilemmas.

AUGUSTINE

Augustine's (354–430) influential writings still animate Christianity today. Augustine lived in a volatile and tumultuous time.[1] He was born in Thagaste in Northern Africa and lived in Carthage, Rome, and Milan before becoming the Bishop of Hippo. He lived through dramatic political transition as he was born at a time when Christianity was legal, and his life spanned the rules of various emperors, including Theodosius I, who outlawed Roman worship practices. Before converting to Christianity, Augustine was a rhetoric professor in Carthage and a member of the church of Manichee. In Milan, Ambrose converted him through his intellectual rigor and inviting personality. Augustine became an official and confessing member of the Christian church in 387. Once he was a committed Christian, he teased out and clarified Christian positions through his debates with the Donatists and Pelagians. Augustine also defended Christianity from accusations that the Roman Empire fell because of Christianity. He took an allegorical approach to reading biblical texts, although at some points he adhered to literal interpretations of scripture.

For Augustine, the highest good is love of God.[2] In his view, we are called to love temporal goods in right order, but sin has corrupted the way we love those goods.[3] Grace comes through the Word and through the Holy Spirit.[4] For Augustine, "life eternal is the supreme good, death eternal the supreme evil, and that to obtain the one and escape the other we must live rightly."[5] Augustine's *Confessions* reveals his recognition of the difficulty inherent in following one's will.[6] For Augustine, original sin is pride, and the effects of the Fall manifest as concupiscence.[7] Concupiscence perverts our desires so that we put power, domination, sensuality, or materiality ahead of our love for God.[8]

Augustine feels deeply the difficulties of life and the tyranny of sin. He laments the woes of this life: "slights, suspicions, quarrels, war," "treachery" in relationships, judges compelled to torture, and "lamentable ignorance."[9] He bemoans the "misery of these necessities."[10] His sensitivity to these harsh realities may explain his enduring appeal.

Augustine develops an ethics of war following Ambrose, and it is later influentially promulgated by Aquinas. Augustine argues that war is justified when determined by right authority, done for just cause (peace), and performed with right intention.[11] He argues against war in the name of self-defense.[12]

Augustine also defends marriage against proponents of exclusive celibacy. He makes space for a view where both marriage is upheld as a good and celibacy is valorized.[13] He famously derives the three goods of marriage: procreation, fidelity, and sacrament.[14] In his view, procreation within marriage is good since procreation was part of Eden.

Augustine does not put forward a category of moral or tragic dilemmas, but he does have an appreciation for hard cases and life's difficulties, which is why it is interesting to consider what his thought offers on the topic. The scholarship on the relationship between Augustine and moral dilemmas tends to focus on what Augustine's judge suggests for the possibility of moral dilemmas. I use the case of the judge to investigate what Augustine contributes to the philosophical notion of "ought implies can," which has major implications for the categories of moral and tragic dilemmas. After addressing this, I call attention to Augustine's ambivalent anthropology revealed by comparing his sexual ethics and ethics of war. I suggest these inconsistencies are indicative of how his inability to properly name moral dilemmas disrupts the coherency of his work.

Augustine's Judge

In Book XIX of *City of God,* Augustine famously reflects on the "wise judge" who must torture the accused in order to gain information.[15] The judge is described as free from sin and yet unhappy. Lisa Sowle Cahill and Jesse Couenhoven offer analyses of this passage that are important for assessing how Augustine's judge relates to debates about moral dilemmas. Cahill focuses on the judge's unhappiness, while Couenhoven places the judge within a broader discussion of Augustine's view of the philosophical claim "ought implies can" (OIC).[16]

Augustine bemoans that torture is both a "misery" and a "necessity" in which the judge must partake due to both human ignorance and the demands of being a judge.[17] Augustine explains that the judge is tasked with determining the truth, but certainty is unlikely. Augustine draws out the reality that torture may bring about truth, or it might produce a false confession and an erroneous death sentence. Even in the best scenario, Augustine deplores that the accused person will be acquitted after having to suffer torture. For Augustine, lament is the most appropriate response to this stark reality.

In Augustine's view, the judge bears the weight of his noble and necessary profession. Augustine is clear that the judge does not sin, that this is the only way to perform the duties of a judge, and that it would be worse for the judge to refuse to participate in these duties. Augustine writes:

These numerous and important evils he does not consider sins; for the wise judge does these things, not with any intention of doing harm, but because his ignorance compels him, and because human society claims him as a judge. But though we therefore acquit the judge of malice, we must none the less condemn human life as miserable. And if he is compelled to torture and punish the innocent because his office and his ignorance constrain him, is he a happy as well as a guiltless man? Surely it were proof of more profound considerateness and finer feeling were he to recognize the misery of these necessities, and shrink from his own implication in that misery; and had he any piety about him, he would cry to God *"From my necessities deliver me."*[18]

In this passage, Augustine makes two crucial points of contact with the debates on dilemmas: the wise judge is guiltless and the wise judge is unhappy.

Cahill focuses on the judge's unhappiness to argue for the possibility of moral dilemmas within Augustine's thought. She writes, "If the judge is unhappy, he must be a man of compromised virtue."[19] She argues this is evidence for the possibility of a moral dilemma because in Augustine's moral system, virtue and happiness are aligned. As such, rightly ordered loves result in happiness. Why would the judge be unhappy, then, if he did the right thing? For Cahill, the judge's lack of guilt indicates that he acted rightly, yet his unhappiness indicates something is amiss. In Cahill's view, this decoupling of happiness and virtue points to the possibility of moral dilemmas.

It is necessary to unpack Augustine's description of the judge as lacking guilt. Augustine explicitly states that the judge does not commit a sin, he does not commit "malice," and he is "guiltless." Recall from chapter 1 of this book that moral and tragic dilemmas involve at least one moral obligation that remains in some way, even when the moral agent is unable to fulfill the obligation while acting in the best way possible. Recall, also, that there are discrepancies between different scholars regarding whether moral or tragic dilemmas involve moral transgressions or guilt. I have emphasized transgressions and great harm or marring as constitutive of, specifically, tragic dilemmas. Given the terrain of the debates around dilemmas, the judge could be guiltless *and* have participated in a moral or tragic dilemma. Does Augustine chart a path where the judge's obligations are unable to be eliminated *and* yet he is without guilt or sin? If so, this could suggest that the judge participates in a dilemma of some sort. Or does the lack of sin and guilt indicate that the judge does not participate in a dilemma? If so, does Augustine assume that the unmet moral obligations are lifted, thus denying the possibility of a dilemma?

The judge partakes in a dilemma if he is unable to fulfill all his obligations *and* if all his duties remain obligatory. Augustine's position on OIC will shed light on whether this is possible within his thought. As I discuss in chapter 1, while not all moral dilemma theorists deny OIC, many do deny OIC.

Augustine's wise judge navigates competing obligations, but the nature of those obligations is, at least initially, somewhat unclear. In his role, the judge is obligated to pursue justice by determining the truth of accusations. This is likely to involve torture, and it may even involve putting to death some innocent people. Are torturing innocent people and putting innocent people to death moral transgressions in Augustine's view? They seem to be, because Augustine calls them "numerous and important evils." Given this, the path to achieving justice will likely involve evils. The actions are evil because the judge is doing things he should not do—he should not torture the innocent, and he should not put to death the innocent. Yet he must perform these actions. He is therefore unable to fulfill all his obligations to determine the truth, to not torture the innocent, and to not kill the innocent.

The question for the topic of moral and tragic dilemmas is whether the unfulfillable obligations—not torturing the innocent, not putting the innocent to death—remain obligatory despite being impossible to fulfill all at once in the pursuit of justice. Or are these obligations lifted after the judge tries his best and determines the best course of action? The former makes way for the judge's participation in a dilemma, while the latter pushes against that possibility. Augustine's position on OIC can help unlock the answers to these questions.

Recall from chapter 1 that the force of OIC in the debate on dilemmas is that moral agents can only be morally obligated to actions that are achievable.[20] This can play out in a variety of ways. One way this happens is that OIC limits what counts as a moral obligation to begin with so that agents are never morally responsible for absurdities. For instance, following OIC, there is no obligation to deter an asteroid from hitting the earth if that requires technologies we don't have. Another way OIC influences ethical analyses is that OIC contends that obligations are lifted when they are impossible to fulfill due to the circumstances. So if one is obligated to perform both actions A and B but doing action A prevents one from doing action B (and vice versa), the moral agent is not morally obligated to perform both actions. After determining what action to perform, the obligation to the other action is lifted because it is impossible to do it after having performed the chosen action. So if someone determines that pursuing obligation A is the best course of action, obligation B is no longer an obligation because it is impossible to fulfill. On the contrary, denying OIC in that situation means that obligation B remains. While this is not the only way to argue for moral and tragic dilemmas, denying OIC creates the conditions for dilemmas by arguing that even after performing the best action possible, an obligation still remains unfulfilled.

The importance of OIC to the concept of moral dilemmas can be seen in the first case study in the introduction regarding the limited supply of ventilators during the coronavirus pandemic. Many patients need ventilators in order to have a chance to survive, but there are not enough for all who need them. If one affirms OIC, then so long as the hospital system acts in the best way possible (perhaps following the ethical advice of Daly or Emanuel and colleagues, as described in the introduction), the obligation is lifted to save those who need a ventilator but who do not receive one due to supply limits. The obligation is lifted because it is simply impossible to give every patient a ventilator. However, if one denies OIC, then the obligation to save those patients remains even if the task is impossible.

As it relates to Augustine, if Augustine denies OIC, then the judge is likely facing some kind of dilemma because all of his obligations remain despite his inability to fulfill them. But if Augustine accepts OIC, then the judge is not facing any kind of dilemma because he is not beholden to the unmet, impossible obligations—in fulfilling his duty as judge and deciding the best course of action, he has properly fulfilled all his obligations and he is not morally bound to obligations that are impossible to fulfill.

Couenhoven explains that Augustine debated with the Pelagians and Julian on the issue of OIC, with Augustine usually denying it and the Pelagians and Julian supporting it. Couenhoven explains that the main theological issues at stake in the debate as expressed by Julian are (1) whether or why God would demand something that is impossible to fulfill, and (2) whether ethical demands are useless for guiding ethics if people can't follow them.[21] Augustine argues for what Couenhoven describes as the "pedagogical function" of impossible obligations.[22] Augustine writes: "The Pelagians think that they know something great when they assert that 'God would not command what He knew could not be done by man.' Who can be ignorant of this? But God commands some things which we cannot do, in order that we may know what we ought to ask of Him. For this is faith itself, which obtains by prayer what the law commands."[23] As Couenhoven explains, according to Augustine, given our weaknesses and fallen state and our lack of "willpower or wisdom," we often find ourselves in situations where we are unable to do what is required of us.[24] Nevertheless, as Couenhoven interprets Augustine, the obligations often remain and are important because the obligations teach us how to behave, even if we cannot achieve them.[25]

This is famously echoed in Augustine's *Confessions*.[26] Augustine describes his difficulty with chastity, but it is certainly not the case that the demands of chastity are reduced or eliminated in response to Augustine's personal weaknesses. Rather, the unmet demands of chastity are instructive for how Augustine ought to live.

Couenhoven regards Augustine's description of the wise judge's predicament as one of a variety of ways that Augustine is not committed to OIC (the others being "volitional necessity" and "unavoidability").[27] Couenhoven contends that the situation of the judge is an example of "moral dilemmas" wherein Augustine seems to be saying that, no matter what, one acts "badly."[28] Couenhoven argues that "Augustine may have believed that the use of torture was acceptable in such situations, yet he was uncertain whether the judge who tortures can be absolved of all wickedness even if the judge acts with good intentions."[29] This interpretation suggests that the judge's obligations remain and that this is indicated by the existence of "wickedness" that cannot be totally undone. Couenhoven emphasizes Augustine's contention that the judge should ask God, "'Deliver me from my necessities'."[30] I take it that Couenhoven presumes that if the judge's actions were completely justified, then the judge would not have to pray for deliverance. I concur, and this suggests to me that some of the judge's unmet obligations retain their moral force.

However, there are other times that Augustine seems to gesture toward OIC, in Couenhoven's view.[31] For instance, Couenhoven notes that Augustine remarks on a situation when the dead are not buried because the city was sieged. Augustine says, "This is neither the fault of the living, for they could not render them; nor an infliction to the dead, for they cannot feel the loss."[32] So, then, no one is guilty or "at fault" for not burying their dead when it is impossible to do so. I suggest this is a qualification of OIC. Like the case of the judge, those who do not fulfill all their demands—in this case, those obliged to bury the dead—are not guilty. So there is no guilt, but do the obligations still remain? A key to figuring this out is the category of lament.

It is important to note that, unlike the situation involving the judge, in this scenario of being unable to bury the dead, Augustine does not lament. While the judge is miserable and ought to cry, that is not the case here. This seems to be because Augustine believes there is no great harm incurred. His belief in the lack of harm is indicated by his determination that the action is "nor an infliction to the dead, for they cannot feel the loss."[33] In Augustine's view, there is no great harm caused presumably because the dead have no idea they are not buried. The lack of lament here suggests to me that the obligation to bury the dead is completely lifted. This indicates a qualification for when obligations can be lifted: when they are impossible to fulfill *and* when no great harm occurs by not fulfilling the obligation. As it relates to the wise judge, the judge's obligations cannot be lifted because they involve great harms—not ascertaining the truth, torture, and death.

When thought of in terms of Tessman's distinction between negotiable and nonnegotiable obligations that I discuss in chapter 1, I contend that the situation with the judge involves nonnegotiable obligations that simply cannot all be met, yet that all remain. These are the nonnegotiable obligations to protect truth, not to torture, and not take innocent life. The judge's sadness is evidence of the fact that not all of the nonnegotiable obligations can be fulfilled, and yet they remain as obligations.

Importantly, Augustine laments in other places, such as when he justifies war. Augustine says of war, "Let every one, then, who thinks with pain on all these great evils, so horrible, so ruthless, acknowledge that this is misery. And if any one either endures or thinks of them without mental pain, this is a more miserable plight still, for he thinks himself happy because he has lost human feeling."[34] The lament that Augustine associates with war suggests that it involves great harm wherein the obligations cannot be lifted.

This qualification of OIC is particularly relevant to tragic dilemmas, which by definition cause great harm or personal marring. This suggests that OIC holds true for Augustine when no harm is done, but when great harm is done, an obligation cannot be lifted. Importantly, it is harm that differentiates nonnegotiable obligations from negotiable ones. This suggests that the obligations that define tragic dilemmas cannot be negated. Augustine's judge resonates with the theory of tragic dilemmas, specifically, in that certain obligations cannot be lifted when great harm ensues. Furthermore, Augustine's view of justified war as something to lament suggests that war resonates with tragic dilemmas and must be investigated further.

Augustine's Inconsistencies: Within Ethics of War

In addition to her interpretation of Augustine on the judge, Cahill also makes way for moral dilemmas in Augustine's thought because she regards his internal arguments about war to be inconsistent.[35] Augustine's predicament when developing a just war ethic is to defend war in light of Jesus's command in the Sermon on the Mount to love the enemy. As Cahill explains, Augustine develops two different modes of argumentation to overcome that challenge.

Cahill explains that Augustine offers a line of reasoning where war can be justified when it is out of love, analogous to "the loving father punishing his son."[36] In this view, Cahill explains, sometimes love requires harsh and even violent intervention and correction, and so war can fulfill the demands of the Sermon on the Mount to love the enemy. But elsewhere, as Cahill observes,

Augustine puts forward an alternate view wherein he says the Sermon on the Mount requires "not a bodily action, but an inward disposition."[37] Thus, in this second view, action and intention separate. This is problematic for Cahill because it is unclear what limits war and violence if only good intention matters. And if love justifies war, according to Augustine's view of loving punishment, why does Augustine go on to relegate the demands of the Sermon of the Mount to intention only?

Cahill suggests these tensions indicate that, when dealing with the problem of war, Augustine is implicitly dealing with moral dilemmas. Cahill writes, "The reality of moral dilemmas that cannot be satisfactorily resolved is attested by both Augustine's ambiguous views of killing in war and torture and the flawed analysis by which he squares them with Christian virtue."[38] Augustine's inability to offer a coherent justification of war suggests to Cahill that he is dealing with an ethical category he does not effectively attend to—moral dilemmas. I contend that there are additional inconsistencies in Augustine's work that support Cahill's claim, and I address them in the next section.

Augustine's Inconsistencies: Differing Theological Anthropologies for Sexual Ethics and War Ethics

When defending his ethics of war, Augustine employs a distinction between mind and body that is not found in his sexual ethics. Augustine's competing anthropologies are interesting in and of themselves, but what is crucial to dilemmas is the fact that Augustine uses contrasting anthropologies to deal with sexual ethics and ethics of war. I argue that these anthropological inconsistencies reveal a deep flaw within Augustine's ethics: that without a category of moral or tragic dilemmas, Augustine has no coherent way to deal with the problem (i.e., dilemma) of killing in war. To justify killing in war, Augustine develops a vision of the human person distinct from that which supports his views on sexual ethics. This, I argue, indicates the need for a category of dilemmas.

Let's take a closer look at these competing anthropologies, starting with the theological anthropology that informs Augustine's sexual ethics. Augustine is suspicious of sex. In Book XIV of *City of God*, he contrasts sex before and after the Fall, idealizing sex before the Fall.[39] Before the Fall, sex would have been under the control of will.[40] But according to Augustine, the will is impaired as a result of the Fall. Consequently, after the Fall, intention and reason can do little to control lust. This is why sex is so troubling to Augustine. He explains that sexual lust is the immediate aftermath of the Fall described in Genesis by the line "'the eyes of them both were opened.'"[41] As a result, Augustine believes that the error of the Fall is recapitulated in sexual lust.[42]

At times it seems as if Augustine suggests that it is impossible to have sex without uncontrollable lust. This is evident in *City of God* when Augustine describes the state of sex and procreation and the power of lust: "But even those who delight in this pleasure are not moved to it at their own will, whether they confine themselves to lawful or transgress to unlawful pleasures."[43] Augustine's pessimistic attitude toward sex is not lost on his interlocuters. Historian Peter Brown describes Augustine's sexual theology from Julian's point of view, a contemporary of Augustine who saw that Augustine's ideas are undergird by a belief in "a permanent derangement of the sexual urge."[44]

Yet, at other times, Augustine seems to maintain that non-lustful sex (and therefore non-sinful sex) is possible but under particular circumstances. For instance, in *The Excellence of Marriage* he explains that sex in marriage is "blameless" so long as it is for procreation.[45] But sexual activity that is narrowly focused on procreation without falling into lust seems unlikely, or at least rare, given Augustine's understanding of lust.

The overall thrust of Augustine's sexual ethics is to defend the close relationship between what one's body does and what one's mind intends. This is evident in *The Excellence of Marriage* when Augustine writes that celibacy is not simply a disposition but also a behavior: "They see that the virtue of celibacy ought always be present as a habitual disposition of mind, but it has to manifest itself in behavior according to the demands of different times and circumstances."[46] In these ways, Augustine sears together the bodily act of sex with lust.

With the threat of sexual lust looming, it is unsurprising that in *The Excellence of Marriage* Augustine devises a thorough scheme of sexual ethics denoted by various hierarchies of sexual activities.[47] For instance, he asserts that sex with one's spouse for pleasure is a "venial sin," but this is less sinful than sex outside of marriage.[48] Fornication and adultery are "mortal sin[s]."[49] However, of adulterers, adulterous acts with the same partner are better than adulterous acts with different partners.[50] Non-procreative sex in marriage is better than sex with a concubine in order to have a child.[51] And he suggests not to draw ethical conclusions from the behavior of the patriarchs of the Hebrew Scriptures because they had different expectations.[52] Non-procreative sex with one's wife is better ("a venial sin") than non-procreative sex with a mistress ("a mortal sin").[53] And kinky sex with one's wife is worse than sex of the same kind with one's mistress, in Augustine's view.[54]

But in matters of war and killing, Augustine has a different approach. As with sex, Augustine knows temptation is present and sin is likely. However, here the actions of the body—fighting and killing—do not easily lead to participation in sin. Unlike in matters of sexual ethics, in the case of war,

Augustine is optimistic about the possibility for intention and circumstance to temper the action of the body in order to prevent lust. As a result, he promotes a rather permissive ethics of war.

As with sex, Augustine worries about what kind of sinful dispositions war can produce. In *Contra Faustum* Augustine writes, "The real evils in war are love of violence, revengeful cruelty, fierce and implacable enmity, wild resistance, and the lust of power, and such like."[55] He calls these problematic dispositions the "evils of war" rather than the loss of lives being the evils of war. And in *City of God* he worries about the ways the *libido dominandi*—lust for domination—drives the actions of the earthly city.[56]

Augustine recognizes that one can experience *libido dominandi* on the battlefield, but this does not steer his ethics of war. Rather, he focuses on the goods at stake. For Augustine, war has the potential to bring earthly peace, which all people on Earth can enjoy as an approximation of the peace in the city of God.[57] Cahill explains that, in Augustine's view, the good of war comes about when war is enacted out of love and according to the proper criteria: "The peace of this world, even when requiring force or violence, is of instrumental value to members of the heavenly city in their earthly journey."[58] Unlike his treatment of sex, Augustine emphasizes the good of war with less focus on the pernicious dispositions it can encourage.

Given that sin is less imminent in the situation of war as opposed to sexual intercourse, in his estimation, Augustine's war ethics are somewhat vague and lack the many prescriptions found in his sexual ethics. Augustine's criteria for just war are well known and are discussed earlier in this chapter: legitimate authority, right intention, and just cause. His defense of war is tied to his understanding of the role of the Christian to love so that it may be appropriate to use war to punish if it is for the good of society.[59] Outside the just war framework, he offers very few rules. There is a restriction where he disavows self-defense, but otherwise his war ethics are disturbingly permissive.[60] For instance, he offers no recommendations for curbing government behavior, and he finds coercion to be a reasonable method of governing, saying little on the limits and bounds of coercion.[61]

Unlike Augustine's approach to sexual ethics, in his approach to war ethics the actions of the body are not so closely related to sin. He says this clearly in the quote previously noted, when he tells Faustus that the Sermon on the Mount is not about behavior but about disposition. Recall that, in that response, Augustine says of Jesus's exhortation to turn the other cheek: "What is here required is not a bodily action, but an inward disposition."[62] So an agent's body can kill and yet be so focused on God as to avoid experiencing lust or love of violence. But, according to Augustine, during an act of sex it is almost impossible for the will and mind to prevent sinful, lustful thoughts. While the bodily act of sex is generally connected to a corrupted disposition, killing is not. In this way, his approach to determining the ethics of war is in tension with his approach to sexual ethics. Augustine offers a very optimistic view of what actions are possible without falling into lust amid war, whereas this is close to an impossibility when dealing with sex.

Culling his system for how he deals with hard cases reveals that Augustine possesses divergent anthropologies to deal with sexual ethics and war ethics. This indicates a shortcoming within his systematic thought. I argue this occurs because he is circling around the problem of tragic dilemmas—killing in war—but without acknowledging a category of dilemmas. Without an explicit concept of tragic dilemmas to deal with the problem of killing in war, Augustine is forced to rework his anthropology to justify killing. As a result, he has two divergent anthropologies for treating the ethics of sex and war. While one does not necessarily need to ascribe to Augustine's anthropology in order to confirm (or deny) moral and tragic dilemmas, the mere existence of the inconsistency reveals the limits of his ethical system and its inability to properly attend to killing in war. The anthropological assumptions he makes in order to justify killing in war are contrary to the anthropological assumptions in his sexual ethics. This demonstrates that his framework cannot adequately deal with the problem of tragic dilemmas.

Augustine's approach differs from that of Aquinas, who implements various strategies to deal with hard cases, such as the hierarchy of goods and what would become the principle of double effect. These are taken up in the next chapter.

RAMSEY

Ramsey (1913–88) was an American Protestant ethicist who wrote prolifically from around the 1940s until near his death. Ramsey was greatly influenced by Augustine. His ethics are rooted in Christian neighbor-love, and early in his career he focused on the power of love to transform justice. His writing explores the ethics of war and bioethics, and within those applied ethical areas he frequently explores hard cases.

Ramsey's writings are numerous. He entered into various debates of his day but never put forward a systematic theology or ethical system. Within his vast writings, a few key texts mark major ideas and developments of his thought.[63] In *Basic Christian Ethics*, Ramsey develops his approach to

Christian ethics that is fundamentally rooted in Christian neighbor-love as exemplified by Jesus.[64] In *Nine Modern Moralists*, Ramsey uses Fyodor Dostoevsky's example of how Rodion Raskolnikov's character in *Crime and Punishment* devolves as evidence of the idea that actions lack meaning without Christ.[65] Later, in *War and the Christian Conscience*, Ramsey unpacks how *agape* guides the ethics of war, showcasing the ways Christ makes a difference to ethics.[66] In this text Ramsey follows Augustine's focus on love in war but emphasizes noncombatant immunity and what Cahill describes as "love for the innocent victims of aggression."[67] Ramsey goes on to apply *"fidelity to covenant"* to bioethics in *Patient as Person*.[68] And *Speak up for Just War or Pacifism* is Ramsey's return to the ethics of war toward the end of his career, and the work showcases his pastoral concerns.[69]

Ramsey argues that Jesus had an "apocalyptic outlook," meaning that Christian ethics should be focused on neighbor-love and obedience to God as determined by the demands of the kingdom of God.[70] From this eschatological view, Christianity serves as "a criticism of any civilization, religious or otherwise," and Jesus shows us how to live.[71]

Ramsey permits killing in order to save the life of the neighbor. This is because the demands of love that arise out of his eschatological vision are absolute demands. Ramsey writes, "That Jesus Christ is the standard for measuring the reign of God among men is essentially a correct however astounding a claim."[72] For Ramsey, this is lived out as radical love of the neighbor.

David Smith offers an analysis of Ramsey's approach to certain kinds of cases—hard cases of the sort that Smith calls "'conflict' cases."[73] As Ramsey is primarily concerned with the ethics of war and bioethics, the conflict case framework essentially captures much of Ramsey's writings. Framing Ramsey's work as Smith does highlights the enormous overlap with theories of moral and tragic dilemmas insofar as Ramsey deals head on with the problem of conflicting obligations, even though Ramsey himself does not use the lens of moral or tragic dilemmas as defined here.

Smith's critiques of Ramsey point to areas that Ramsey treats insufficiently. For instance, Smith argues that Ramsey does not offer a systematic way to assess various gradations of force and coercion in war.[74] Smith explains that this does not mean Ramsey does not recognize a moral difference between different kinds of force but rather that he offers little to assess specific cases. Smith criticizes Ramsey's definition of love as "radically altruistic" in its expectation of "absolute covenant fidelity to the neighbor."[75] Smith points out that a less extreme view of love, such as Aquinas's idea of love as friendship, is able to set limits on neighbor-love by determining what is required to properly love

God and oneself. In this view, Smith explains, one can't save a friend's life if it requires committing a sin. Smith also criticizes Ramsey's view for lacking an appreciation of sin. Smith says, "He never explicitly says that sin *causes* conflict."[76] This critique is interesting because it is likely that Ramsey's Augustinian worldview and its emphasis on sin is in part what leads him to address hard cases. Nevertheless, the implication of Smith's critique is that Ramsey fails to recognize the sins and sinful social structures that often create conflicts.

While Ramsey does not explicitly lay out a theory of moral or tragic dilemmas, he recognizes those times when the demands of love and justice seem incompatible, and he recognizes the complex demands of the Christian politician. I suggest that these are the closest approximations to moral and tragic dilemmas in Ramsey's thought.

Ramsey on Love and Justice

Ramsey does not deal explicitly with the topic of moral or tragic dilemmas. Presumably, in his thought, following the demands of Christian neighbor-love and justice will ensure that there are no unmet moral obligations. Yet, at times, when employing love and justice in real-life cases such as abortion, Ramsey acknowledges their limits. This suggests that hard cases cannot all be neatly solved in his system. I argue that Ramsey approximates moral and tragic dilemmas by hinting at the possibility for some uncleanliness that can occur when acting in hard situations even after love transforms justice.

Ramsey deals with the categories of love and justice to varying degrees throughout his career.[77] Charles Curran notes that while in the 1950s and early '60s Ramsey emphasizes love and justice, in the '60s and '70s Ramsey shifts to focus more on order, force, and sin.[78]

Nevertheless, Ramsey is known for his belief in the power of love to transform justice. Ramsey understands justice through Jesus: "Jesus Christ must be kept at the heart of all Christian thinking about justice."[79] Thus, the demands of justice are made known through Christ. For instance, in his work on war, Ramsey interprets just war theory and its potential to restrain war not in terms of natural law, as just war is classically articulated, but rather as a requirement of love.[80] In doing so, he stakes a position that is appreciative of natural law and what it can offer Protestant ethics but that is not wholly dependent on a natural law approach.

For Ramsey, sometimes love and justice align, and other times justice puts forward a minimum threshold for behavior while love expects more, but there are still other times when he recognizes that love and justice split apart.[81] In fact, Ramsey contends that at these times love may seemingly require the opposite of justice. This is when love transforms justice, in Ramsey's view, because love requires a totally new vision of what is right and just.

Within his optimism for the compatibility of love and justice, Ramsey notes that right action will not always be easy. This is seen in his early work when he recognizes the existence of hard cases: "Participation in regrettable conflict falls among distasteful tasks which sometimes become imperative for Christian vocation. Only one thing is necessary: for love's sake it must be done."[82] Ramsey rejects standing on the sidelines and trying to avoid messy conflicts; instead he advocates for action. As such, he believes that Christian convictions should impel one to get involved, even (especially) when right action is hard or uncomfortable.

The difficulty of action and the limits of love and justice are seen when Ramsey turns to a difficult abortion case in *War and the Christian Conscience*. Ramsey analyzes the very rare event where a fertilized egg from an ectopic, tubal pregnancy moves and begins to grow in the woman's abdomen.[83] The woman's life is in danger, and it is unlikely that the growing fetus will thrive. Ramsey takes on the Roman Catholic view as represented by theologian T. Lincoln Bouscaren, who argues for using the principle of double effect and concludes that there is no way to indirectly terminate the fetus in such a case. As a result, there are no licit interventions available until the fetus is viable and can be removed, or until the placenta detaches naturally, prompting interventions to prevent likely fatal hemorrhaging in the woman.

Ramsey thinks the prohibition against direct killing is problematic here because inaction may lead to the death of both the fetus and the woman. The prohibition is squarely rooted in justice, and this troubles Ramsey. He writes, "I suggest that it would be *wrong*, and not only exceedingly regrettable and a suffering to be referred to the providence of God, for a physician to stand by and, by failing to take indirect or, if need be, direct action, for him to allow both to die."[84] This mistake happens, according to Ramsey, because relying solely on the natural law does not make space for "divine charity."[85] In this case, Ramsey claims love and justice split apart. He writes:

> At the point of decision in a concrete case there takes place a convergence of judgments guided in these ways, a convergence in which sometimes love does what justice requires and assumes its rules as norms, sometimes love does more than justice requires but never less, and sometimes love acts in a quite different way from what justice alone can enable us to discern to be right.[86]

In light of this, Ramsey argues that something new is required—a reimagining of what is right—and this is how love transforms justice. Ramsey is very clear that this should not be thought of as doing wrong in the name of right, nor is it that the end justifies the means. Rather, it is that the demands of charity in relation to a specific case require a reimagining of what is right and wrong: "It is, therefore, worth repeating here that what I have suggested means a fresh determination of what is right in a given context in which the requirements of love prevail, and that right should not be determined by the natural law alone."[87] If inaction in the name of righteousness permits someone to die, then Ramsey proposes that there must be rethinking of what is "right."

This is akin to a tragic dilemma because life is at stake, and saving the mother involves an action that some consider a transgression. Recall that within the theory of moral and tragic dilemmas, obligations remain even after discerning the right course of action. In a tragic dilemma, a transgression is performed and great harm or marring occurs. For Ramsey, on the other hand, the category of wrong as determined by natural justice is reimagined so that it no longer holds in its prior form. Ramsey revises ethics in a particular situation so the act previously thought of as a transgression— directly killing the fetus to the save this woman, in this case—is no longer a transgression. This solves the issue of a possibly lingering moral obligation because all obligations are fulfilled when the demands are totally reworked.

Even though the obligations are theoretically satisfied within his system by reimagining what is right, Ramsey's language in this case hints at the impossibility of fully transforming the transgression. He explains that getting involved when love and justice separate requires the physician to dirty his hands according to natural law ethics: "One thing charity will never allow him to do namely, to stand by idle while two of the companions God has given him inevitably die from 'natural' causes or processes when one might have been saved had he been willing to soil his hands by performing an action which, according to his view of natural-law means, was defined as wrong."[88] Presumably, for Ramsey, the physician is misguided in thinking the action is wrong and will taint him. But the metaphor of soiled hands is curious and suggests to me something about the obstinate nature of the obligation—perhaps that the transgression isn't totally transformed since it may involve uncleanliness. This is further supported in how Ramsey discusses the politician, which I discuss in the next section. This gives the sense that Ramsey does not necessarily think love transforms all wrongs, but this is not something he takes up at length. The possibility for soiled hands even when justice is transformed by love is important for the notion of moral or tragic dilemmas because it suggests that Ramsey hints at the possibility that love does not metamorphosize everything, so love cannot ensure that all obligations are fulfilled. This has resonance with the theories of moral and tragic dilemmas, which claim there are "leftovers" when adjudicating cases of dilemmas.

Ramsey's Christian Politician

Ramsey attempts to navigate the tensions between Christian demands and secular demands when it comes to the Christian politician. His view of the politician is presumably informed by his understanding of the relationship between Christianity and politics. Ramsey is adept at adapting his arguments to his audience. As James T. Johnson highlights, Ramsey argues on Christian grounds when addressing Christians and on secular grounds when addressing secular persons.[89] Johnson asserts that Ramsey's position relies on Augustinian thought, and he explains Ramsey's view in this way:

> The presence of love in earthly politics is what makes it *right* politics, and it is this *right* politics, transformed internally by love, to which Ramsey appeals as the basis for "inherent," "systemic" restrains on warfare. It is not necessary for this conception of the work of charity that it be visible for all to see; yet for Ramsey faith knows that it is there when justice is being done and the world is thereby being transformed.[90]

So then, according to Ramsey and lived out in his approach to ethics, Christians can work for Christian ideals using secular reasoning to build a consensus in a pluralistic society.

But political consensus building is a lengthy and complex process. As such, Ramsey contends that the Christian politician may find herself in a situation where it is judicious to support the "nation's preparations for unjust warfare" as a tactic to achieving a greater goal.[91] In this case, Ramsey says, "Meantime, repentance may have to be deferred, if only to gain the time necessary to persuade public opinion to support that action which a statesman may wish to take."[92] In this way, Ramsey indicates that it is sometimes impossible to be a shrewd politician and satisfy Christian demands *at the same time*. This is because a politician may have to accept both a compromise agreement and a compromised position that she knows she will have to repent for later. But she accepts the deal at the present time as a means to a greater goal.

Dirtying oneself in politics is better than abandoning politics completely, according to Ramsey. He writes, "This may be better than keeping personal conscience clean by getting out of office."[93] For Ramsey, politics requires moral compromises that dirty one's conscience.

Invoking cleanliness yet again to describe the fallout of hard cases further suggests that Ramsey recognizes that not all conflicts are neatly solved. In the previous description of love transforming justice, the moral agent may perceive her hands to be dirty. In the case of the politician, no obligations are transformed, but the prudent and effective politician must perform some transgressions on the way to achieving a greater goal. As a result, her conscience is dirtied. She knows she will repent, but she will wait to repent until her ultimate goal is achieved. This tracks moral dilemmas generally because it is impossible for the politician to fulfill all her Christian obligations at once while in office. This tracks tragic dilemmas when the compromise involves a transgression and causes great harm or marring, such as when lives will be inevitably lost in war. As such, the politician makes moral concessions in order to accomplish her goals, and these concessions are very much like the moral transgressions that occur in a tragic dilemma.

In this chapter, I have drawn out ways that Augustine and Ramsey hint at moral and tragic dilemmas in cases where moral conflicts are not adequately solved. Augustine's judge laments the misery of the necessities that he must perform as judge. I suggest that lament, for Augustine, arises from obligations that cannot be negated because not fulfilling the obligations causes great harm. Obligations that cannot be lifted in a situation that causes great harm are the defining marks of a tragic dilemma. Thus, Augustine's wise, lamenting judge makes connections with concepts in moral and tragic dilemmas.

Furthermore, the theological anthropologies that undergird Augustine's views of sexual ethics and ethics of war are in tension. These inconsistencies reveal that Augustine makes unconvincing and strained arguments to justify killing in war. This is perhaps because it is very hard to make sense of killing in war without a category of tragic dilemmas. War should be considered akin to a tragic dilemma insofar as it involves lament and great harm.

Ramsey preaches the power of Christian love, yet the details within his arguments betray the possibility for unsolved hard cases and dirty hands. While love and justice can be mutually informing, he explains that that is not always the case. He explains that sometimes the demands of love and justice direct one in opposite ways. And during those times, love transforms what was previously thought to be "wrong," in Ramsey's view. But, while this should solve hard cases, one may be left wondering if this truly does. This resonates with moral and tragic dilemmas insofar as Ramsey is grappling with the nature of conflicting obligations.

Ramsey's description of the Christian politician illustrates his recognition that agents may make moral compromises in an effort to achieve a greater goal. He offers no explanatory theory for how this moral conundrum is solved, other than through repentance. This suggests that Christian politicians may face moral or tragic dilemmas. These are akin to tragic dilemmas when they involve transgressions and great harm or personal marring.

NOTES

1. Brown, *Augustine of Hippo*; and O'Donnell, "Augustine: His Time and Lives." I rely on these scholars for the information in this paragraph.
2. Augustine, *On the Nature of Good*, 1.
3. Augustine, *City of God*, 15.22.
4. Augustine, *On Grace and Free Will*.
5. Augustine, *City of God*, 19.4.
6. Augustine, *The Confessions of St. Augustine*.
7. Burns, "Augustine on Evil," 24.
8. Augustine, *City of God*, 14.28.
9. Augustine, 19.5, 19.6.
10. Augustine, 19.6.
11. In *ST* II-II q.40 a.1, Aquinas attributes these just war criteria to Augustine according to the following sources: Augustine, *Contra Faustum*, 75 (right authority); Augustine, QQ. in Hept., qu. x, super Jos (just cause); Augustine, *Contra Faustum*, 74 (right intention). Note that the just cause criteria can be found in Augustine, "Sixth Book—Questions on Joshua the Son of Nun."
12. Augustine, *On Free Choice of the Will*, Book 1, Chapter V.
13. Augustine, *The Excellence of Marriage*, 10.
14. Augustine, 32.
15. Augustine, *City of God*, 19.6.
16. "Ought implies can" and its connection to moral dilemmas is first discussed in chapter 1 of this book. I also take up Cahill on Augustine and dilemmas elsewhere. See Jackson-Meyer, "Just War, Peace, and Peacemaking," 91–92.
17. Augustine, *City of God*, 19.6.
18. Augustine, 19.6.
19. Cahill, *Blessed Are the Peacemakers*, 103.
20. Chapter 1 of this book. See also McConnell, "Moral Dilemmas"; and Couenhoven, "Indicative in the Imperative." The work of McConnell and Couenhoven inform the understanding of OIC that I describe here.
21. Couenhoven, "Indicative in the Imperative," 74–79.
22. Couenhoven, 75.
23. Augustine, *On Grace and Free Will*, Chapter 32. For where Couenhoven takes up this quote, see Couenhoven, "Indicative in the Imperative," 74.
24. Couenhoven, "Indicative in the Imperative," 79.
25. Couenhoven, 79.
26. Augustine, *Confessions*, VIII.
27. Couenhoven, "Indicative in the Imperative," 79.
28. Couenhoven, 77.

29. Couenhoven, 77.
30. Couenhoven, 77.
31. On this point, see Couenhoven, 74–78, especially 75. Note that Couenhoven goes on to argue for "an Augustinian alternative to OIC," what he calls "ought implies apt" or "OIA," Couenhoven, 84. Essentially, in this view, moral agents are not obligated to duties that are outside their "design plan," and this limits what can even be considered obligatory, independent of the circumstances, Couenhoven, 84. More attention to this view is beyond the scope of this book. For more on this, see Couenhoven, 84–90.
32. Augustine, *City of God*, 1.13. See also Couenhoven, "Indicative in the Imperative," 75.
33. Augustine, *City of God*, 1.13. Note that the position Augustine takes seems to contradict ancient ideas of the importance of burying the dead, evident in texts such as Sophocles's *Antigone*. A discussion of how Augustine's view coheres with other ancient literature is beyond the scope of this book. The main point for this work is that Augustine clearly states that the dead do not experience an "infliction" when they are not buried in a situation where it is impossible to bury them. Thanks to David Cloutier for pointing out the need to clarify this.
34. Augustine, *City of God*, 19.7.
35. Cahill, *Blessed Are the Peacemakers*, 91–137.
36. Cahill's description in Cahill, *Blessed Are the Peacemakers*, 112. See also Augustine, "Letter 138, to Marcellinus," 14; and Augustine, "Sermon on the Mount," 1.20.63.
37. Augustine, *Contra Faustum*, 22.76. See also Cahill, *Blessed Are the Peacemakers*, 114.
38. Cahill, *Blessed Are the Peacemakers*, 91.
39. Cahill, "Using Augustine in Contemporary Sexual Ethics," 26–27. For a fascinating interpretation that shows how Augustine's view of sex before the Fall may have been welcomed in his time, see Cavadini, "Feeling Right," 204–8. Cavadini offers a sympathetic view of Augustine in relation to sex and pleasure.
40. Augustine, *City of God*, 14.24.
41. Augustine, 14.17.
42. Brown, *The Body and Society*, 387–427.
43. Augustine, *City of God*, 14.16.
44. Brown, *Body and Society*, 412. Brown's description of Julian's understanding of Augustine.
45. Augustine, *The Excellence of Marriage*, 11.
46. Augustine, 26.
47. On this point, I owe my gratitude to Francine Cardman, whose course at Boston College School of Theology and Ministry prompted a discussion on Augustine's ranking approach to sexual activities.
48. Augustine, *The Excellence of Marriage*, 6, 12.
49. Augustine, 6.
50. Augustine, 4.
51. Augustine, 16.
52. Augustine, 18.
53. Augustine, 12.
54. Augustine, 12.
55. Augustine, *Contra Faustum*, 22.74.
56. Augustine, *City of God*, Preface, 1, and 14.28.
57. Augustine, 19.17.
58. Cahill, *Blessed Are the Peacemakers*, 102.

59. Augustine, *City of God*, 19.7. See also Augustine, *Contra Faustum*, 22.74.

60. Augustine, *On Free Choice of the Will*, Book 1, Chapter V.

61. Cahill, *Blessed Are the Peacemakers*, 109–21.

62. Augustine, *Contra Faustum*, 22.76; Cahill also discusses this passage, as I discuss earlier. See Cahill, *Blessed Are the Peacemakers*, 114.

63. For a good analysis of this, see Davis, "Paul Ramsey and Augustinian Ethics." Davis's article has greatly informed my understanding of Ramsey's various works as I describe them in this paragraph.

64. Ramsey, *Basic Christian Ethics*.

65. Ramsey, *Nine Modern Moralists*, 11–55.

66. Ramsey, *War and the Christian Conscience*.

67. Cahill, *Blessed Are the Peacemakers*, 115. Cahill discusses Ramsey's position on noncombatant immunity in Cahill, 33.

68. Ramsey, *The Patient as Person*, xlv.

69. Ramsey, *Just War or Pacifism*.

70. Ramsey, *Basic Christian Ethics*, 44.

71. Ramsey, 44.

72. Ramsey, 44.

73. Smith, "Paul Ramsey, Love and Killing," 3.

74. Smith, 6–7.

75. Smith, 8.

76. Smith, 7.

77. Kaveny, *Ethics at the Edges*, 141.

78. Curran, "Paul Ramsey and Natural Law Theory," 55.

79. Ramsey, *Basic Christian Ethics*, 17.

80. Carnahan, *Reinhold Niebuhr and Paul Ramsey*, 199–230.

81. Ramsey, *War and the Christian Conscience*, 178.

82. Ramsey, *Basic Christian Ethics*, 184.

83. Ramsey, *War and the Christian Conscience*, 172–86. Note that I discuss the principle of double effect in the next chapter. The main point here is that this hard case causes Ramsey to delve into how love transforms justice in a way pertinent to my discussion.

84. Ramsey, *War and the Christian Conscience*, 176.

85. Ramsey, 176.

86. Ramsey, 178.

87. Ramsey, 185.

88. Ramsey, 179.

89. Johnson, "Just War in the Thought of Paul Ramsey," 191–93. For a different view of Ramsey on Christianity and politics, particularly as it relates to the law, see Kaveny, *Ethics at the Edges*, 138–68.

90. Johnson, "Just War in the Thought of Paul Ramsey," 194.

91. Ramsey, *War and the Christian Conscience*, 311.

92. Ramsey, 311.

93. Ramsey, 311.

3

PROBLEMS WITH THOMISTIC APPROACHES TO MORAL AND TRAGIC DILEMMAS

This chapter examines moral and tragic dilemmas from the theological perspective of Thomas Aquinas and the Thomistic tradition. I argue that while Aquinas and traditional interpretations of Thomistic thought deny moral and tragic dilemmas, Aquinas's treatment of mixed actions admits the ambiguity of hard cases. Aquinas is a formidable interlocutor because his work raises theological challenges for the concepts of moral and tragic dilemmas. As with much philosophical literature, the focus of Aquinas and Thomistic scholars is often on moral dilemmas generally, without major special attention to tragic dilemmas. As such, this chapter first attends to moral dilemmas with the understanding that this has important implications for the existence of tragic dilemmas. Toward the end of the chapter I make connections between Aquinas's work and tragic dilemmas specifically.

This chapter explores Aquinas's claim that moral dilemmas are the result of an agent's sinfulness. Aquinas is optimistic that hard cases can be solved and, following suit, Thomists have navigated apparent moral dilemmas primarily using Aquinas's hierarchy of goods and the principle of double effect. But I argue that these solutions are unsatisfying because they do not account for the incommensurability of goods and what it means to sacrifice one good for another. I also show how the principle of double effect is limited. I then identify undeveloped points of contact and departure between Aquinas and philosophical thought on the issue of moral and tragic dilemmas. I argue that Aquinas's reference to "repugnance of the will" provides an expanded account of intention that challenges present-day usage of the principle of double effect, and I contend that Aquinas's attention to mixed actions provides new ground to reflect on moral and tragic dilemmas within Thomistic ethics.

TRADITIONAL VIEWS OF AQUINAS ON MORAL DILEMMAS

Writing as Dominican friar in the thirteenth century, Aquinas (1225–74) approaches ethics with God at the center. This is evidenced by the fact that his ethical reflection is found in the second part (*Secunda pars*) of the *Summa Theologiae*, preceded by questions on God and God's creations and followed by questions on Jesus Christ and the sacraments, thus following a structure known as "*exitus-reditus*."[1] According to the *exitus-reditus* pattern, the world is created out of God's love in order to return to God in love. In Aquinas's view, humans are created for friendship with God; grace perfects our nature, and the infused virtues orient us to God.

Building on his philosophical and theological predecessors and synthesizing Christianity with Aristotelian thought, Aquinas declares God as the highest good. Aquinas explains that humans are destined by God to be happiest when in friendship with God, which is *caritas* (or love or charity).[2] Because we are created for happiness, Aquinas contends that right action is typically accompanied by joy—not an ecstatic happiness but a sense of internal peace.[3] For Aquinas, virtues orient one to the good. Virtues, in his view, are not handed down like principles but are fostered through habituation and practices to become "stable dispositions."[4] The cardinal virtues are prudence, justice, fortitude, and temperance, and the theological virtues are faith, hope, and *caritas*.[5] All humans have the capacity for the acquired cardinal virtues, but it is only through grace that we receive the infused theological virtues and the infused cardinal virtues.[6] Grace elevates and heals, justifies and sanctifies.[7] The theological virtues perfect the cardinal virtues; grace perfects nature, charity perfects the will, and faith perfects reason.[8] Aquinas defines the virutes and their role in the moral life. Prudence applies right reason to contingent situations.[9] Justice is the will to render each her due.[10] Fortitude is firmness, especially in things that are difficult.[11] Temperance is right ordering of one's desires.[12] While the cardinal virtues are important, the theological virtues are at the heart of the Christian life for Aquinas. Aquinas defines faith as assent of the intellect, hope as hope in our final end with God, and *caritas* as union or friendship with God.[13] Faith and hope precede *caritas* in Aquinas's writings in the *Summa*, but Aquinas contends that *caritas* is the highest virtue.[14]

According to Aquinas, without grace, we have the capacity only for natural happiness; but with grace, we are given supernatural happiness, or friendship with God. For Aquinas, like Aristotle, true friendship is a friendship between equals. Grace is the gift that furnishes us with a nature raised to a "supernatural" level, thus providing humans with a nature capable of

God's friendship.[15] In this view, a real change in our nature translates into real change in the moral life. Thus, through grace, we receive the infused theological virtues, and in turn we also receive the infused cardinal virtues, which are expressions of the theological virtues.[16]

The language of infused virtues intends to indicate that these virtues are gratuitous gifts from God and modes of conversion as opposed to the acquired cardinal virtues that are products of habit and personal growth. Yet the language of "infusion" gives the false impression that we are instantly and permanently zapped into virtuous persons by God's mighty grace infuser. As experience demonstrates, this is hardly the case. This raises questions about the role of virtue and whether grace leads all moral agents to right action all the time. While we may experience conversion of our hearts and a change in our nature, the infusion of the virtues does not simply undo all prior bad behaviors and dispositions. Instead it seems as if recalcitrant habits impede our full cooperation with grace. Aquinas realizes this and says, "Sometimes the habits of moral virtue experience difficulty in their works, by reason of certain ordinary dispositions remaining from previous acts."[17] Elsewhere he says, "But here grace is to some extent imperfect, inasmuch as it does not completely heal man, as stated above."[18]

In contemporary adaptions of this view, friendship with God can be thought of as a "dynamic" relationship.[19] The paradigm of dynamism highlights humans' ongoing relationship with God, offering flexibility to explore the many modes and mediums through which humans receive grace in the movement toward becoming better people.

According to Aquinas, human moral acts are composed of object, intention, and circumstance.[20] The object is the action itself—*finis operis*, "material" action, as specified by what the will determines is the end of the action and related to the intention.[21] Intention, or *finis operantis*, is the formal part of the action, or the "heart" of the morality of an action.[22] Aquinas explains that "intention, properly speaking, is an act of the will."[23] So, then, object and intention are related to the will. The will is oriented to the universal good, which is why humans desire good and not evil.[24] The circumstances are the context of the action.[25] Take the example of an impoverished father who steals food for his family. Stealing is the object, stealing food to feed the family is the intention, and poverty and hunger are the circumstances. Right actions possess a good or neutral object, are done with good intentions, and are fitting given the circumstances.[26] An action with a good or neutral object but performed with bad intention is immoral.[27] Actions with bad objects, even ones done with good intentions, are also immoral, in Aquinas's view.[28] So, in the case of the father stealing, the theft is not justified. In any situation, according to Aquinas, it is always possible, in principle, to discern and to choose the highest good, which is why Aquinas rejects the possibility of actions that are both good and bad.

Aquinas and subsequent Thomists offer an ethical framework that does not have space for moral and tragic dilemmas. In their view, moral dilemmas are a result of sin or are not dilemmas at all.[29] According to them, these cases can be solved with the hierarchy of goods, the principle of double effect, the principle of lesser evil, or the notion of intrinsic evil. Importantly, according to Aquinas, hard cases should be accompanied by sadness when appropriate.

Perplexus as a Result of Sin or a Mischaracterization

For Aquinas, any apparent moral dilemmas either are not dilemmas because there is a clear solution or are problems brought on by an agent's own sinfulness.[30] Aquinas's position can be determined by assessing various parts of his great body of work, but there is no specific question in the *Summa* or elsewhere on "*perplexus*," which is Latin for "perplexity."[31] Records indicate that toward the end of his life, Aquinas was asked directly about *perplexus* during a public debate—a quodlibetic disputation now referred to as *Quodlibet XII* that occurred in 1272 at the University of Paris.[32] His answer to the question, unfortunately, was not recorded.

The primary work on Aquinas and dilemmas is based on Alan Donagan's interpretation of four Thomistic texts that use the term *perplexus*: *ST* I-II q.19 a.6 ad.3; II-II q.62 a.2 obj.2; III q.64 a.6 ad.3; and *de Veritate*, q.17 a.4 ad.8.[33] Donagan explains that Aquinas builds on Saint Gregory the Great's analysis of the issue.

Donagan, hailing from a Kantian point of view, interprets Aquinas to hold the view, like Kant, that a coherent moral system should never leave an agent without recourse or limited to only wrong actions.[34] Donagan explains that Aquinas distinguishes between two potential categories of dilemmas: "perplexity *simpliciter*," which are not the agent's fault, and "perplexity *secundum quid*," which are the agent's fault.[35] Donagan explains that because dilemmas are, in fact, always and only *perplexus secundum quid* in Aquinas's system, perplexity about how to act is the result of an agent's sin, not the result of a true conflict in the order of goods or among goods. For as Aquinas writes, "And there is no difficulty in saying that, if some condition is presupposed, it is impossible for a man to avoid sin."[36] Although there has been some debate on what he means by this, Donagan's interpretation is that it is logical for one sin to lead to more sins and thus dilemmas.[37]

M. V. Dougherty builds on Donagan's work and expands the list of Aquinas's relevant texts on moral dilemmas to include eighteen texts that, according to Dougherty, refer to an agent in *perplexus*.[38] Dougherty divides the eighteen cases into the following categories: "*Malformed Conscience Dilemmas, Wayward Cleric Dilemmas, Evil Intention Dilemmas, Layperson Dilemmas, Infelicitous Oath Dilemmas,* and finally, *Hidden Option Dilemmas*."[39]

With the inclusion of these extra texts, Dougherty adds evidence for the impossibility of *perplexus simpliciter* in Aquinas's thought. Dougherty shows that sometimes Aquinas repeats this position clearly. For instance, in *II librum Sententiarum*, Aquinas says, "No one is *perplexus simpliciter*, absolutely speaking, but given a certain supposition, it is not *inconveniens*, on that assumption, that someone would be *perplexus*."[40] Dougherty points out that elsewhere Aquinas says, "For nothing prohibits someone to be *perplexus* given some supposition, although no one is *perplexus simpliciter*."[41] Dougherty also calls attention to a Thomistic text of questionable origin that states there is no such thing as *perplexus simpliciter* "because no one is in such a state that he is not able to take care of his salvation."[42] Based on this evidence, it is clear that Aquinas believes *perplexus* results from an agent's sinfulness.

Dougherty points out examples from Aquinas that further support this interpretation in illustrious ways.[43] Dougherty explains that in some cases the dilemmas are resolved when sinners stop sinning. These are cases of *perplexus secundum quid*. For example, the conscience of a fornicator tells him to fornicate, but it is a sin to fornicate; or vanity motivates the man of "vainglory" to give alms, but he sins out of vanity when giving alms.[44] Once the agents abandon desires for fornication or praise, the dilemmas are solved. However, one will remain in a dilemma if one refuses to stop sinning. Aquinas repeats this judgment elsewhere when describing a scenario of a priest who needs to perform sacraments yet is in a state of sin: "But there is nothing unreasonable in his being perplexed, if we suppose that he wishes to remain in sin."[45] So, then, *perplexus* is a result of sin.

In other cases, Dougherty shows that Aquinas rectifies *perplexus* by showing that there is no real dilemma and that the agent misunderstood the situation. For instance, there seems to be a moral dilemma after revealing a truth that hurts another's reputation.[46] The problem here is that harming a reputation with a truth makes it impossible to achieve restitution, which is necessary for salvation, because one can't restore the person's reputation without lying. However, Aquinas points out that this is not a dilemma because the action is permissible when one justifiably speaks a truth about something that damages a person's reputation.[47] But if one ruined another's reputation by lying, then Aquinas explains that one must recant the lie. If the reputation was ruined by revealing a truth that was unjust to reveal, then the truth-teller must do her best to repair the other's tarnished reputation, according to Aquinas. These are ways Aquinas solves these potential problems.

Elsewhere, Aquinas solves another apparent dilemma when he clarifies that an excommunicated cleric is not caught between obligations to celebrate the Eucharist (in his role as priest) and not celebrate the Eucharist (in light of his excommunication) since the excommunication nullifies the obligation to consecrate the Eucharist.[48] And Aquinas clarifies that one is not in a dilemma after pledging an oath to commit a sin, such as adultery or murder, because an oath to commit sin is not a binding oath.[49]

In another instance, Aquinas addresses the perceived dilemma of a priest saying mass and discovering that the wine in the chalice is potentially poisoned by a toxic substance or by "a fly or a spider."[50] The priest must drink the wine for mass, but this would put him danger. If this occurs before consecration, Aquinas recommends pouring out the wine and replacing it. If the wine is consecrated, Aquinas says that it must be stored with the relics and the bug should be burned and put into the sacrarium. In these ways, Aquinas argues that dilemmas are either the result of an agent's sin or not actually dilemmas. In all cases, there is a clear solution that resolves the issue.[51]

Hierarchy of Goods

Aquinas's hierarchy of goods is a strategy for determining right action, especially when goods conflict. This is particularly relevant to moral dilemmas. For Aquinas, all goods are ordered toward our ultimate end—beatitude, union with God.[52] In this view, human happiness is composed of various goods that cannot always be easily compared, yet goods exist in a hierarchy in relation to our highest good, God.[53] For Aquinas, the hierarchy of goods dictates what goods should be chosen when goods seem to be in competition. In the strongest understanding of the hierarchy of goods, choosing the highest good also secures the interests of the lower good at stake.[54] Daniel McInerny takes this point of view and argues that because the hierarchy of goods should guide discernment, the reality of the hierarchy prevents Aquinas from regarding certain hard cases as tragic because choosing the highest good satisfies the demands of morality.[55] Thus, while goods may conflict in concrete situations, goods are not at odds in a tragic way, and there is no "tragic conflict" because the hierarchy of goods demands an order such that certain goods take precedence over other goods.[56] It is always right to choose the highest good; this is never a sin.

For Aquinas, the human good exists as a "multiplicity" and an "ordered unity" in which there exists a hierarchy.[57] Aquinas introduces the basic framework of the hierarchy when arguing for the "precepts of the natural law": that all humans have the propensities to do good and to avoid evil, to procreate and educate the youth, to live in community, and to learn the truth about God.[58] McInerny explains the three different types of goods within Aquinas's hierarchy of goods: "instrumental goods" that are used to achieve another good, "final goods" that have inherent value, and "a most final good" to which the other goods are ordered.[59] McInerny says of Aquinas, "The basic structure of the human good is a *duplex ordo*, an order of goods to one another and to an absolutely ultimate end."[61] Goods cannot all be easily compared by some shared quality, yet they can still be ordered, and while there is one ultimate good, people can manifest the particularities differently in their own lives.[61] The hierarchy is determined by nature while prudence discerns how the hierarchy ought to be perceived in particular situations.[62] John Bowlin explains that Aquinas does not put forward "a simple set of rules" for determining right action, but rather Aquinas believes that prudence can discern the hierarchy by focusing on the common good and relying on the advice of friends.[63] Importantly, here, goods should be evaluated by how they contribute to the common good.

McInerny explains, for instance, nature determines that talents must be used for the good of the community, while prudence decides how to do that in specific cases.[64] So then, because goods are contingent at the practical level, doing x in one situation may be right, and doing y in another situation will be right. According to McInerny, "For Aquinas ... all intrinsically valuable goods exist in *per se*, that is necessary, relationships of the prior and posterior."[65] Goods are also contingent because at certain times some goods are ends in themselves, and at other times they are useful for another good. On this point McInerny gives the example of someone who plays piano for her own enjoyment ("intrinsic" good) and then plays piano to raise money for a charity ("instrumental" good).[66]

Bowlin stresses Aquinas's appreciation for the contingent nature of goods, making the point that in a situation where goods conflict, their contingency means that one can ignore, dismiss, or have "silenced" certain goods.[67]

Aquinas acknowledges the challenge of living this out in concrete situations. He gives the example of "a judge [who] has a good will" when sentencing a thief to death because this is what is best for the common good.[68] Because the thief's wife is primarily concerned with the good of her family—a private good—she does not want the thief to die. In this sense her will "is also good."[69] And this is how "various wills of various men can be good in respect of opposite things."[70] But for Aquinas, willing a particular good is only right insofar that the common good is the end. Ultimately, the human will ought to be "conformed to the Divine will," which is ordered to the universal good.[71]

As in the case of the wife of the thief, this is hard to enact. As Bowlin explains, right action will involve the "silencing" of the good of her husband.[72] Right action coheres with what is best for the common good, thus eliminating the possibility of a dilemma here for Aquinas.

In this way, the hierarchy of goods can guide action in a moral dilemma. For example, in the case of the priest holding the poisoned chalice, it is apparent that it is more important to protect life than to avoid disrupting mass. McInerny claims that according to the hierarchy of goods, lower goods are served by acting for higher goods in a way that directly contradicts the possibility for tragic outcomes: "The relationship between two goods, one of which is for the sake of the other, is in no way a relationship of competition—in the way goods can turn out to be according to the tragic view. The hierarchy of goods implies that superiority of a good in the hierarchy does nothing to undermine, in fact does everything to promote, the intrinsic worth of a good subordinate to it."[73] In this view, lower goods tend to serve higher goods and are regulated by higher goods aiming for the ultimate good. McInerny gives the example of a scholar who wants to "pursue truth and wisdom" and in doing so must navigate familial commitments and the academic study of philosophy.[74] While the goods of philosophy and family seem to be at odds, McInerny says they are not at odds if they are properly ordered—truth is a higher good that organizes both family relations (where family is also an intrinsic good) and scholarship, and some aspects of both can aid the scholar in pursuing the truth.

Principle of Double Effect

Another highly influential strategy for dealing with hard cases is found in Aquinas's reflection on self-defense, which would become the principle of double effect.[75] When assessing the ethics of the difficult case of a death that occurs as a result of self-defense, Aquinas says, "Nothing hinders one act from having two effects, only one of which is intended, while the other is beside the intention."[76] In this case of self-defense, defending oneself is the intended effect and the death of the aggressor is "beside the intention."

Contemporary formulations of the principle of double effect allow for the possibility (when in accordance with certain criteria) of justifying actions that have both a desired effect and an unfortunate, undesired effect. The desired effect is regarded as "intended" while the undesired, unwanted, and unfortunate effect is regarded as "unintended." The principle of double effect permits actions that adhere to the following conditions: (1) the act is good or neutral, (2) the evil is unintended (as defined above), (3) the evil effect is not the means to attaining the good, and (4) the good effect is proportionate to the evil caused.[77] Importantly, the agent must account for the unhappy, unintended consequences using the criteria of proportionality. In this way, good or neutral actions done with good intentions and with proportionate ill side effects can be justified.

The principle of double effect is used in cases that many would consider to be moral or tragic dilemmas, especially in war. For instance, the principle of double effect would be used to approach the drone warfare case in the introduction, where a little girl would likely be killed during a strike targeting terrorists nearby to her who are plotting an attack. According to the principle of double effect, the strike is permissible so long as killing the terrorists is intended and the death of the girl satisfies the criteria of being unintended, not the means of stopping the terrorist attack, and proportional.[78]

Other Thomistic Approaches to Dilemmas

The principle of lesser evil and the importance of sadness are other ways Aquinas's interpreters deal with hard cases. In *On Kingship to the King of Cyprus* Aquinas offers what would become the principle of lesser evil: "When a choice is to be made between two things, from both of which danger impends, surely that one should be chosen from which the lesser evil follows."[79] This does not mean that there are situations with only two evil options; rather, it means that when accounting for the side effects of different choices, one must avoid the greater evil. This interpretation was powerfully put forward by the Thomistic defender Johannes Capréolus.[80] The principle of lesser evil does not justify sinning and only means that one should "avoid a greater evil" when making a decision.[81]

Although there is debate about the principle of lesser evil, many contemporary commentators interpret the principle in a similar way, affirming that it is not about two bad moral choices but about side effects.[82] In contemporary ethics, the principle of lesser evil can be used when choosing between equally effective medical interventions, and when used this way it requires one to implement the method with the least bad side effects.[83] This complements the principle of double effect because it guides proportionality, clarifying that when the other criteria are met, the action with the least bad side effects should be chosen.

Finally, Aquinas acknowledges that sorrow may be appropriate in certain cases, especially after a hard decision. Right emotion is a sign of a virtuous agent for Aquinas.[84] What is troubling to Aquinas, however, is "inordinate" or excessive amounts of any appetite, for this misguides the will.[85] It is clear that Aquinas knows life is not always rosy, so appropriate sadness is virtuous.

CHALLENGES TO AQUINAS

In this section I critique the arguments made by Aquinas and Thomists that all moral dilemmas are a result of sin, that the hierarchy of goods is always operative, and that the principle of double effect is effective. As a result of these problems, I argue that Aquinas does not sufficiently deal with the issue of dilemmas.

Dilemma as Sin

Aquinas's determination that dilemmas are the result of sin—*perplexus secundum quid*—focuses on the extent to which individual sinfulness leads to complicated ethical issues, but it ignores the extent to which structural sin (as opposed to personal sin) causes *perplexus*.

For instance, the first case in the introduction raises the issue of resource allocation during the coronavirus pandemic. Some have argued that ventilator and personal protective equipment shortages are a result of lack of planning, slow action, lack of coordinated efforts, and the hollowing out of federal disaster agencies.[86] These structural issues led to hard choices. Many other dilemmas in bioethics, such as the case in the introduction about the mother in the Philippines faced with crushing health care costs for her son, arise from the reality that poor and marginalized communities do not have access to many health care resources that are more readily available to privileged groups and wealthy countries. These dilemmas are a result of structural injustices and structural sins.[87]

While Aquinas is somewhat aware of how society shapes character, his treatment of *perplexus* is narrow and does not acknowledge how structural injustices can put people in dilemmatic situations. In Aquinas's work, the moral dilemmas in which moral agents find themselves arise from personal sin or confusion. However, the origins of many dilemmas are not necessarily the result of individual sinfulness but rather social sinfulness.

Hierarchy of Goods

I disagree with the assertion that a hierarchy of goods rectifies the problems at stake in moral dilemmas. I am skeptical of whether a hierarchy of *all* goods truly exists. Many proponents of the existence of moral dilemmas argue that at least some goods are incommensurable.[88] In this view goods are far too diverse to possess a shared quality to justify *all* comparisons. Thus, it seems unlikely that *all* goods can be ordered. It seems even more unlikely that even if all goods could be ordered, we would be capable of discerning this order to a degree adequate to resolve all dilemmas.

There may be a very broad hierarchy of goods that we intuit when we protect humans over animals, or animals over objects, or when we judge that health is a higher good than wealth and claim God as the highest good. And even if allegiance to the common good can guide the thief's wife to see the wisdom and rightness of her husband's execution, a hierarchy of goods does nothing to solve dilemmas where goods are of seemingly equal value (symmetrical). Such are the difficulties presented in some of the cases in the introduction. For instance, how does the hierarchy guide the decision of who receives the one available ventilator when two COVID-19 patients of the same age and with equal prognoses need it? Or cases where parents are deciding the fate of their children and have to choose one child over another?

And then there are other dissimilar goods that are rather difficult to order, such as the value of tennis lessons versus swimming lessons, braces versus tennis lessons, freedom versus protection, or spending resources on preventing disease x versus disease y.

Finally, it is certainly not the case that aiming for a higher good clearly guides one's actions, as McInerny argues. For instance, despite McInerny's claims, one only has to meet a few brooding philosophers (or theologians) to know that it is challenging to serve both the demands of academia and the family even when organized by the pursuit of truth.

This is especially unlikely when agents are in constrained situations. Recall from chapter 1 Martha Nussbaum's predicament—what she calls "minitragedies"—of (seemingly) needing to attend a regular Harvard philosophy seminar as a junior faculty member and the seminar taking place in the evening when she had to take care of her daughter.[89] This problem homes in on the reality in which many working parents find themselves, where it is almost impossible to meet both familial and work obligations and where even the best solutions do not serve all the goods at stake. It is noteworthy that Nussbaum explains that her problem was finally articulated when Robert Nozick voiced his need to leave an evening lecture early in order to pick up his son from hockey practice. As Nussbaum points out, Nozick was a well-respected and tenured philosopher who had significantly more power and agency in the philosophy department than Nussbaum. The issue of agency will be taken up in more detail in the next chapter. The main point here is that Nussbaum faced two competing goods, and she could neither voice her problem nor change the situation. This example shows that McInerny's solution for how a higher good guides action is simply not always obvious or feasible for a variety of reasons.

Principle of Double Effect

As previously discussed, the principle of double effect, used today, assigns culpability according to intention, distinguishing between intended and unintended consequences.[90] When adhering to contemporary notions of the principle of double effect, the agent must account for and mitigate unintended bad consequences but is only culpable for intended consequences. However, scholars such as Lisa Sowle Cahill and Rosemary Kellison are wary of the usefulness of this.

Cahill takes up the case recounted in the introduction of the mother in the Philippines.[91] Recall that the mother is reluctant to remove the expensive apparatus keeping alive her seventeen-year-old son at a financial cost the family cannot withstand. The analysis from the bioethics text that cites this case says that the mother should be "reassured" that removing the treatment is the "best" decision.[92] Cahill explains that double effect reasoning justifies the ethics of this decision, and she worries that the principle of double effect used in this way allows for a razor-sharp focus on the mother's action and intention, obscuring the structural issues that cause burdensome health care costs. Cahill calls this use of the principle of double effect "not only futile but inhumane" and "a self-deceiving abdication of responsibility for the larger factors of unjust resource distribution that forced her [the mother's] choice."[93] In this way, Cahill illuminates that the setup of the principle of double effect means that it can be implemented in such a way that the immediate, pressing issue may appear to be solved, yet the social conditions causing the problem remain not only unresolved but also unidentified and unnamed.

Kellison expresses skepticism for the possibility of a meaningful distinction between intended and unintended consequences when both carry foreseeable effects. She summarizes philosopher Elizabeth Anscombe's contribution to this issue: "When one knows with certainty that an act will cause the death of an innocent person, then causing the death of an innocent person is part of the act."[94] Kellison cites William O'Brien on the almost-assured death of noncombatants that just war theorists usually characterize as unintended: "The death or injury to those noncombatants is certainly 'intended' or 'deliberately willed,' in the common usage of those words."[95] O'Brien is suggesting that if an agent knows a consequence is likely, then the consequence is not "unintended" but rather a "deliberate" aspect of the action, and this unwanted, foreseeable consequence is so crucial to the action that the moral agent experiences it as part of what is intended, even when it is unwanted.

How the principle of double effect falls short of offering a solution to dilemmas is seen clearly when reflecting on the case in the introduction where the innocent girl will likely be killed in the strike against terrorists planning an attack. As I previously stated, the principle of double effect regards the death of the terrorists as intended while the girl's death is regarded as unintended but foreseeable and proportionate—and therefore justified. But it seems hard for agents to claim to not intend to kill the girl when they understand that her death is an almost-guaranteed consequence of their actions. The film the case is based on, *Eye in the Sky*, portrays the ambivalence and hesitancy that various leaders, and especially the drone pilot, display over the action because of the likely death of the girl.[96] This indicates that it is not so easy to take such a narrow understanding of intention amid real-life trials.

Aquinas understands intention as an activity of the will.[97] In real life, it is almost impossible for some moral agents to home in on the intended effects of an action without also seeming to "will"—and so intend—the undesired but likely consequences that the principle of double effect claims can be siloed as "unintended." I return to the problems with principle of double effect later in the chapter when I assess Aquinas's view of mixed actions.

Intrinsic Evil

An issue related to nonnegotiable moral requirements is the concept of "intrinsic evil." Building on Aquinas, Catholic moral theology posits that intrinsic evils are those actions whose object is always bad and so the action is always wrong, regardless of the intention and circumstances.[98] This includes actions such as abortion, euthanasia, and lying.[99] As Cathleen Kaveny points out, sometimes an intrinsically evil act is not as horrendous as another non-intrinsically evil, wrong act. She gives the example of a man burning his building in order to receive money from insurance while knowing that it is likely a mother will die in the fire. Kaveny explains that this is not "intrinsically evil" because burning a building is not inherently wrong, that is, the object is not always bad. But as Kaveny points out, this is a horrible act and arguably worse than other acts.[100] For instance, it is worse than lying to your best friend that you love her new wallpaper even though you do not think any wallpaper is ever tasteful.[101] This demonstrates the limited usefulness of the category of intrinsic evil.

Furthermore, there is much debate about which intrinsic wrongs ought to be legislated by the law and whether and how this should influence voting.[102] As such, how this concept should influence politics is a contentious and charged issue. For these reasons, I find the category of intrinsic evil too fraught to be helpful.

The limits of these strategies—the hierarchy of goods, the principle of double effect, and intrinsic evils—call into question whether it is possible to solve hard cases as neatly as the Thomistic tradition claims. As I have shown, Aquinas has not adequately dealt with moral dilemmas that are a result of structural sin. And the hierarchy of goods seems to offer little practical value when the hierarchy is difficult to discern, especially when an agent is dealing with symmetrical goods or acting in constrained situations. The principle of double effect assumes a distinction between intended likely consequences and unintended likely consequences that is not always borne out in moral experience. And the notion of intrinsic evil is limited in its usefulness.

AQUINAS ON MIXED ACTIONS

As I have explained, Aquinas and Thomists deny the possibility of moral dilemmas and, by implication, tragic dilemmas. But in this section I point to areas of Aquinas's thought that have been generally ignored in discussions on the possibility for moral and tragic dilemmas. I argue that in his discussion of mixed actions, Aquinas opens the door to the possibility of situations in which an agent's freedom is limited, intentionality is mixed, and culpability can be reduced to a certain extent.[103]

Aquinas expresses his views on mixed actions in I-II q.6 of the *Summa* and in Book III of the *Commentary on Nicomachean Ethics* (hereafter, *CNE*), both referring to Book III of Aristotle's *Nicomachean Ethics*. At times it will be illuminating to refer to Aristotle's text for a better sense of Aquinas's aim.

Intention and Repugnance of the Will

The special trait of humans is that we freely choose and reflect on our actions, giving our actions a moral quality. Yet sometimes our freedom is limited. Following Aristotle, Aquinas describes three categories of actions—voluntary, involuntary, and mixed—that are determined by how the will is moved.[104] Voluntary actions are those actions that come from within with "knowledge of the end."[105] Aquinas explains, "Voluntary is what proceeds from the will."[106] But involuntary actions, such as those performed out of ignorance or by force, are not internally motivated; they are contrary to one's will. Violence is an external force that can cause involuntary action.[107]

Following Aristotle and Gregory of Nyssa, Aquinas explains that actions done out of fear of evil "are of a mixed character" in that they are both voluntary and involuntary.[108] According to Aquinas, they are voluntary because the agent knowingly acts, but they are involuntary because the agent would not perform such actions if the situation were different. The will is oriented to the good, but Aquinas explains that sometimes the constraints of a fearful situation require that, for the best outcome possible, the will must be drawn to an object to which it is not usually attracted. Aquinas explains this when he discusses the voluntary aspect of an action performed in fear: "The will is moved towards it, albeit not for its own sake, but on account of something else, that is, in order to avoid an evil which is feared."[109] Because the will participates, the action is not totally involuntary, according to Aquinas, but the action contains an involuntary aspect because the moral agent would rather not perform the action and would not perform it in ideal circumstances. Aquinas uses Aristotle's example of throwing cargo overboard during a storm to explain this: Acting out of fear of the danger of the storm, one throws cargo overboard, but in other circumstances one would not do such a thing.[110]

In *Summa* I-II q.6 a.6 Aquinas describes mixed actions as those actions performed out of fear, while in Book III of *Nicomachean Ethics* Aristotle describes mixed actions more broadly as "things that are done from fear of greater evils or for some noble object."[111] Aristotle gives two examples of mixed actions: an agent is asked to do something "base" by a tyrant who threatens to kill his family, and an agent throws cargo overboard during a storm. Aristotle sees both examples as getting at something similar, for after providing the first example he says, "Something of the sort happens also with regard to the throwing of goods overboard in a storm."[112] Both are mixed actions in Aristotle's view because in both cases the agent chooses the action yet would prefer not to perform those actions and would not perform them in ideal circumstances. In *Summa* I.II.6 Aquinas refers only to the cargo scenario, but in *CNE* he refers to both scenarios.[113]

Aquinas supplements Aristotle's analysis by adding that mixed actions performed in fear are "repugnant to the will."[114] After explaining the cargo incident, Aquinas says, "But if we consider what is done through fear, as outside this particular case, and inasmuch as it is repugnant to the will, this is merely a consideration of the mind."[115] The importance of "repugnance of the will" is clarified in the following article when Aquinas explains how the will's repulsion when acting out of fear is the involuntary aspect of the action and so is crucial to the action being ultimately characterized a mixed action.[116] According to Aquinas, if the will enjoyed the object, the person would be acting out of concupiscence and the action would no longer be considered "mixed." Aquinas explains: "He who acts from fear retains the repugnance of the will to that which he does, considered in itself. But he that acts from concupiscence, e.g. an incontinent man, does not retain his former will whereby he repudiated the object of his concupiscence; for his will is changed so that he desires that which previously he repudiated."[117] Importantly, this establishes that actions done out of fear occur with repugnance of the will. As I established earlier, actions done out of fear are mixed actions for Aquinas. So, then, mixed actions are often enacted with repugnance of the will. Using "repugnance of the will" here is very telling about Aquinas's view of the will in these cases. In a mixed action, the will both cooperates in the action and finds the action repugnant, which is how a mixed action takes on both a voluntary and involuntary status. But when the will cooperates without repugnance and according to concupiscence, the action is voluntary and, by implication, sinful.

This suggests that even for Aquinas, the hierarchy of goods does not mean that acting for the higher good always serves a lower good at stake, as McInerny argues, which I explain earlier in the chapter. This also calls into question Bowlin's claim that goods are contingent, so in certain cases they can be "silenced," which I also explain earlier in the chapter. Repugnance of the will would not be necessary in mixed actions if the goods were somehow served or silenced by the act. Repugnance of the will also raises questions for how particular goods are ordered to the common good and ultimate good, for repugnance of the will would not be necessary if the ultimate good takes precedence in a full and final way.[118]

Repugnance of the will also has implications for other parts of Aquinas's thought, particularly what informs the principle of double effect, which hinges on the meaning of intention. How, then, are the principle of double effect and repugnance of the will related to each other? Crucial to this question is whether Aquinas's primary example of a mixed action—throwing the cargo overboard—possesses similar features to, and so can be compared to, Aquinas's example of loss of life in self-defense, which leads to the principle of double effect. In the case of throwing the cargo overboard, the unfortunate effect (losing the cargo) is the means to achieve the desired effect (protecting the people on board the ship during the storm). This is unlike actions considered using the principle of double effect in today's form because in today's usage the unwanted effect(s) cannot be the means of achieving the desired effect. But this is not the case in Aquinas's text, from which the principle of double effect originates. In Aquinas's question on self-defense, the unwanted effect *is* the means of achieving the desired effect because self-defense is achieved through the death of the aggressor.[119] This indicates that throwing the cargo overboard with repugnance of the will can be compared with the scenario of self-defense. So, then, Aquinas's view of how will and intention function during the cargo incident and other mixed actions may be illuminating for how he views the will and intention to be functioning during loss of life in self-defense.

When relating Aquinas's views of mixed actions and self-defense, a cru-cial question is whether repugnance of the will refers to all the consequences the agent foresees. It is clear that in the cargo incident the agent foresees the loss of the cargo, which is why the agent's will is repugnant to the action. Does repugnance of the will refer to consequences the agent does not intend, or does it refer to consequences the agent sadly intends? Recall that, for Aquinas, "intention, properly speaking, is an act of the will."[120] From this it follows that repugnance of the will would not be necessary for actions that the agent does not intend. So, then, repugnance of the will refers to an unfortunate and foreseeable consequence that the agent intends. The agent intends the unfortunate, foreseeable consequences, which is why the will is implicated and the agent acts with repugnance.

As it relates to the article on self-defense, which I discuss earlier, Aquinas very clearly states that an action can have two effects: an intended effect and an effect that is "beside the intention" (what Thomists have called an unin-tended effect).[121] The question, then, is what counts as unintended effects for Aquinas and what does repugnance of the will illuminate about the nature of these unintended effects? As has already been discussed, the Thomistic tradition has asserted through the principle of double effect that unintended effects include foreseeable or highly likely effects of an action that are unde-sired or unwanted; these are not the means of the good effect(s), and the bad effect(s) are proportionate to the good caused. However, repugnance of the will, as I describe it, challenges this idea. Repugnance of the will denotes that an agent abhors the consequences of her action that are intended, forseeable, and unwanted. The consequences are foreseeable or highly likely given that, in the primary example of a mixed action, the person throwing the cargo overboard knows the cargo will be destroyed by this action. The action leads to undesired or unfortunate effects as specified by the repugnance that marks the will. And the unwanted consequences are intended as stipulated by their being of the will—that is, repugnant to the will. So repugnance of the will suggests that intention includes the highly likely or foreseeable consequences of an action even when the consequences are unwanted.

Recall that on the question on self-defense, Aquinas maintains that an action can have both intended effects and effects that are beside the intention. I have used Aquinas's notion of repugnance of the will to widen the classical scope of intention to include effects that are both foreseeable and unwanted. This leaves open the question of what Aquinas would count as effects that are beside the intention. I suggest that effects that are beside the intention are accidental effects—these are effects that are unknowable, unforeseeable, or so unlikely to occur that the agent could not have anticipated them. This is in line with Aquinas's example of self-defense, for if I am defending myself from a violent assailant, the event would be chaotic and fast and reactive, so it would be improbable that I would be able to calculate the likely effects of my actions.[122] For instance, if I am throwing my arms around wildly and kicking wherever and whenever I have an opportunity, it is unlikely that I could foresee that one particular kick in a vulnerable area that I happen to hit will lead to death. The assailant's death that happens in self-defense is beside the intention in this scenario insofar as I did not foresee it. Therefore, the death that occurs in light of the action of self-defense is unintended because the death is accidental.[123]

Gregory Reichberg essentially disagrees with this line of interpretation, arguing that because Aquinas takes up "accidental homicide" in the article after self-defense, the article on self-defense must not also be about accidents.[124] However, given Aquinas's penchant for distinctions and clarifications, I am not sure why that need be the case.[125] As I see it, in *ST* II-II q.64 a.7 (the article on self-defense), Aquinas raises the major point that an action can have intended effects and effects that are beside the intention, and then in the next article, *ST* II-II q.64 a.8, he goes on to further explain this by clarifying that effects that occur by chance can be included as effects that are beside the intention. In *ST* II-II q.64 a.8, Aquinas then further clarifies his understanding of accidental actions and effects. He asserts that actions are not accidental when one is doing something illegal or without "sufficient care," thus providing a full picture of how to understand accidental actions.[126]

Within article 8 Aquinas articulates an objection that raises the problem of hitting a pregnant woman who then miscarries, which causes the woman to die, but the death of the woman occurs "without any intention of causing her death."[127] The objection claims, "Therefore one is guilty of murder through killing someone by chance."[128] In his reply to that objection, Aquinas explains why that is not murder by chance. He first discusses how the deaths of the fetus or the woman are not accidental because it is unlawful to hit a pregnant woman.[129] Unlawful acts cannot be considered accidental in Aquinas's view, as I note above, therefore the assailant is guilty of homicide. This coheres with what has already been said about chance. Then Aquinas adds something interesting. He says, "He will not be excused from homicide, especially seeing that death is the natural result of such a blow."[130] So the foreseeable nature of the death of the fetus or the woman is part of what makes the assailant guilty of homicide. This suggests that the foreseeable aspect of consequences is ethically relevant. Given the topic of the article, this indicates that what is foreseen is not also accidental, which is why it is taken up in this article. This further demonstrates that Aquinas does not consider foreseen consequences as unintended.

Reichberg, on the contrary, regards this as Aquinas using "double-effect reasoning" and thus sees Aquinas's response to the example of the pregnant woman as offering additional support for the classical interpretation of Aquinas on this issue.[131]

When trying to make sense of these competing views—mine and Reichberg's—a source of confusion is that the pregnant woman scenario is brought in by way of an objection, so it is unclear what to make of the term *intention* as it is used in the objection. The objection claims it was not the assailant's "intention" to kill the woman. It is unclear whether the objection is using *intention* in the sense that Aquinas carefully and precisely uses it in the previous article (article 7), or if the objection and the use of *intention* is a colloquial version of *intention* used casually, sloppily, and incorrectly by the person who wages the objection. If it is the latter, then Aquinas's reply may be a challenge not only to the claim that the death was by chance but also to the claim that the death was unintended. While the objector claims that the assailant does not intend to kill and worries that the assailant will be guilty of an act caused by chance, Aquinas's reply indicates that the death of the woman or the fetus is not a death that happens by chance and, perhaps also, that it is not a death that is unintended.

Kellison's work further supports the Thomistic view of intention that I propose here. She points to a part of the *Summa* where Aquinas focuses on the distinction between foreseen and unforeseen consequences, and she uses this to undermine the emphasis on the "foreseen/intended distinction" that characterizes much current thought on the principle of double effect.[132] Kellison calls attention to where Aquinas writes the following: "The consequences of an action are either foreseen or not. If they are foreseen, it is evident that they increase the goodness or malice."[133] Aquinas then goes on to discuss what to do about foreseen and unforeseen consequences.

If foreseeable consequences are important for whether an action grows "in goodness or malice," as Aquinas states there, then it seems as if they must be included in determining the moral worth of an action, and so must be accounted for through one's intention. I argue that the main takeaway in that passage is that Aquinas proposes two categories of consequences: foreseen and unforeseen. This is important because, in the article on self-defense, he also proposes two categories of consequences: intended and unintended.[134] It is logical to conclude that these groupings are parallel to each other so that in Aquinas's view there are two categories of effects or consequences: (1) those effects that are foreseen and intended, and (2) those effects that are unforeseen and unintended. This aligns with the concept of repugnance of the will I suggest wherein a moral agent intends via the will the bad foreseen consequences of an action and so acts with repugnance in light of the undesired consequences.

This is also precisely what happens in dilemmas—actors make choices for actions that have foreseen, unfortunate consequences. These effects are intended according to the more expanded view of intention I argue for. As such, they occur with repugnance of the will because the moral agents do not desire all the effects of the action. For instance, in the case of the drone pilot in the introduction, he seemingly bombs the terrorists' compound with repugnance of the will. He intends the girl's death insofar as it is a likely consequence of the action, and so he acts with repugnance of the will insofar as he despises that the girl will likely die when bombing the compound.

I also suggest that repugnance of the will speaks to the same phenomenon Bernard Williams tries to describe through the concept of a remainder. However, the remainder is a feeling, while repugnance of the will is not a feeling but a posture of the will. Yet it could be possible that repugnance of the will informs a feeling that manifests as a remainder and a feeling of regret. For instance, the drone pilot acts with repugnance of the will and so experiences Williams's remainder in the form of regret. This is not what Aquinas is saying explicitly, but it is a way to think about the concepts together.

A New View of Aquinas on Moral and Tragic Dilemmas

In *CNE*, Aquinas reflects extensively on Aristotle's claim that agents acting in fear may be "praised," "blamed," or "pardon[ed]."[135] While he does not refer to repugnance of the will in this section, I speculate on how it could function in each category. Aristotle explains that one can be "praised" if the action is for something "noble," "blamed" if it was not for something "noble," or receive "pardon" when acting wrongly under "pressure which overstrains human nature and which no one could withstand."[136] To explain this, Aquinas interprets Aristotle to offer three "grades" of actions performed under fear.[137] Aquinas's description of these grades illuminates ways that Aquinas tries to handle hard choices.

The first grade refers specifically to mixed actions and to when one can receive praise or blame.[138] It is praiseworthy to perform an action that is not sinful but is "dishonorable," for the sake of a great good.[139] But if someone performs a dishonorable action for "little or no good," Aquinas explains that the person ought to be blamed.[140] The key to Aquinas's interpretation lies in the following line: "No one suffers any evil to preserve a good unless that good is of greater value in his estimation than the other goods to which the evil he suffers are opposed."[141] "Suffer evil" means endure evil. Thus, an action is permissible as long as a higher good is protected through the loss of a lower good(s).

Thinking about this in terms of repugnance of the will, as I qualify it earlier to account for foreseeable unwanted effects, suggests that the virtuous agent may experience repugnance of the will in light of the dishonor and evil endured and the goods lost in order to spare the higher good. The very fact that the action is "dishonorable" indicates that the object of the action is not something that normally attracts the will. The action should be praised when it is appropriate for the situation. While Aquinas does not refer to the case of the cargo here, throwing the cargo overboard is a fitting example of this type of praiseworthy action. In the case of the cargo, the competing obligations are the obligation to protect the precious cargo and the obligation to protect the people on the ship. The agent does something she wishes she did not need to do (forfeit cargo) in order protect a higher good (human lives on board the ship). I suggest that repugnance of the will is an appropriate posture for the virtuous agent and does not suggest blame here.

This grade seems to fulfill the criteria of moral dilemmas according to many of the philosophers discussed in chapter 1, for even after one throws the cargo overboard, the obligation to protect the goods remains applicable and valid. But this does not seem to fulfill any philosopher's idea of a tragic dilemma. As I describe in chapter 1, for Rosalind Hursthouse, a tragic dilemma produces horrible results that mar a life, but this is not applicable to this category. Recall, that for Christopher Gowans, moral tragedy involves great harm to persons, but here only cargo is lost. Furthermore, a moral agent does not do something obviously wrong when throwing cargo overboard.

The second grade that Aquinas discusses is doing something bad out of extreme fear and, due to the circumstances, one should receive pardon.[142] While the emphasis on the first grade is on protecting a good and how much evil one can endure to protect the good, the second grade emphasizes that wrong action might be understandable in certain circumstances. Aquinas explains that in this grade one does "certain things he ought not do, such as actions unbefitting his state" because "of the fear of evils beyond human endurance."[143] Aquinas gives the example of one who "tells a jocose lie" or does a "menial task" in order to avoid "punishment by fire."[144] In the first grade, Aquinas clarifies that the actions are not sinful. In the second grade, Aquinas does not use the language of "sin," but he seems to assume the actions are sins because he uses the example of a "jocose" lie. Aquinas believes all lies are sins, and a jocose lie is a type of lie whose sinfulness is "diminished" because it is a lie performed for the sake of enjoyment.[145] So, then, using a "jocose lie" as an example of the actions in this grade clarifies that these actions are somehow "sinful." Aquinas takes an interesting approach here, claiming that the person should be both "pardon[ed]" and "not be blamed."[146] The lack of blame indicates that the person is not morally culpable for this action, yet the need for pardon and the reference to the jocose lie indicate that the agent performs a transgression. Aquinas also claims that the action "should not be considered seriously binding."[147] While the meaning of this is unclear, I suggest it indicates that this one-time offense does not necessarily produce a vice.

The key here is that Aquinas believes the circumstances mitigate a transgression, for it is understandable why someone would give in to these unfitting actions when threatened by fire. The transgression, while wrong, is a pardonable reaction given the threat. But, for instance, lying about your report card because you fear your parents would be disappointed would not be a pardonable offense.[148] Angry parents do not fulfill the mitigating criteria of "fear of evils beyond human endurance."

The second grade is as close as Aquinas gets to moral ambiguity and tragic dilemmas, for here Aquinas admits that what is at stake renders sinful actions pardonable and the moral agent not blameworthy. When the obligation to protect oneself is in conflict with the obligation to remain virtuous, even Aquinas acknowledges that it is a hard decision. Unlike a praiseworthy mixed action, however, this involves a sin. The distressing circumstances and the relatively mild transgression (as opposed to the next grade, where the action is "so evil") mitigate the action for Aquinas so that the agent should not be blamed and should be pardoned.

While Aquinas does not consider this to be a tragic dilemma, it fits with the definition of a tragic dilemma. Here the competing obligations are the obligation to right action (truth telling, no unbefitting tasks, etc.) and the obligation to protect oneself. Aquinas seems to suggest that the moral agent commits a transgression, which also occurs in a tragic dilemma. And this category has resonances with tragic dilemmas given the threat of "fear of evils beyond human endurance." While in a tragic dilemma great harm is caused no matter how the situation is adjudicated, here great evil is avoided when one performs a transgression. In one sense this seems to limit the extent of the tragedy since a small wrongdoing is able to thwart the tragedies caused by great evil. But it doesn't necessarily eliminate the possibility of one's life being marred. It remains open whether the agent could experience marring in the way Hursthouse describes the effects of a tragic dilemma. While the contemporary person would be unlikely to experience even any second thoughts at having to commit a jocose lie in order to stave off great evil, the gravity of committing a sin within Thomistic thought would likely make way for a strong response similar to how Hursthouse describes marring. And like

Hursthouse, Aquinas is clear that the person is not blameworthy. Interestingly, Hursthouse on tragic dilemmas and Aquinas (by inference) on this grade do not think the event causes a vice.[149] In sum, like a tragic dilemma, this category involves transgression and marring. The category of tragic dilemmas demands that we linger on the effects of a hard case for a moral agent, but Aquinas moves on quickly.

The third grade Aquinas describes involves actions of extraordinary evil that can never be justified, which indicates there is a limit to how much circumstance can mitigate an action.[150] For Aquinas, these evil actions are not permitted or pardoned, even out of fear. Aquinas says, "He [Aristotle] states that other actions are so evil that no amount of force can compel them to be done."[151] The phrase "other actions are so evil" that Aquinas uses to distinguish the third grade is crucial. Presumably there is no higher good that can justify these actions.

Aquinas does not specify the criteria that qualify an action as "so evil" as to be impervious to mitigating circumstances; he only affirms that such bad actions exist. He believes it is rather obvious that one should not perform these evils, no matter the circumstances. Aquinas says this grade relates to Aristotle's example of Alcmaeon, a character depicted in a work of Euripides.[152] Aquinas explains that Alcmaeon killed his mother as commanded by his father prior to his father's death; the father died fighting a war his wife recommended that he fight. Aristotle says of this: "But some acts, perhaps, we cannot be compelled to do . . . for the things that 'compelled' Euripides' Alcmaeon to slay his mother seem absurd."[153] Killing for revenge and whatever else was going on strikes Aquinas and Aristotle as unjustifiable behavior.

I suggest that this grade does not qualify as a moral or tragic dilemma according to anyone's standards because wrong action is apparently fairly obvious and not justifiable in any view. This action should not be praised or pardoned but punished. The agent who gives into these kinds of "absurd" external forces should receive blame for the wrong actions.

Aquinas then goes on to discuss the difficulties Aristotle sees in discernment.[154] While these difficulties do not constitute a moral or tragic dilemma in Aquinas's view, his sensitivity to times when discernment is foggy speaks to concerns expressed by dilemma theorists and so should be lifted up. Aquinas is responding to where Aristotle writes: "It is difficult sometimes to determine what should be chosen at what cost, and what should be endured in return for what gain, and yet more difficult to abide by our decisions; for as a rule what is expected is painful, and what we are compelled to do is base, whence praise and blame are bestowed on those who have been compelled or have not."[155] In response, Aquinas identifies these two challenges to moral reflection: "The judgment of reason" and "the stability of the affection."[156] To the first issue, Aquinas explains that Aristotle recognizes it can be challenging to discern both how to evade evil and when to accept evil for a greater good. To the second issue, Aquinas says that Aristotle knows the threat of pain is difficult to overcome. There is no set procedure for how to proceed because the particulars are important.[157] This demonstrates Aquinas's attunement to the challenges of the moral life and should be emphasized when determining how to apply Aquinas's thought to real-world issues.

In this chapter, I have shown that the literature on Aquinas and moral dilemmas generally contends that Aquinas offers little on the matter beyond the idea that all dilemmas are *secundum quid*—the agent's fault—and that the hierarchy of goods guides all action. These responses remain unsatisfying to those who believe that goods are incommensurable and that structural sin poses many moral dilemmas. The principle of double effect is meant to address hard cases, but it relies on a troubling assumption that one does not intend all likely foreseeable consequences. However, Aquinas's thought on mixed actions offers a fresh theological look at the possibility for moral ambiguity. I highlight Aquinas's concept of repugnance of the will, and I use that to argue for a broadened view of intention in Aquinas's thought wherein an agent intends both the foreseeable wanted and the foreseeable unwanted effects of an action. While Aquinas does not argue for moral or tragic dilemmas, I have shown how his discussion on mixed actions can be pushed to make contact with the notions of moral and tragic dilemmas.

NOTES

1. Pope, "Overview of the Ethics of Thomas Aquinas," 30.
2. *ST* II-II q.23.
3. Wieland, "Happiness (Ia IIae, qq. 1–5)."
4. Pope, "Overview of the Ethics of Thomas Aquinas," 34.
5. *ST* II-II q.1–170.
6. Pope, "Overview of the Ethics of Thomas Aquinas."
7. *ST* II-II q.109 a.3; *ST* II-II q.113 a.1–10; and *ST* II-II q.111 a.1–5.
8. Pope, "Overview of the Ethics of Thomas Aquinas," 37.
9. *ST* II-II q.47–56.
10. *ST* II-II q.57–122.
11. *ST* II-II q.123–40.
12. *ST* II-II q.141–70.
13. *ST* II-II q.1–46.

14. *ST* II-II q.1–22; II-II q.23 a.6.

15. *ST* I-II q. 62 a.1; ST II-II q.23 a.1; *ST* II-II q.26 a.2; and *ST* II-II q.109 a.3.

16. O'Meara, "Virtues in Thomas Aquinas," 254–85. For a fascinating look at the possibility for "pagan virtue" in Aquinas, see Decosimo, *Ethics as Work of Charity*.

17. *ST* I-II q.65 a.3 ad.2.

18. *ST* I-II q.109 a.9 ad.1.

19. Cahill, *Global Justice, Christology and Christian Ethics*, 172.

20. *ST* I-II q.6–21.

21. *ST* I-II q.8.

22. *ST* I-II q.12.

23. *ST* I-II q.12 a.1.

24. *ST* I-II q.8.

25. *ST* I-II q.7.

26. *ST* I-II q.18 a.4.

27. *ST* I-II q.19.

28. *ST* I-II q.20. The distinct but related topic of intrinsic evils is taken up later in the chapter. Note that modern usage of these terms—*object, intention, circumstance, intrinsic evil*—is mired in a contentious scholarly debate that is beyond the scope of this book. The magisterium holds that physical acts considered in themselves (the object) can be defined as "intrinsically evil" and thus prohibited, regardless of the circumstances. But proportionalists argue that it is impossible to characterize an act totally separate from the circumstances. In response, the "new natural lawyers" devised a list of incommensurable goods that could not be violated. This is controversial, however, because it equates goods such as procreation, life, and play. It is not obvious that the good of life is equal to the good of play. As it relates to the current discussion, the debates around these terms demonstrate that there is no consensus on how to define or interpret these terms. More discussion of this is beyond the scope of this book. To read more on this, see Keenan, *History of Catholic Moral Theology*, especially 155–58; see also Kaveny, "Intrinsic Evil and Political Responsibility."

29. For another view, Cahill argues that Aquinas holds an "ambivalent" view toward killing in war, and this makes way for thinking about "irreducible moral dilemma[s]" in his thought. On this, see Cahill, *Blessed Are the Peacemakers*, 139–72, quote at 158. For my views on Cahill's position, see Jackson-Meyer, "Just War, Peace, and Peacemaking," 92–93.

30. This interpretation was influentially made by Alan Donagan. See Donagan, *The Theory of Morality*, 144–46; and Donagan, "Consistency in Rationalist Moral Systems." For a take on Donagan's influence on this issue, see Dougherty, *Moral Dilemmas in Medieval Thought*, 115–17. For an alternative interpretation of Aquinas, see Mann, "Jephthah's Plight," 617–47.

31. Dougherty, *Moral Dilemmas in Medieval Thought*, 113.

32. Aquinas, *Questiones de quodlibet XII* q.22 a.3, referred to in Dougherty, *Moral Dilemmas in Medieval Thought*, 112–13.

33. For Donagan's interpretation, see Donagan, *The Theory of Morality*, 144–46, and 144n3.

34. Donagan, 144–57.

35. Donagan, 144.

36. Aquinas, *Questiones Disputatae de Veritate* q.17 a.4 ad.8. Donagan uses this quote to build his argument; see Donagan, *The Theory of Morality*, 144–45.

37. Donagan, *The Theory of Morality*, 144–45. See also Dougherty, *Moral Dilemmas in Medieval Thought*, 133–36.

38. Dougherty, *Moral Dilemmas in Medieval Thought*, 117–46.

39. Dougherty, 118.

40. Aquinas, *II librum Sententiarum* d.39 q.3 a.3 ad.5, quoted in Dougherty, *Moral Dilemmas in Medieval Thought*, 138.

41. Aquinas, *Super Romanos* cap. 14, 2, para. 1120, quoted in Dougherty, *Moral Dilemmas in Medieval Thought*, 139.

42. Aquinas, "Articuli additi in codici F," *Questiones de quolibet*, quoted in Dougherty, *Moral Dilemmas in Medieval Thought*, 144.

43. Dougherty's interpretation informs this paragraph, as well as the following paragraphs in this section, along with my understanding of Aquinas on these points. See Dougherty, *Moral Dilemmas in Medieval Thought*, 118–32.

44. Aquinas, *Questiones Disputatae de Veritate* q.17 a.4 ad.8. Note that both Donagan and Dougherty invoke this passage.

45. *ST* III q.64 a.6 ad.3. Note that both Donagan and Dougherty invoke this passage.

46. *ST* II-II q.62 a.2 obj.2. Note that both Donagan and Dougherty invoke this passage.

47. *ST* II-II q.62 a.2 ad.2.

48. *ST* III q.82 a.10 ad.2. Note that Dougherty invokes this passage to make his case.

49. *ST* II-II q.98 a.2 ad.1. Note that Dougherty invokes this passage to make his case.

50. *ST* III q.83 a.6 ad.3. Note that Dougherty invokes this passage to make his case.

51. In light of the fact that Aquinas presents only resolvable dilemmas, Dougherty investigates whether Aquinas could imagine a category of "irresolvable prior-fault dilemmas," concluding that Aquinas could not. See Dougherty, *Moral Dilemmas in Medieval Thought*, 168–97.

52. *ST* I-II q.3 a.8.

53. This interpretation was famously debated between Ralph McInerny and John Finnis. McInerny believes Aquinas assumes a hierarchy of goods, while Finnis believes certain goods are incommensurable and there is no hierarchy. However, Finnis also believes that these goods cannot genuinely conflict. See McInerny, "Principles of Natural Law"; and Finnis and Grisez, "Basic Principles of Natural Law: A Reply to McInerny."

54. McInerny, *The Difficult Good*, 34–54; 109–32.

55. McInerny, 109–32.

56. McInerny, 109.

57. McInerny, 52.

58. *ST* I-II q.94 a.2.

59. McInerny, *The Difficult Good*, 110.

60. McInerny, 51.

61. McInerny, 53–54.

62. *ST* II-II q.47.

63. Bowlin, *Contingency and Fortune*, 79.

64. McInerny, *The Difficult Good*, 44.

65. McInerny, 44.

66. McInerny, 43. I—and Amber Herrle, who proofread drafts of this book—enjoyed what seems to be McInerny's pun here on "instrumental."

67. Bowlin, *Contingency and Fortune*, 75.

68. *ST* I.II q.19 a.10. I am indebted to an anonymous reviewer for the *Journal of the Society of Christian Ethics* who pointed out the importance of including this passage. Bowlin also takes this up. See Bowlin, *Contingency and Fortune*, 73–76.

69. *ST* I.II q.19 a.10.

70. *ST* I.II q.19 a.10.

71. *ST* I.II q.19 a.10.

72. Bowlin, *Contingency and Fortune*, 76.

73. McInerny, *The Difficult Good*, 112.

74. McInerny, 113–14.

75. There is scholarly debate as to whether the principle of double effect truly originates with Aquinas. See Keenan, *History of Catholic Moral Theology*, 45n58.

76. *ST* II-II q.64 a.7.

77. Connell and Kaczor, "Double Effect," 396.

78. Baker, "*Eye in the Sky* and Moral Dilemmas."

79. Aquinas, *On Kingship to the King of Cyprus*, 6.36.

80. Dougherty, *Moral Dilemmas in Medieval Thought*, 168. Dougherty explains that Capréolus is known as the "'Prince of Thomists'" who finished, in 1432, *Arguments Defending the Theology of St. Thomas Aquinas*, written at the beckoning of some Dominicans in order to defend Aquinas against critics.

81. Dougherty, *Moral Dilemmas in Medieval Thought*, 187.

82. Honnefelder, "The Evaluation of Goods," 433.

83. Dougherty, *Moral Dilemmas in Medieval Thought*, 193.

84. Aquinas, *Commentary on the Book of Job*.

85. *ST* II-II q.125 a.1.

86. Herper, "The Coronavirus Outbreak"; and World Health Organization, "Shortage of Personal Protective Equipment."

87. Structural injustices are taken up in more detail in the next chapter.

88. Hsieh, "Incommensurable Values."

89. Nussbaum, "Costs of Tragedy," 1015.

90. A related issue is cooperation, which also hinges on intention. Formal cooperation is when the agent intends the wrongdoing her action causes or aids; this is always wrong. Material cooperation is when the agent does not intend the evil her action knowingly or unknowingly causes or aids; this may or may not be wrong depending on the circumstances and the centrality of the aid to the evil action. A full discussion of cooperation is beyond the scope of this book. For an introduction on these concepts, see Cieslak, "FAQs from the 2011 CMA Annual Conference," 71–91.

91. Cahill, *Theological Bioethics*, 118–20. The case is referenced in the introduction of this book.

92. Lumitao, "Death and Dying," 99.

93. Cahill, *Theological Bioethics*, 119.

94. Kellison, "Impure Agency and Just War," 329.

95. O'Brien, *Conduct of Just and Limited War*, 47. See also Kellison, "Impure Agency and Just War," 329n13.

96. Hood, *Eye in the Sky*, film.

97. *ST* I-II q.12 q.1.

98. John Paul II, *Veritatis splendor*, 80. See also Keenan, *History of Catholic Moral Theology*, 45 and 45n59. Keenan argues that Aquinas never puts forward a notion of "intrinsic evil."

99. Kaveny, "Intrinsic Evil and Political Responsibility."

100. Kaveny.

101. My example.

102. Kaveny, "Intrinsic Evil and Political Responsibility."

103. Special thanks to Jen Lamson-Scribner, who suggested during a Boston College Ethics Colloquium meeting that I should look more at Aquinas's view of mixed actions.

104. *ST* I-II q.6.

105. *ST* I-II q.6 a.1.

106. *ST* I-II q.6 a.3.

107. *ST* I-II q.6 a.5.

108. *ST* I-II q.6 a.6.

109. *ST* I-II q.6 a.6 ad.1.

110. *ST* I-II q.6 a.6.

111. *ST* I-II q.6 a.6; and Aristotle, *Nicomachean Ethics* (hereafter, *NE*) 1110a4-5.

112. *NE* 1110a8-10.

113. *CNE* Book III, Lecture 1.388, 389.

114. *ST* I-II q.6 a.6. See also *ST* I-II q.6 a.8; and *ST* I-II q.6 a.7 ad.2, where Aquinas says, "repugnance of the will." Aquinas also discusses what is "repugnant to the will" elsewhere, see especially *ST* I q.82 a.1; *ST* I q.83 a.1 ad.5.

115. *ST* I-II q.6 a.6.

116. *ST* I-II q.6 a.7 ad.2.

117. *ST* I-II q.6 a.7 ad.2.

118. Reference to earlier discussion on *ST* I.II q.19 a.10.

119. *ST* II-II q.64 a.7. For a somewhat similar interpretation of the unwanted effect being the means for achieving the wanted effect in Aquinas's example, see Matthews, "Saint Thomas and the Principle of Double Effect," 68. Cahill also makes this point in Cahill, *Blessed Are the Peacemakers*, 163.

120. *ST* I-II q.12 a.1.

121. *ST* II-II q.64 a.7.

122. For a similar description of this possibility, see Matthews, "Saint Thomas and the Principle of Double Effect," 68.

123. Kellison comes to a similar conclusion: "For Aquinas, double-effect reasoning functioned primarily as a way to morally evaluate accidents and unforeseen effects of one's actions." Kellison, "Impure Agency and the Just War," 328.

124. Reichberg, *Thomas Aquinas on War and Peace*, 177.

125. For a discussion on the content of *ST* II-II q.64 a.7 and *ST* II-II q.64 a.8, see Cavanaugh, *Double Effect Reasoning*, 1–14. Cavanaugh argues that article 8 is about unforeseen, accidental consequences, so article 7 is about foreseen "risked consequence." For a rebuttal to this, see Reichberg, *Thomas Aquinas on War and Peace*, 177n12.

126. *ST* II-II q.64 a.8.

127. *ST* II-II q.64 a.8 obj.2.

128. *ST* II-II q.64 a.8 obj.2.

129. *ST* II-II q.64 a.8 ad.2.

130. *ST* II-II q.64, a.8, ad.2.

131. Reichberg, *Thomas Aquinas on War and Peace*, 177n12.

132. Kellison, "Impure Agency and the Just War," 328.

133. *ST* I-II q.20 a.5. See also Kellison, "Impure Agency and the Just War," 328.

134. *ST* II-II q.64 a.7.

135. *CNE* Book III, Lecture 2.392–405. See also *NE* 1110a20–26.

136. *NE* 1110a20, 22, 24–26.

137. *CNE* Book III, Lecture 2.392–405.

138. *CNE* Book III, Lecture 2.393.
139. *CNE* Book III, Lecture 2.393.
140. *CNE* Book III, Lecture 2.393.
141. *CNE* Book III, Lecture 2.393. Aquinas's focus on one who "suffers . . . evil to preserve a good" indicates that this category is about both protecting a good and avoiding a bad.
142. *CNE* Book III, Lecture 2.394.
143. *CNE* Book III, Lecture 2.394.
144. *CNE* Book III, Lecture 2.394.
145. *ST* II-II q.110 a.2.
146. *CNE* Book III, Lecture 2.394.
147. *CNE* Book III, Lecture 2.394.
148. My example.
149. Hursthouse, *On Virtue Ethics*, 73n8. I take this up in chapter 1.
150. *CNE* Book III, Lecture 2.395.
151. *CNE* Book III, Lecture 2.395.
152. *CNE* Book III, Lecture 2.395.
153. *NE* 1110a26–29.
154. *CNE* Book III, Lecture 2.396–97.
155. *NE* 1110a29–35.
156. *CNE* Book III, Lecture 2.396, 397.
157. *CNE* Book III, Lecture 2.399.

4

A PROPOSAL FOR A CHRISTIAN VIEW
OF TRAGIC DILEMMAS

Chapter 1 assesses the philosophical debate on moral and tragic dilemmas. Within this literature, I highlight the definition of moral dilemmas, which states that moral dilemmas are situations where moral requirements remain even after adjudicating a moral event. Weaving together various philosophical views, tragic dilemmas are a kind of moral dilemma that involve transgressions causing great harm or marring agents' lives. In chapters 2 and 3, I investigate the limits of Augustinian and Thomistic approaches to hard cases and the relevance of their thought to moral and tragic dilemmas.

In this chapter, I develop a definition and understanding of moral and tragic dilemmas in Christian ethics. I apply Lisa Tessman's distinction between "negotiable" and "non-negotiable" moral requirements to a Christian context.[1] I argue that, for Christians, nonnegotiable moral requirements are rooted in others' sacred humanity and vulnerabilities and recognized by Augustinian lament. These situations are inherently wrong and tragic, so what constitutes moral dilemmas in the Christian view are by definition tragic dilemmas. I argue that culpability is often twofold, including both personal moral responsibility and social moral responsibility whenever tragic dilemmas arise from unjust social structures. Moral agents are culpable even when the best decisions are made; however, culpability is mitigated when agents act with Thomistic repugnance of the will. I then build on Hursthouse's proposition that tragic dilemmas "mar" agents' lives.[2] I argue that the possible devastating personal effects of tragic dilemmas are revealed in evidence from veterans returning from war and suffering from moral injury.

Tragic dilemmas are often the result of harmful social conditions, and moral agents may experience additional hurt from being involved in tragic dilemmas. But these conditions and the harms they cause are frequently overlooked by ethical systems and strategies that claim to settle hard cases.

This chapter develops a Christian definition of tragic dilemmas that brings to light these dangers and their resultant wounds. The category of tragic dilemmas indicts the unjust social structures that are often the cause of these harmful events.

A CHRISTIAN THEOLOGICAL ACCOUNT OF WHY SOME OUGHTS REMAIN

Coherent with many of the definitions of moral dilemmas I present in chapter 1 and following Tessman's distinction between negotiable and nonnegotiable moral requirements, my definition of tragic dilemmas first accounts for nonnegotiable moral obligations. I look at these in a Christian context and in light of what constitutes a dilemma. I argue that from within the Christian tradition, oughts produced by others' humanity and vulnerabilities cannot be eliminated.

Tessman's distinction between negotiable and nonnegotiable requirements is helpful because it makes sense of moral experience, as described by the cases in this book's introduction, without falling prey to a view where the moral life is overwhelmed by dilemmas because no obligation can ever be eliminated. Recall from chapter 1 that Tessman proposes that some obligations are negotiable in that they are able to fall away when in conflict with another requirement that one determines should take precedent. Tessman explains that this occurs when abandoning the requirement produces a loss that can be replaced, or when an irreplaceable and non-substitutable loss is permissibly small; these requirements follow "ought implies can."[3] For instance, my cuddly Cockapoo shrieks and cries at the vet when she is spayed, but my obligations as a good dog mother to keep her free from pain and discomfort are overridden by the various health benefits and other benefits that spaying produces.[4] But according to Tessman, who develops ideas from Christopher Gowans and Martha Nussbaum, deciding against nonnegotiable moral requirements involves losses of a "unique value" that are so high they are "a cost that no one should have to bear"; these requirements do not follow "ought implies can."[5] Tessman argues that these nonnegotiable moral requirements are recognized by our intuition (as opposed to our reasoning pathways) and are often, relying on Philip Tetlock's theory, "'sacred values.'"[6] Recall that Tessman asserts that sacralization keeps those values out of reach of evaluation because they are beyond reason.

Tessman develops a view of nonnegotiable moral requirements founded on her constructivist convictions.[7] Even though she uses the language of "sacred" at times, she does not rely on theological premises. However, I think it is possible to use her distinction between negotiable and nonnegotiable requirements without using her constructivist building blocks. In my view, Christian theological commitments can arrive at a similar conclusion and recognize that some moral requirements are so fundamental and sacred that they are nonnegotiable. I argue that Christian commitments to protecting life and the vulnerable are so foundational that they should be viewed as nonnegotiable requirements in the Christian view. Following Tessman's understanding of nonnegotiable moral requirements, these requirements—protecting life and the vulnerable—serve goods that are unique and whose loss would be intolerable.

In my view, there is a consensus between some secular thought and the Christian view I propose here on both the possibility for nonnegotiable obligations and the content of those obligations. While I argue for protecting human life and the vulnerable as nonnegotiable according to the Christian tradition, the ethical demands of these nonnegotiable obligations are commensurate with unwavering ethical demands articulated by Tessman and some of the scholars who inform her thought—Gowans and Nussbaum. The nonnegotiable obligations I propose cohere with Tessman's account of ethical demands that arise from others' vulnerabilities, Gowans's notion that "responsibilities to persons" are unwavering, and Nussbaum's idea of what counts as acceptable loss versus tragic loss.[8] But I argue for the nonnegotiable obligations to protect human life and the vulnerable as they arise from Christian commitments.

While other Christian duties are important and should be accounted for, I argue that they dissolve after determining the appropriate course of action when in conflict with each other or when in conflict with a foundational commitment. However, commitments to protect life and the vulnerable are indissolvable and nonnegotiable.

Protecting human life is a central Christian principle. It is supported in various biblical texts from the imagery of the *imago Dei* at the Garden of Eden to the example of Jesus's life to the demands of the beatitudes.[9] Prisco Hernández offers four concrete reasons for why killing is a major problem for Christians.[10] First, he explains that the prohibition against killing exists as an "*a priori* moral intuition" written on our hearts as part of the natural law, our human participation in God's law.[11] Second, he explains that killing is offensive to humans because we are fundamentally social, so there is an especially great loss when a person is removed from community and relationships. Third, he asserts there is an immeasurable cost to killing, for the world misses out on unknown potential and talents. And fourth, Hernández argues that killing presents "eschatological" problems.[12] In Hernández's view, killing is a major transgression against God because it destroys a human into whom God has breathed life. As such, this destroys another human's freedom that is created by God, and it interrupts the person's ongoing relationship with God. In this way, Hernández explains that killing produces an eschatological problem because the killer rejects God and cuts short the victim's efforts to build a relationship with God through the work of her life. Hernández concludes that this jeopardizes the victim's eschatological fate.

It is important to clarify the nonnegotiable moral requirement to protect human life for which I am arguing. Within the Christian tradition, the dignity of human life is respected as part of an eschatological vision such that incumbent death is not feared. This means that life must be protected because there is a moral duty to ensure that life does not end prematurely, and it means that upholding human dignity also requires accepting when one is on the verge of death. This view undergirds the distinction in Catholic health care between "ordinary means" and "extraordinary means" of end-of-life care.[13] According to this distinction, and rooted in patients' "free and informed judgment," patients are obligated to receive "ordinary or proportionate" care, defined as means that "offer a reasonable hope of benefit and do not entail an excessive burden," but patients are not obligated to receive "extraordinary or disproportionate" care and may "forgo" interventions that "do not offer a reasonable hope of benefit or entail an excessive burden."[14] I affirm this distinction. Thus, it is an affirmation of human dignity and not a violation of the requirement to protect life when, for instance, a family makes peace with the reality that their elderly mother is in a coma and dying and, following her advance directive, do their best to keep her comfortable and tended to in hospice care without using aggressive treatments to extend her life. This is, of course, not an instance of killing. Acceptance and letting go are the primary ways of respecting life in such a case.

It is also fundamental to Christianity that we protect the vulnerable. Impelled by Matthew 25, and because we have a vested interest in the common good, we must pay close attention to how the marginalized are treated, for the common good is in jeopardy when some are suffering.[15] The vision that called the Good Samaritan to act should inspire how we interact with and view the world, and a compassionate perception is the first step to recognizing the marginalized and their needs.[16] Catholic social teaching is a rich tradition that gives preference to the poor and vulnerable.[17] Protecting life and protecting the vulnerable are pillars of Christian ethics. Duties for the disciples of Christ always involve these commitments, so the obligations these produce cannot be eliminated even when Christians are unable to fulfill them.[18]

The inability to uphold these nonnegotiable moral obligations leads to a transgression. Tragedy occurs when one is unable to fulfill these fundamental oughts, for at stake are lives and basic needs. The implication of this understanding of nonnegotiable obligations is that this Christian definition of moral dilemmas is also, by default, a definition of tragic dilemmas. This is different from a view such as that proposed by Williams, where many obligations may linger to create moral dilemmas and where tragic dilemmas are a special kind of moral dilemma. I suggest that in the Christian context there is a very narrow scope for what constitutes nonnegotiable moral obligations. Therefore, situations that constitute moral dilemmas in the Christian view are tragic dilemmas because these are cases where, by definition, they involve transgressions that cause great harm, possibly even marring moral agents lives.

Tragic dilemmas in the Christian view ought to be accompanied by lament. Recall from chapter 2 that Augustine laments the wise judge who tortures to get the truth, but he does not lament the situation where one cannot bury the dead when the city is under siege. From Augustine's viewpoint, the judge causes harm, but no harm is done to the deceased.[19] Here lament corresponds with nonnegotiable obligations (as I have defined them) and the harm that arises from not meeting these obligations. Augustinian lament is a profound realization of the tragedy of an event.

Lament, then, may serve as both a guide and a response to tragic dilemmas in the Christian view. For when determining what nonnegotiable obligations to protect human life and human vulnerability demand in particular situations, it is fair to say that these obligations, if not met, will cause lament. And lament is the proper response to not being able to fulfill these obligations.

It will be helpful to turn to a case. Recall from the introduction the case about the innocent girl who happens to be outside a compound that armed forces are planning to bomb in a preemptive drone strike against terrorists who are inside preparing an attack. The girl will most likely die in the drone strike due to her unfortunate proximity to the compound. When analyzing this as a tragic dilemma, the major nonnegotiable obligations are (1) the nonnegotiable obligation to protect the innocent people who will die in the terrorists' attack, (2) the nonnegotiable obligation to protect other innocent people in that moment, including the girl, and (3) the nonnegotiable obligation to protect all human life, including the terrorists.[20] Despite the fact that not all of these obligations can be met, they all remain even when the best possible choice is made. This may explain the hesitation that various decision-holders have in determining how to proceed. It is very unlikely that they will fulfill the obligation to protect the girl if they go ahead with the strike, but that obligation to the girl remains even though it is impossible to fulfill. Anticipation of Augustinian lament guides many of the decision-makers, particularly the drone pilot who is reluctant to shoot, and then this lament is experienced by many of those involved, evidenced by the array of sober reactions to what is an otherwise successful military mission.

PERSONAL AND SOCIAL MORAL RESPONSIBILITY IN TRAGIC DILEMMAS

In this section I assess moral responsibility for tragic dilemmas on both the personal and social levels. I propose that a moral agent is partially morally responsible for any nonnegotiable oughts that remain. Another way to think about this is that the agent is the perpetrator of, and morally responsible for, the bad consequences of the action. I argue this from a feminist point of view and using Aquinas's understanding of knowledge and action. The agent is blameworthy because, as I show, an agent is responsible to those with whom she is in a special relationship. I argue that this means we are morally responsible for requirements grounded in the sacredness of human life and vulnerability. Importantly, though, constrained situations diminish culpability. Aquinas's concept of repugnance of the will determines when moral responsibility is mitigated. Constrained situations are often the result of unjust social structures, so the category of tragic dilemmas calls for an assessment of the social structures that may have contributed to the problem.

Personal Responsibility According to a Relational Autonomy

Recall from chapter 1 that Hursthouse is unable to fill in the content of the remainder after a tragic dilemma, and she does not determine if a remainder is a product of remorse or of regret.[21] Hursthouse's treatment of the remainder is unsatisfying because she changes the subject rather than solves the issues of why and when regret or remorse is appropriate. Yet the nature of tragic dilemmas and moral responsibility is illuminated by her inability to definitively identify the remainder in these cases. Her ambivalence reveals that the remainder of a tragic dilemma is a mixture of remorse *and* regret. Hursthouse tries to uncover the real-life experience of an agent who feels a magnitude of distress akin to that which is appropriate when the agent is morally culpable, even though it often seems inaccurate to ascribe blame to the agent acting in a tragic dilemma. Blame usually seems inappropriate and unduly harsh in tragic dilemmas when the agent acts in the best way possible. But *is* blame inaccurate?

Regret is usually regarded as a wish that one had acted differently, while remorse signifies guilt.[22] Regret and remorse can also be distinguished along the lines of causal responsibility and moral responsibility.[23] If you are causally but not morally responsible, you feel regret; if you are morally and causally responsible, you feel remorse. For instance, a driver going the speed limit at night hits and kills a pedestrian who is wearing all dark clothing and who darts out into the middle of the road. The driver is causally responsible but not morally responsible because she drove responsibly. She feels regret. However, moral responsibility is appropriately assigned to the inebriated driver in the same scenario who fittingly feels remorse in addition to regret.[24]

I argue that the typical remorse/regret distinction breaks down in a tragic dilemma. This is because participation in a tragic dilemma is more complex, involving deliberation and consent to violate a nonnegotiable moral requirement. While the agent is blameless in the sense of not contributing to the precipitating events, it seems fitting to say that the agent's grief—which Hursthouse can't quite characterize—is somehow related to the sense of moral responsibility the agent feels for having performed terrible action x. This is why regret misses the mark. The agent is justified in doing action x, and she would do it again if placed in the same situation, yet she experiences herself as complicit with evil because she reflected on the choice and in the end does something she considers "bad" even if she thinks it was the best course of action possible. I suggest that causal responsibility through deliberate, albeit necessary, participation in an action that produces ill consequences leads to moral responsibility. Given the constraints of the situation, it is fair to say that the agent does not take on full moral responsibility, but some moral responsibility is fitting.

Along similar lines, Stephen De Wijze argues for the "moral emotion" of "tragic-remorse."[25] He explains that this accompanies instances where wrongdoing is both inevitable and justified, typified in cases of "dirty hands."[26] De Wijze distinguishes tragic-remorse from the more straightforward feelings of remorse and regret, and from Williams's agent-regret, which is not about wrongs. Tragic-remorse is the emotional fallout that occurs when an agent's action is justified, yet "an agent . . . has been morally polluted by events and circumstances outside of her control, and . . . she rightly feels a measure of anguish, guilt and shame in recognition that she has done something wrong."[27] It is marked by feelings of "anguish, pride, and a sense of moral pollution in addition to the usual feelings of guilt and shame that ordinarily accompany moral violations."[28] According to De Wijze, this often occurs when the moral agent's actions are constrained due to other people's immorality.

I suggest that the agent is responsible for an action she carries out but was not complicit in creating. This is because the agent chooses the action and because agency is broad and relational. Relational agency is a common feminist revision of typical "atomistic" ideas of agency that ignore how agents are constituted by relationships.[29]

Rosemary Kellison argues that agency is never about the individual acting alone. She describes feminist Margaret Urban Walker's notion of "impure agency": "Human agency is impure because humans are not completely free or independent."[30] In this view, the idea of a totally autonomous agent is an illusion and contrary to reality due to the web of relationships in which we live. As a result, Kellison says, "We *do* hold one another responsible for things beyond our control."[31] And we ought to. This is particularly true when the good of others close to us is at stake, for "one of the most significant sources of these responsibilities is our relationships."[32] This is important because relationships and our responsibility for others' vulnerabilities are generally what make tragic dilemmas tragic.

Catholic feminist Sidney Callahan makes a similar point, arguing that our relationships produce moral obligations that we do not necessarily explicitly agree to, but they are obligations nonetheless. She reveres the moral agent who recognizes and accepts these obligations: "Responsiveness and response-ability to things unchosen are also instances of the highest human moral capacity."[33] For Callahan, interdependence is essential to what it means to be human, so we ought to accept the demands relationality places on us.

With her revision of autonomy, feminist Claudia Card makes a series of distinctions between different kinds of responsibility. Her most salient point for this discussion is that strict causality does not determine how we orient ourselves to events and their effects. Card distinguishes between responsibility that is "backward-looking," which she says has been the concern of much of recent Anglo-American philosophy, and "forward-looking," which is where she wants to shift the focus.[34] "In the forward-looking senses, when we take responsibility for something, there is no assumption that we produced it," she writes.[35] In Card's view, our responsibility is broader than causality:

> The following seem worth distinguishing: (1) the administrative or managerial sense of responsibility—undertaking to size up and organize possibilities comprehensively, deciding which should be realized and how; (2) the accountability sense of responsibility—agreeing to answer or account for something, or finding that one should be answerable, and then doing so; (3) the care-taking sense of responsibility—committing oneself to stand behind something, to back it, support it, make it good (or make good on one's failure to do so), and following through; (4) the credit sense of responsibility—owning up to having

been the (morally) relevant cause of something's happening or not happening, taking the credit (or blame) for it.[36]

She observes that the first three types look forward, while the fourth type looks backward. Card's concern is how forward-looking notions of responsibility reimagine moral agency so that one exhibits moral agency by taking care of one's character and building "integrity" in the face of bad moral luck, even when one is not morally culpable for the situation.[37]

The main takeaway for my project is that Card challenges the typical relationship between causality and responsibility. She points out ways that an agent takes responsibility after the fact, even if the agent did not cause the event. In my view, this unlocks a cascade of moral obligations, especially when thinking about what this means for our responsibilities to others. For example, if your mother is in a car accident, you don't take care of her only out of a sense of *caritas*, you take care of her also out of a sense of responsibility. It is your task, although it was never explicitly given to you or caused by you.[38]

I am suggesting a slightly different and more encompassing type of responsibility than that proposed by Card, yet still in line with the trajectory of Card's attempt to reimagine our orientation to actions beyond strict causation.[39] I seek to expand how we think about culpability. I suggest that we bear a certain amount of blame for how our actions affect others, particularly those with whom we are in relationship. This is true even if an agent is constrained by limited circumstances outside of the agent's control, as in the case of tragic dilemmas. This is true because after reflection on how to proceed in a tragic dilemma, an agent chooses a certain course of action. Deliberation about an action, even if it is to reflect on a limited number of options, is an act of autonomy. This sliver of autonomy implies a limited amount of participation, which means that the agent incurs some moral culpability for the action. Furthermore, there are levels of culpability so that in tragic dilemmas an agent does not take full blame for the events but does accept a sliver of moral responsibility. I address this in the next section.

Personal Responsibility due to Knowledge of the Act

Knowledge is crucial for what constitutes culpable action. As such, Aquinas's reflection on moral knowledge is helpful here. In Aquinas's terms, I argue that in tragic dilemmas agents perform actions with sufficient knowledge.

To illuminate issues around ignorance and knowledge, Aquinas responds to an objection that describes a man who unknowingly kills his enemy when trying to kill a deer; the man does not feel sad about this because the man had hoped to kill his enemy at some point.[40] Even though the man didn't plan on killing his enemy at that moment, the action is not involuntary because the result is not "repugnant to the will"; thus, the action is acted in accordance with "non-voluntariness."[41] This is "concomitant" ignorance, according to Aquinas, and it occurs when an agent lacks knowledge but the outcome is aligned with her will; having the missing knowledge would not have changed the action.[42] This is wrong.[43]

"Consequent" ignorance is when one voluntarily chooses not to have knowledge, and Aquinas explains that this can happen in a few ways.[44] Actions that involve a lack of knowledge along these lines are not considered involuntary in Aquinas's view because the lack of knowledge is purposeful. This includes "affected ignorance," the voluntary decision to avoid knowledge.[45] Under the category of consequent ignorance, for Aquinas, is also "ignorance of evil choice" and "negligence."[46] Aquinas contends that one is morally responsible for these ignorances.

For Aquinas, ignorance produces an involuntary action when the ignorance arises from what the agent was "not bound to know" or could not or honestly did not know, so long as the effect of the lack of ignorance is not in line with the agent's will.[47] This is "antecedent" ignorance, and to explain this, Aquinas gives the example of a bowman who, after diligently surveying the area, could not have known that a man would walk through the arrow's path and be killed by his arrow.[48] This differs from the previous example because in this case, had the bowman known, he would not have shot the arrow. This is an involuntary action, and so, for Aquinas, the agent is not morally responsible in this case.

In accordance with this, my definition of tragic dilemmas is limited to incidents when the agent chooses an action with sufficient knowledge and so can make a good estimation of what the reasonably foreseeable consequences are. As such, I leave out cases where the consequences of one's actions are utterly unknowable or incredibly uncertain. So this excludes cases where the agent has limited knowledge, such as Sartre's student (discussed in chapter 1), who does not know what the effects of joining the military will be and whether he will die in battle. While that case, and others like it, could constitute a tragic dilemma, it is a borderline case. Like some of the authors before me (discussed in chapter 1), I will avoid a definition that deals with marginal cases. The main point here is that the agent is, to some extent, morally responsible for the unmet nonnegotiable moral obligation because the agent purposely chooses the action with sufficient knowledge.

While the moral agent ought to accept moral responsibility due to the knowledge she possesses when acting, the constrained nature of the situation and the agent's disgust for performing the action mitigates moral responsibility. Recall from chapter 3 that Aquinas uses the phrase "repugnance of the will" to describe mixed actions. This, I argue, describes the proper moral posture of someone acting the best way possible amid the constrained circumstances of a tragic dilemma. Repugnance of the will indicates that the agent is doing what needs to be done but wishes that it didn't have to be done, and she chooses how to act with sufficient knowledge that can foresee the likely consequences of her action. I suggest that repugnance of the will can be used as a marker to determine when an agent takes on diminished moral responsibility, for it signals both the situation of constrained choices and the proper attunement of the will to act in the best way possible while intending the unfortunate consequences, in line with the expanded notion of "intent" that I argue for in chapter 3. Moral agents who act with repugnance of the will in tragic dilemmas take on some, but not total, moral responsibility for acting in the best way possible amid constrained situations and limited options.

Social Responsibility for Tragic Dilemmas

Many tragic dilemmas do not occur in a vacuum but are the result of unjust social structures. Tragic dilemmas demand that we zoom out and look more broadly at the social structures in which the problems occur. The notion of structural sin captures the social aspect of unjust structures and the nature of personal and social responsibility within these structures.

Structural sin is premised on the notion that society and individuals inform one another. Catholic bishops in Latin America took up liberation theology's notion of structural sin in the Medellín Conference of 1968 when they affirmed the existence of "unjust structures" that can only be overcome by systemic change prompted by individual "conversion."[49] The concept was further developed by liberation theologians and was officially adopted into church teaching by Pope John Paul II.[50] Liberation theology emphasizes the structures themselves with a critique of economic and political structures, while Pope John Paul II interprets social sin in light of individual agency and his personalist perspective. While still emphasizing the role of the individual to resist sin, the magisterial concept of structural sin highlights how individuals exist amid and act within unjust structures.

Daniel Daly uses critical realism and theology to investigate the relationship between structures, moral agents, and flourishing. In his view, "structures are webs of relations among social positions" where a position conscribes a range of moral actions and where the structures encourage or discourage licit or illicit actions.[51] In his view, virtuous structures foster virtuous actions and uphold dignity while vicious structures do the opposite. Daly maintains that both kinds of structures allow for moral agency and that, at the same time, acting amid these structures molds the character of moral agents.[52]

Daniel Finn investigates how sinful structures increase the likelihood of sin.[53] Finn's study is rooted in *Caritas in veritate*'s notion that original sin infiltrates even social structures.[54] Finn argues for a dynamic relationship between individuals and structures, urging from the critical realist perspective that "social structures emerge from the activity of individuals, yet have independent causal impact on people through the way structures affect the (free but constrained) choices persons make."[55] To explain this, Finn uses the concept of emergence: "Emergence occurs when two or more 'lower level' elements combine to form a 'higher level' element that has different characteristics."[56] Social structures are gestalt because, as Finn explains, like water or the mind, they are greater than the sum of their individual parts. Importantly, Finn shows that sinful social structures are the result of individual actions, each of which do not necessarily have nefarious intentions but, when taken together, form systems where sin is supported. According to Finn, within these structures certain actions and relations are encouraged, discouraged, thwarted, or made easy. In Finn's view, structures are sinful when they foster sinful choices, although personal agency still exits.

Finn explains that structures are hard to change because those who tend to be the most motivated to change them are those who are disenfranchised by the structures and who thus have the least power to affect change, while those who benefit from the structures and have more freedom in changing them are less inclined to demand change. For example, he notes that higher wages for adjuncts at universities was sparked by the concerns of contingent faculty experiencing poor pay, not by the administrators or tenured faculty who are not in that condition.[57] This understanding is supported by Nussbaum's example of having to decide between attending the evening philosophy seminars and taking care of her child.[58] Nussbaum had a large incentive to change the time of the meetings, but as a junior faculty member, Nussbaum could do little to voice her need or create change. Eventually, the highly respected and tenured philosopher Robert Nozick declared his need to leave an evening lecture early in order to pick up his son. Presumably, Nozick's status gave him the freedom to speak up about the issue in a way Nussbaum could not.

As various theologians who rely on critical realism assert, social structures are supported by and interact with culture in a "reciprocal" way.[59]

Matthew Shadle argues that culture is essentially the "ideas" that society and individuals draw from; these are not monolithic—and in fact can contradict—and they are not abstracted from social structures or real life but refer back to concrete realities.[60] In his view, culture does not extinguish agency. Nevertheless, as Shadle points out, "in most cases one's culture is accepted simply as part of 'the way things are.'"[61] These complexities come to the fore in David Cloutier's discussion of the difficulty of addressing climate change when faced with contradicting cultural ideas about sustainability, on the one hand, and individualism and consumerism, on the other hand, and the competing structures these support.[62]

Finn purposefully does not take up culture in his seminal article, but I think it is worth reflecting on how culture interacts with the university structure in his example of the contingent faculty who argue for better conditions.[63] The cultural ideas that support and reinforce a contingent workforce in the academy (and beyond) are numerous. There is an array of cultural ideas that make changing the system very difficult, including, perhaps, a culture of extreme gratitude that expects gratefulness and dismisses demands for fair pay, as well as cultural idealizations of the professorate. These are coupled with the economic reality that, in the United States, without much of a social safety net, contingent faculty are likely to be reluctant to push back against the university system for fear of jeopardizing their livelihood.

This is all to make the point that culture is an important piece in understanding how injustice works because cultural ideas set the stage for what is possible, and then the unjust structures encourage sinful actions, which reify the cultural ideas. Changing the structures, then, also requires a change in cultural ideas.

Taken together, this view of structural sin and culture is helpful in identifying how individuals contribute to the creation of unjust structures that are often at the heart of tragic dilemmas. Take the case in the introduction about the mother in the Philippines whose family cannot afford life support for the eldest son. That such a situation arises is in part due to unequal distribution of resources, inadequate pay, and policies that do not support the vulnerable. These structures of inequality are supported by behaviors bolstered by a myriad of cultural ideas. For instance, there are contradictory ideas that resources should be distributed and individuals should not have to give up personal resources or goods in that endeavor. Unjust structures may be perpetuated by the idea that inequality is permissible or even desirable. To the extent that individuals embrace the narratives and ideas that support these unjust structures, individuals are part of the problem. So it would then be erroneous for individuals who are not directly involved in tragic dilemmas to see themselves as divorced from the dilemmas. As in the case of this mother, her plight is in part a result of the actions and beliefs of many.

Tessman lays out a variety of ways that oppression causes dilemmas.[64] She gives examples of the many ways poverty forces hard choices, such as between working versus spending time with one's children or paying for rent versus paying for health insurance. She delineates the dilemmas that racism poses for Blacks in the United States, such as wanting the help of the police at times but not trusting the police or the judicial system to act justly. In Tessman's view, the result of this and what it means for working against injustices are profound, leading to "a moral life that is, perhaps relentlessly, troubled by its shortcomings and filled with disturbing moral remainders."[65] This reveals a devastating effect of oppression—how it undermines the moral life by creating situations of dilemmas.[66]

Importantly, this view of the relationship between unjust structures and tragic dilemmas challenges Aquinas's views on dilemmas. Recall from chapter 3 that Aquinas limits *perplexus* to situations that arise from confusion or personal sin. His insight that sin causes *perplexus* is helpful, but he limits his focus to individual actions, whereas I see the problem lying primarily at the level of social structures. Contra Aquinas, I argue that tragic dilemmas are often the result of social sin and unjust social structures.

This highlights a key tragedy of tragic dilemmas—that moral agents find themselves in situations where they must participate in wrongdoing in order to act in the best way possible. This dimension of harm caused by social sin ought to be identified clearly. But this hurt is often obscured by strategies that claim to solve hard cases, for when the cases are declared to be sorted out, there is little in the way to identify the damage that has been done. When the actors are declared morally spared, there is little reason to identify the faulty social context of the situation. This misses the societal critique that hard cases point to and that the category of tragic dilemmas names. Denying the reality of tragic dilemmas is a cultural idea that supports structures of injustice by ignoring and obscuring a facet of harm that structural injustices cause.

Arguing for both mitigated personal and social responsibly for tragic dilemmas highlights the ill effects of unjust social structures. Adding "tragic dilemmas" to the lexicon of cultural ideas works to push against structural injustices by naming the moral harm that the injustices cause. Not only do unjust structures cause destruction through oppression and inequitable allocation of resources so that, for instance, the boy in the Philippines is unable to receive the sustained care that is available to the economically privileged, but unjust structures also cause moral harm because people are forced to make hard ethical decisions in tragic dilemmas. Recognizing mitigated personal moral responsibility for tragic dilemmas reveals the extent of harm of unjust structures. The category of tragic dilemmas demands that we identify personal and social guilt, and this, in turn, is a way to identify social problems that we must overcome.

HOW TRAGIC DILEMMAS CAN MAR AGENTS' LIVES

Importantly, the category of tragic dilemmas alerts us to the possible lifelong challenges of living with the reality of being unable to fulfill a nongegotiable moral obligation. This is what Hursthouse calls attention to when she says that a tragic dilemma "mars" an agent's life. This reality, however, is eclipsed by strategies that claim to solve dilemmas because when the issue is "solved," there is no call to recognize the ongoing personal effects of the hard case. In this section, I use evidence from moral injury studies to show that an agent's life may be marred after a tragic dilemma due to the difficulty of integrating the event into an agent's self-understanding.

As previously discussed, Hursthouse offers a provocative but at times vague claim about tragic dilemmas: "An action is right iff it is what a virtuous agent would, characteristically, do in the circumstances, except for tragic dilemmas, in which a decision is right iff it is what such an agent would decide, but the action decided upon may be too terrible to be called 'right' or 'good.' (And a tragic dilemma is one from which a virtuous agent cannot emerge with her life unmarred)."[67] Yet, what "marring" is remains unclear. Tessman writes that Hursthouse's notion of marring results from "sorrow, a feeling of being haunted, or a lack of peace with oneself."[68] Hursthouse explicitly states that a tragic dilemma does not necessarily cause a vice, indicating that the moral agent's character isn't necessarily harmed.[69] But Tessman suggests that when one's life is marred, "one's character may be in jeopardy," which is a stark and dramatic claim.[70] In sum, the moral repercussions within Hursthouse's view are hazy. It seems as if Hursthouse is trying get at some kind of profound repercussions, but what these are remains unclear. However, it is necessary to identify these repercussions because they draw out a harm that Augustinian and Thomistic approaches to hard cases miss.

I suggest that the field of moral injury provides clarity to Hursthouse's notion of marring. Ultimately, moral injury shows that a tragic dilemma can mar an agent's life because the transgression and harm of a tragic dilemma is hard to integrate into one's self-understanding. This disrupts well-being even (especially) when agents act in the best way possible.

Moral injury comes out of the field of psychology to name a kind of harm experienced by veterans of war. This harm is not properly described by post-traumatic stress disorder (PTSD) because unlike PTSD, which focuses on fear and the repercussions of life-threatening situations, moral injury looks to the damage caused by moral strife; some people who experience PTSD may also experience moral injury and vice versa, but PTSD and moral injury are often regarded as distinct phenomena.[71]

Two major definitions of moral injury originate from the concept's early pioneers, Jonathan Shay and Brett Litz and colleagues.[72] Although the definitions are often cited together, they approach moral injury in distinct ways.[73] Shay focuses on, what Joseph Wiinikka-Lydon describes as, the "institutional context" of moral injury.[74] As such, Shay argues that the moral shortcomings of leaders can cause moral injury in their subordinates.[75] Shay contends that moral injury possesses these three components:

1. Betrayal of what's right
2. by someone who holds legitimate authority (in the military— a leader)
3. in a high stakes situation.
All three.[76]

He writes, "It [moral injury] deteriorates their [agents'] character; their ideals, ambitions, and attachments begin to change and shrink."[77]

Litz and colleagues, on the other hand, focus on individual actions.[78] While defending certain therapeutic interventions for moral injury, they define "potentially morally injurious experiences" as

> perpetrating, failing to prevent, bearing witness to, or learning about acts that transgress deeply held moral beliefs and expectations.... Moral injury requires an act of transgression that severely and abruptly contradicts an individual's personal or shared expectation about the rules or the code of conduct, either during the event or at some point afterwards.... The event can be an act of wrongdoing, failing to prevent serious unethical behavior, or witnessing or learning about such an event. The individual also must be (or become) aware of the discrepancy between his or her morals and the experience (i.e., moral violation), causing dissonance and inner conflict.[79]

Importantly, these different views taken together demonstrate that moral injury arises from situations of moral transgressions of some kind. Litz and colleagues' definition offers myriad ways in which one may be involved in moral transgressions—as perpetrator, as witness, as one who fails to act. Shay's definition, on the other hand, focuses on leaders who betray subordinates.

A crucial part of Litz and colleagues' definition of moral injury is that it occurs when the person is faced with "the discrepancy between his or her morals and the experience (i.e., moral violation), causing dissonance and inner conflict." This definition involves an event (some kind of moral violation), an awareness of the moral violation, and consequent internal harm. They go on to explain that veterans who are unable to incorporate these actions into their self-understanding may feel "shame, guilt, anxiety," and they advocate for "self-forgiveness" (among other things) as part of the healing process.[80]

While Shay goes so far to impugn character damage into moral injury, Litz and colleagues do not. But both Litz and colleagues and Shay argue that moral injury manifests as emotional disruption: despair, suicidal tendencies, and being prone to violence.[81]

Also, to be clear, both definitions do not exculpate blame for how veterans act because of moral injury. Agents are morally responsible for how they act in light of moral injury. So if a morally damaged soldier goes on to commit offenses in her personal life, she is morally responsible for those actions, and she is responsible for seeking ways to change.

It is important to recognize that there are limits to using moral injury literature in my study. Importantly, not all cases of moral injury are caused by tragic dilemmas. As the aforementioned definitions show, morally injurious events include a range of actions from maliciously motivated actions where the agent is not striving to act in the best way possible and knowingly hurts or abandons others, abuses power, and so on, to situations where right action is difficult to discern or where an action is justified according to accepted ethical theories and notions of just war. Furthermore, the moral injury literature, for the most part, has not focused on offering ethical analyses of the variety of events that can cause moral injury. This is evident in Litz and colleagues' use of "guilt" and "self-forgiveness," which seemingly apply to the wide array of morally injurious events without specification. In light of this, it is my view that moral injury literature would benefit from increased ethical analysis, and moral injury healing programs would benefit from incorporating more tools and strategies to help moral agents understand the ethical nature of morally injurious events in order to examine their own moral culpability, partial moral culpability, or innocence. This lacuna in current moral injury literature means that it is necessary to proceed carefully when evaluating the ethical implications of moral injury. As a result, I identify and focus on only a particular kind of morally injurious event, situations that are notably ethically challenging.

I suggest that what I call tragic dilemmas in a Christian context, scholars of moral injury often describe as situations where right action is "ambiguous."[82] Not all of these cases constitute tragic dilemmas, but many do. These are cases where lives are at stake, the agent experiences limited options, and right action may be difficult to determine or is ambiguous. Often the agent performs an action that is considered "justified" according to the Rules of Engagement, but the agent feels guilty because she violated a moral principle.

For instance, Litz and colleagues note that current developments in war are likely to create situations that lead to moral injury via "ethically ambiguous situations," such as guerrilla warfare, war in cities, and unmarked combatants.[83]

Psychologists Irene Harris and colleagues discuss helping patients come to terms with what they call "morally ambiguous situations," defined as times where "no response could be completely characterized as 'good' or 'bad.'"[84] For them, "morally ambiguous situations" include a case where a child wearing a suicide vest approaches a group of soldiers. In this incident soldiers ask the child to leave, then they fire warning shots, to no avail. The soldiers want to protect themselves, and they do not want to kill a child. In another case from Harris and colleagues, soldiers find an aggressor located in a medical building who is shooting rockets into an open market. The soldiers want to protect the people in the marketplace, but they wonder how to proceed for fear of hurting patients or even damaging the hospital.

Shay gives an example of a Marine sniper tasked to kill an enemy sniper who is found with a baby slung onto himself.[85] The Marine thinks the baby is acting "as a 'human shield.'"[86] The Marine shoots the sniper. He believes the act is justified because it was in accordance with both the Law of Land Warfare and the Rules of Engagement, yet the event stays with him forever (according to Shay's telling). The Marine is distressed by his actions presumably because he violated a moral code to not kill children, even though in that case it was lawful to do so. These cases are instances of tragic dilemmas because obligations to protect human life and the vulnerable will inevitably be unmet and tragedy ensues.

Evidence from moral injury cases shows how participation in these kinds of events have detrimental effects. For instance, moral injury is evident in the final case in the introduction. Nick has a difficult time coping with having killed an Afghan boy who was shooting at Nick and his fellow Marines. Of the event Nick says, "You know it's wrong. But . . . you have no choice."[87] Nick turns to alcohol and is cited for driving under the influence. Eventually Nick finds himself unable to continue his service as a Marine and is honorably discharged. And while he eventually lands a stable job, he can't escape his past.

Research on moral injury indicates that Nick is not alone in his experience. Moral injury causes devastating shame, guilt, anxiety, and anger that can manifest in a variety of ways, including self-isolation, self-harm, or harming others. Based on interviews with clinicians, Kent Drescher and colleagues put together an in-depth list of the effects of moral injury.[88] They categorize the effects into groups: "Social problems, trust issues, spiritual/existential issues, psychological symptoms, and self-deprecation."[89] These can manifest as

> social withdrawal, sociopathy, problems fitting in; legal and disciplinary problems, and parental alienation from their child. Loss of trust or a sense of betrayal . . . giving up or questioning morality, spiritual conflict, profound sorrow, fatalism, loss of meaning, loss of caring, anguish, and feeling haunted . . . depression; anxiety; anger; reenactment; denial; occupational dysfunction; and exacerbated preexisting mental illness . . . guilt, shame, self-loathing, feeling damaged, and loss of self-worth.[90]

Litz and colleagues' influential article offers a theory for why this harm occurs, arguing that it occurs because a coherent sense of the self is disrupted. They explain that moral injury "creates dissonance and conflict because it violates assumptions and beliefs about right and wrong and personal goodness."[91] They describe how this manifests as agents' inability to make sense of the events because the events are counter to how they think about themselves and how they think the world works. In their view, veterans may have troubling reconciling their actions with a sense of their own goodness. In this way, the agents cannot "assimilate," "accommodate," or "integrate" the events.[92] Litz and colleagues and Shay both stress that trust is ruptured: trust in oneself, trust in others, trust in how the world works. Thus, moral agents have trouble making sense of their actions and the world around them.

Soldiers who are involved in making choices about a threatening child soldier or a marketplace shooting often live with long-term psychological distress, even when they believe their choice was justified. I believe these are instances of tragic dilemmas. The soldiers' deliberate involvement in the loss of a life (or lives) implicates them, even though their moral responsibility is lessened due to their constrained options, as I discuss earlier. As many of these cases show, such as the case of Nick, these agents act with repugnance of the will insofar as they do what needs to be done, but do so with revulsion. As a result of their actions, these moral agents often withdraw, alienating themselves from their communities and support systems. These agents act in ways that are antithetical to their prior selves. The emotional harm prevents them from participating in activities and relationships, and it stays with them, souring their lives long after the incident.

It might seem strange that a solider finds herself morally tormented about taking a life. For if killing a combatant is so antithetical to the soldier's worldview, why is she a soldier? But I see that a great contribution of moral injury studies is precisely this point—that even so-called trained killers find themselves suffering from moral qualms about their actions in war, even in cases where the action is justified according to just war theory or the Rules of Engagement. These soldiers find that actual combat and killing adds a profundity to what it means to take a life. The work of moral injury theorists is important in that it illustrates that moral principles such as taking a combatant's life, taking an innocent life, or taking a life in self-defense might not be as easily justified as previously thought. This has important implications, for just war theory operates on the pretense that the obligation not to kill can, in the right circumstances, fall away. I believe the existence of the phenomenon of moral injury calls this into question.

It is important to note that the claim for the existence of tragic dilemmas and my understanding of nonnegotiable moral requirements are not rooted in the moral experiences of veterans coming back from war feeling guilty and damaged. Rather, they corroborate Hursthouse's philosophical concept of marring. Furthermore, moral responsibility is not determined by their feelings of guilt but according to the ethical concepts I develop throughout this book and attend to in this chapter—the existence of nonnegotiable obligations in accordance with Christian moral demands, lament, repugnance of the will, relational autonomy, mitigated responsibility, and social structures.

In this chapter I have developed an understanding of tragic dilemmas in a Christian context. I have argued that a tragic dilemma occurs when an agent is faced with two (or more) nonnegotiable moral requirements as determined by the Christian commitments to protect human life and the vulnerable. The unmet moral obligation is a duty to protect precious goods, so it is a transgression and a tragedy when that duty cannot be fulfilled. This is marked by Augustinian lament. Deliberation with sufficient knowledge in light of relational autonomy means that agents are morally responsible for the foreseeable consequences of actions they choose, so agents bear some moral responsibility for having acted in a tragic dilemma. Moral responsibility, however, is diminished when acting with repugnance of the will. Structural injustices often cause situations of tragic dilemmas. It is a sad and tragic consequence of unjust social structures that moral agents find themselves facing dreadful choices. As such, members of society must accept responsibility for the existence of many tragic dilemmas. A tragic dilemma has the power to mar the agent's life, as evidenced by some cases of moral injury. Healing is the appropriate Christian response to this tragedy, and it is the topic of the next chapter.

NOTES

1. Tessman, *Moral Failure*, 1. See also 27–28 and her section on negotiables and nonnegotiables, 31–44. See also chapter 1 of this book where I introduce Tessman's distinction.
2. Hursthouse, *On Virtue Ethics*, 74. I discuss this in chapter 1.
3. Tessman, *Moral Failure*, 31–44. See also chapter 1 of this book where I discuss Tessman on this point.
4. My example. I do not, in fact, have a dog now, but I grew up with dogs.
5. Tessman, *Moral Failure*, 44.
6. Tessman, *Moral Failure*, 94. For Tessman's view of Philip Tetlock's theory, see Tessman, 94–98. See also chapter 1 where I explain Tessman's view of this.
7. Tessman, *Moral Failure*, 99–149.
8. For where Tessman discusses nonnegotiable moral requirements in terms of vulnerability, see Tessman, *Moral Failure*, 223–56. See also chapter 1 of this book where I describe Tessman's view of negotiable and nonnegotiable obligations. For Gowans on "responsibilities to persons" and moral tragedy, see Gowans, *Innocence Lost*, 117–54, 218–36. See also chapter 1 of this book where I discuss Gowans. For Nussbaum on tragic loss, see Nussbaum, "Costs of Tragedy." See also chapter 1 of this book where I discuss Nussbaum.
9. Genesis 1 and 2; John 13:1–17; Matthew 5:2–12; and Luke 6:20–26.
10. Hernández, "Killing in War." Alternatively, pacifism offers a slightly different approach for coming to the conclusion that killing is fundamentally opposed to Christianity. However, Christian pacifism is not monolithic, and there are debates within it about what kind of force and coercion are permissible and why. A full discussion of Christian pacifism is beyond the scope of this book.
11. Hernández, "Killing in War," 204, 206. Note that there is debate as to whether the Decalogue prohibits all killing or only murder. A full discussion of this is beyond the scope of this book. For more, see Scola, "You Shall Not Kill."
12. Hernández, "Killing in War," 208.
13. Kelly, "The Duty to Preserve Life."
14. United States Conference of Catholic Bishops, *Ethical and Religious Directives*, nos. 59, 56, 57. See also no. 58.
15. Matthew 25:31–46. In *Gaudium et spes*, the common good is defined as "the sum of those conditions of social life which allow social groups and their individual members relatively thorough and ready access to their own fulfillment." Second Vatican Council, *Gaudium et spes*, 26. For a highly influential text on the preferential option for the poor, see Gutiérrez, *A Theology of Liberation*.

16. Farley, *Compassionate Respect*. See also Spohn, *Go and Do Likewise*.
17. Himes, *Modern Catholic Social Teaching*. See also *Catechism of the Catholic Church*, nos. 2444, 2448.
18. For a related discussion on intrinsic evils, see chapter 3 of this book.
19. Note that while his seems to be a somewhat idiosyncratic view for his time period, Augustine suggests that there is no harm caused in the case where one is unable to bury the dead. For more on this, see chapter 2 of this book.
20. To see how this is handled using the principle of double effect, see chapter 3 of this book.
21. This is addressed in chapter 1 of this book. For Hursthouse's position, see Hursthouse, *On Virtue Ethics*, 76.
22. Hursthouse, 76. Bernard Williams does not seem to use regret exactly in this way, as his usage indicates a feeling about the lingering obligation. For more on Williams's view, see chapter 1 of this book. See also, Williams, "Ethical Consistency."
23. For more on this, see Eshleman, "Moral Responsibility."
24. Recall from chapter 1 that Williams introduces a third category to this typical understanding with his notion of "agent-regret." He gives the example of a responsible lorry driver who accidently runs over someone. In his view, agent-regret prompts the responsible driver to want to make up for the death even though it was an unfortunate, unpredictable crash. Williams is specifically not discussing wrongdoing, distinguishing it from my focus. See Williams, "Moral Luck," 28.
25. De Wijze, "Tragic Remorse."
26. De Wijze, 454–58. The topic of dirty hands was discussed in chapter 1 of this book.
27. De Wijze, "Tragic Remorse," 464–65. Note that DeWijze thinks that in some cases atonement is impossible.
28. De Wijze, 470.
29. Stoljar, "Feminist Perspectives on Autonomy."
30. Kellison, "Impure Agency and Just War," 322.
31. Kellison, 327, my emphasis.
32. Kellison, 327.
33. Callahan, "Abortion and the Sexual Agenda," 235.
34. Card, *Unnatural Lottery*, 25.
35. Card, 29.
36. Card, 28.
37. Card, 32–34.
38. My example.
39. Many feminists, including Card, want to move away from the concept of guilt, at least partly because oppressed groups tend to be assigned an unfairly large amount of blame when this category is operative. But it seems to me it is possible to correct that while still using the concept of guilt. Extending the realm of culpability could even serve some feminist goals, in my view—for example, to use a strong sense of guilt to indict various individuals and social structures culpable for patriarchy and its harms.
40. *ST* I-II q.6 a.8 obj.3, and Aquinas's response, *ST* I-II q.6 a.8. For Aquinas's view of types of ignorance, see McCluskey, *Thomas Aquinas on Moral Wrongdoing*, 88–91.
41. *ST* I-II q.6 a.8.
42. *ST* I-II q.6 a.8.
43. *ST* I-II q. 76 a.3, which clarifies Aquinas's view on this.
44. *ST* I-II q.6 a.8.

45. *ST* I-II q.6 a.8.

46. *ST* I-II q.6 a.8.

47. *ST* I-II q.6 a.8.

48. *ST* I-II q.6 a.8.

49. Daly, "Structures of Virtue and Vice," 344. See also Second General Conference of Latin American Bishops, *Transformation of Latin America*. For a good introduction to the development of this concept, read more of Daly's article. See Daly, "Structures of Virtue and Vice," 341–52.

50. John Paul II, *Reconciliatio et paenitentia*; John Paul II, *Sollicitudo rei socialis*; For more on the development of this, see Daly, "Structures of Virtue and Vice"; Gutiérrez, *A Theology of Liberation*; Finn, "What Is a Sinful Social Structure?"; and Shadle, "Where Is Structural Sin in *Laudato Si'*?"

51. Daly, *The Structures of Virtue and Vice*, 166.

52. Daly, 168–91.

53. Finn, "What Is a Sinful Social Structure?"

54. Finn. See also, Benedict XVI, *Caritas in veritate*.

55. Finn, "What Is a Sinful Social Structure?," 138.

56. Finn, 149. Daly also uses the concept of emergence. See Daly, *The Structures of Virtue and Vice*, esp. 180–81, 186–88.

57. Finn, "What Is a Sinful Social Structure?," 149–50, 153, 154–55.

58. Nussbaum, "Costs of Tragedy," 1015. I raise this example in chapters 1 and 3.

59. Shadle, "Culture," 50. See also Cloutier, "Critical Realism and Climate Change."

60. Shadle, "Culture," 50.

61. Shadle, 47.

62. Cloutier, "Critical Realism and Climate Change." 64–67.

63. Culture is addressed at length in Finn's later edited volume, particularly in the chapters already cited here. See Shadle, "Culture"; and Cloutier, "Critical Realism and Climate Change." A full discussion of contingent faculty is beyond the scope of this book. For some great recent discussions on this topic, see Keenan, "Vulnerable to Contingency,"; and Keenan, "University Ethics and Contingent Faculty."

64. Tessman, "Against the Whiteness of Ethics," 200–202. Note that when she discusses dilemmas here, she does not address a distinction between moral dilemmas and tragic dilemmas and uses the term "moral dilemmas."

65. Tessman, 202.

66. Tessman makes a similar point in various works. See Tessman, *Moral Failure*, 175–203; and Tessman, *Burdened Virtues*, 89. *Burdened Virtues* offers an excellent analysis, working from an Aristotelean framework, for how oppression can impede virtuous behavior and undermine flourishing.

67. Hursthouse, *On Virtue Ethics*, 79.

68. Tessman, *Burdened Virtues*, 28.

69. Hursthouse, *On Virtue Ethics*, 73n8.

70. Tessman, *Burdened Virtues*, 89. Note that the position I am taking is not as extreme as the possibility suggested by Tessman.

71. Brock and Lettini, *Soul Repair*, xii–xv.

72. Shay, "Moral Injury"; and Litz et al., "Moral Injury and Moral Repair."

73. Wiinikka-Lydon, *Moral Injury and the Promise of Virtue*, 156–60; and Wiinikka-Lydon, "Moral Injury as Political Critique."

74. Wiinikka-Lydon, *Moral Injury and the Promise of Virtue*, 158.

75. Shay, "Moral Injury," 57–66. For Shay's early work on this, see Shay, *Achilles in Vietnam*.

76. Shay, "Moral Injury," 59.

77. Shay, 59.

78. Wiinikka-Lydon, "Moral Injury as Political Critique," 222.

79. Litz et al., "Moral Injury and Moral Repair," 700.

80. Litz et al., 700, 704.

81. Shay, "Moral Injury," 60; and Litz et al., "Moral Injury and Moral Repair," 697.

82. Litz et al., "Moral Injury and Moral Repair," 696; and Harris et al., "Moral Injury and Psycho-Spiritual Development."

83. Litz et al., "Moral Injury and Moral Repair," 696.

84. Harris et al., "Moral Injury and Psycho-Spiritual Development," 260.

85. Shay, "Moral Injury," 58–59. Shay does not call this a "morally ambiguous situation," but it clearly follows the pattern of the aforementioned cases.

86. Shay, 58–59.

87. Wood, "Moral Injury."

88. Drescher et al., "An Exploration of Moral Injury."

89. Drescher et al., 11.

90. Drescher et al., 11.

91. Litz et al., "Moral Injury and Moral Repair," 698.

92. Litz et al., 698.

5

CHRISTIAN APPROACHES TO HEALING
AFTER TRAGIC DILEMMAS

In this chapter I construct a modest framework for a Christian approach to healing from tragic dilemmas where healing occurs within a Christian community setting. As I argue in the prior chapter, the only kind of plausible dilemma in the Christian view is properly considered a tragic dilemma. This is because, as I argue, in the Christian view, nonnegotiable moral obligations arise from the sanctity of life and human vulnerabilities. Tragedy occurs when these obligations are not upheld. Moral agents who act in tragic dilemmas may experience personal moral repercussions, which is why healing is crucial and should be offered by Christian communities.

I propose that the recovery process should take place within the context of the Christian story and allow for moral discernment. Healing must draw moral agents out of distress and must reconnect the moral agent to the community. Because we are social beings and because society often bears some blame for the occurrence of tragic dilemmas, healing must also happen in, with, and among the community members. As I show in this chapter, healing in this way is a practice because it invites God's healing grace while forming the Christian community to live in a way that is attentive to harm, adaptive to moral agents' needs, patiently committed to the healing process, and open to authentic lament and God's presence.

In the previous chapter, I investigate the relationship between moral injury and tragic dilemmas. In this chapter, I begin with a moral injury case study that illustrates what is at stake in healing from tragic dilemmas. I then turn to various healing approaches from different contexts to garner insights into healing that are applicable to tragic dilemmas. I learn from current and ancient approaches to healing after war, insights from experiences of struggle, healing according to restorative justice models, and healing using trauma-informed approaches. Based on these, I develop ten considerations to guide community-based healing for tragic dilemmas, where healing is a Christian practice.

THE CASE OF CAMILO AND THE DIFFICULTY OF HEALING AFTER A TRAGIC DILEMMA

The case of Camilo reveals not only the challenges inherent to recovery after tragic dilemmas but also the ways traditional therapeutic models fall short when dealing with tragic dilemmas. Recall the case of Camilo presented in the introduction.[1] Camilo is a veteran of the Iraq war. He was raised Roman Catholic and has been influenced by liberation theology. Camilo participated in a range of activities while at war—he killed enemy combatants according to the rules of war, and he was involved in some nefarious activities. He suffers from both PTSD and moral injury, and as scholars Rita Nakashima Brock and Gabriella Lettini explain, "Camilo stresses very adamantly that his PTSD is a breach of trust with the world. Moral injury, however, is the violation of a moral agreement he had with his own internal world, his moral identity."[2] I am concerned specifically with Camilo's involvement in a particular morally injurious situation that I believe is akin to a tragic dilemma.

While on tour, Camilo was confronted with a young man threatening those around him with a grenade. Camilo's reflection indicates he believes he was morally obligated to protect the crowd, and he believes he was morally obligated to protect all lives, even the man with the grenade. Despite his military training and even though targeting the man would ensure safety for others around him, Camilo is distressed about taking the young man's life. Of the aftereffects of the event Camilo says, "That day I knew something had forever changed inside me. I felt a hole within me that had no bottom, an infinite void that could never be replenished. For weeks after the incident, my mind could not shake off the images of the young man walking, and breathing, and then down on the ground, bloody, and dead."[3] Camilo knows his action is justified according to traditional rules of war, yet he feels, essentially, as if he violated a moral principle.

The previous chapter provides theoretical underpinnings for how and why his feelings can be justified. That is, his feelings are a result of being faced with nonnegotiable moral obligations. And even though he makes the "right" decision, he leaves a nonnegotiable obligation unmet, so he is morally responsible for this. Camilo suffers from this event. Coherent with my defense of marring in the prior chapter, Camilo's life is seemingly marred as a result of participation in this tragic dilemma.

In an attempt to heal, Camilo seeks help from a therapist. Camilo describes his experience with the man with the grenade to the therapist, but the therapist cannot grasp what Camilo finds morally troubling about the event. Camilo recounts the session with the therapist:

> He [the therapist] told me that I shouldn't be so hard on myself. The young man had actually thrown a grenade that could have killed people from the crowd or, at a later time, he might have ended up killing other soldiers or civilians. I had followed a lawful order, and I had not opened fire until I was convinced that he was indeed going to throw a grenade. I sat that day with that therapist, and on a certain level I had to agree with him. The problem was that as I observed that young man through the sight of my rifle, when he was still alive, there was something inside me, a voice one could say, that was telling me not to squeeze the trigger. And I knew, without a shred of doubt, that I should not disobey that voice, and that if I did, there would be serious consequences to face. . . . When I opened fire that day, I violated that law and desecrated the most sacred sanctuary of my being.[4]

The therapist unhelpfully dismisses Camilo's conscience. While Camilo agrees with the therapist that he acted lawfully, Camilo observes that he transgressed a fundamental and deeply held moral principle to not kill. The therapist's inclination to ignore Camilo's ethical concerns thwarts his healing because the therapist is unable to deal with the ethical issues at hand. Healing is elusive without proper engagement with Camilo's ethical qualms. Essentially, Camilo desires healing from a tragic dilemma. The Christian community can and ought to offer that healing.

COMMUNITY AND PRACTICE

This section provides a theoretical underpinning for understanding the relationship between community, healing, and practice that informs the rest of the chapter and the healing approach I suggest. I argue for an approach to healing where healing from tragic dilemmas is a communal, Christian practice.

This understanding of healing builds on Alasdair MacIntyre's influential work on practice. MacIntyre defines practice as follows:

> By a "practice" I . . . mean any coherent and complex form of socially established cooperative human activity through which goods internal

to that form of activity are realized in the course of trying to achieve
those standards of excellence which are appropriate to, and partially
definitive of, that form of activity, with the result that human powers
to achieve excellence, and human conceptions of the ends and goods
involved, are systematically extended.[5]

While goods that exist "externally" to an activity, such as wealth and fame, can
be acquired a variety of ways, MacIntyre explains that "goods internal to the
practice" are only attainable through that practice.[6] To explain this, MacIntyre
gives the example of a young child who learns chess. If the child plays chess
only to win candy, she acquires an external good but not an internal good.
However, the child embodies chess as a practice if she plays to master the
specific, internal goods of chess, such as a "particular kind of analytical skill,
strategic imagination and competitive intensity."[7] MacIntyre explains that
these goods are both particular to chess and known to the excellent chess
player who plays chess well. A feature of this that I want to draw out is that
chess is a practice when viewed as a game in its entirety, not simply taken as
a discrete move or two. So while a strong opening move alone—the Sicilian
Defense, let's say—is not a practice in and of itself, a game that involves a
series of plotted attacks, defensive plans, and positional plays done for the
sake of excellence in the game is a practice.[8] MacIntyre teaches that chess is a
practice because it has specific goods known to and achieved by the excellent
chess player.

   A few of MacIntyre's concepts are crucial to the notion of community
healing as a Christian practice that I propose: a practice is performed in community, a practice possesses internal goods, and a practice arises from a series
of excellent actions. I will build from, augment, and adapt MacIntyre's notion
of practice to develop a concept of healing from tragic dilemmas as practice.

   Craig Dykstra and Dorothy C. Bass argue for a Christian understanding
of practices that both builds on and departs from McIntyre.[9] I follow their
emendation that Christian practices are "normed not only internally but also
through the responsive relationship of Christian practices to God."[10] As such,
"Christian practices address fundamental human needs and conditions."[11]
Dykstra and Bass explain that identifying human "needs" requires understanding what God wants for humans and for creation. Healing is a practice
in their view because it "develops in practitioners certain skills, habits, virtues,
and capacities of mind and spirit" that translate into living in and understanding the world in a new, more authentic way.[12] Thus, they teach that healing can
be considered a practice when it provides deeply needed recovery and when it
is enacted within a community context in a certain, intentional way.

While moral healing is not exactly what Dykstra and Bass describe, it operates in a similar way to the healing they discuss in that it also involves specific modes of being, the content of which comes out later in this chapter with the ten considerations I offer. Taken together, the considerations foster the goods that are internal to the practice of healing from tragic dilemmas. This is similar to how the rules of chess set the parameters of the game and, consequently, the conditions for the internal goods of chess. For those offering support, healing shaped by the considerations cultivates the goods of emotional and spiritual attunement with another through accompanying someone who is experiencing emotional and moral strife. For the person healing, the considerations cultivate the good of openness to receiving support. And for all those involved, the considerations build the goods of patience, steadfast commitment to healing, and recognizing God's presence.

Healing from tragic dilemmas as a practice is evidenced convincingly by the contrast of the example of Camilo's therapist. Those engaged in community-based healing for tragic dilemmas will approach people like Camilo in a radically different way from Camilo's therapist, who was emersed in a different kind of healing based on secular, individual therapeutic ideals.

Furthermore, my understanding of healing as a practice relies on the power of community, asserting that God's healing comes through the community. The communal aspect takes on a special role when seen through Jennifer Beste's view that God's grace is ushered in through relationships.[13] Beste is not discussing tragic dilemmas, but her insights about the connection between God's grace and relationships are valuable and applicable to my project. Beste crafts her view using trauma theory and Karl Rahner's ecclesiology. She argues that the severe harm of incest, when viewed through trauma theory, shows that personal relationships can cause devastating harm to the point of potentially undermining a moral agent's freedom and ability to choose God in the fundamental option.[14] Beste argues that in this type of experience, personal relationships thwart grace. Conversely, she argues, trauma theory elucidates how personal relationships are instrumental in healing from trauma when they provide a way for victims to feel safe, reimagine their narratives, and reestablish agency. As Beste describes, this kind of healing is commensurate with descriptions of the work of grace. Because this kind of healing occurs through personal relationships, she argues that personal relationships can be a vehicle for grace. Beste shows how the power of relationships to both harm and heal reveals the centrality of personal relationships in receiving God's grace. Beste uses concepts from Rahner's ecclesiology to argue for the possibility of a Rahnerian "theological conviction that God mediates grace interpersonally."[15] According to Beste, "God depends on us to love our neighbor in order to mediate God's love and foster each other's freedom to respond positively to God's grace."[16] Beste points out that this is a demanding ethic, for it crystalizes the importance of relationships for oneself and for others. As it relates to Beste's project, Christian communities ought to be sites for healing from sexual violence.[17] Her important insight relevant to my project is that loving God and letting God's love flow from oneself requires being in community. In light of this, it is incumbent on church communities to create and foster opportunities for many kinds of transformative personal relationships that usher in grace's healing power.

This view has profound implications for healing from tragic dilemmas because it shows that the healing power of grace occurs through personal relationships and thus is radically social. Healing from tragic dilemmas is a Christian practice because it is a communal activity normed and informed by God. Healers and the healed involved in this practice embody and achieve the goods internal to this practice: accepting support (for those healing); being attuned to another person's emotional, spiritual, and physical needs and incorporating approaches that are adaptive to specific needs (for those offering support); and exhibiting patience, lament, and an openness to God's presence amid strife (for all involved in the healing process). These goods are developed through the ten considerations for healing that I discuss in this chapter. How the considerations are lived out will vary by community and context, which is why their excellence is known by those who are able to live them out well.

LESSONS FROM VARIOUS APPROACHES TO HEALING

The ten considerations for healing come out of insights from various perspectives: scholars writing from moral injury and war studies, experiences of suffering, the perspective of restorative justice, and North American church-based healing after trauma. These approaches do not specifically deal with tragic dilemmas, but they are areas of thought where theory and praxis intersect to provide healing after a difficult event. I have chosen approaches that characterize different contexts in order to be sensitive to how location is an important aspect of healing. In this section I briefly introduce these various approaches to healing, and then I spend the remainder of the chapter crafting the considerations drawn from these approaches.

Healing after Participation in War

Helping veterans to heal after participation in warfare has been a concern since ancient times. Currently, moral injury studies offers a promising, albeit limited, approach that can be augmented by the wisdom of ancient and medieval societies. A modern-day "Liturgy of Reconciliation" for veterans offers a blueprint for how to do this.[18]

As I discuss in chapter 4, moral injury studies originates from a military context and addresses moral pain. Brett Litz and colleagues, among others, have developed a theory around moral injury and a plan for psychological healing from moral injury.[19] Their approach to healing, and the contribution of moral injury studies in general, is different from other psychotherapeutic models represented by Camilo's therapist primarily because moral injury proponents tend to take seriously agents' moral evaluations of their actions.

However, the healing approach of Litz and colleagues has limited applicability here both because they do not distinguish between tragic dilemmas and other nefarious actions (as I describe in the prior chapter) and because of their limited engagement with Christian ideas and presuppositions. Litz and colleagues acknowledge that "spirituality," defined as "an individual's understanding of, experience with, and connection to that which transcends the self," can be an avenue for healing.[20] And while they recognize that religious and spiritual communities can encourage forgiveness and serve as places where veterans can experience healing and wholeness, how that works is not fleshed out in their work.[21]

Furthermore, as Warren Kinghorn points out, because Litz and colleagues lack a teleology, "they are unable to distinguish between meaningful and non-meaningful moral suffering," where meaningful suffering encourages or leads to flourishing, while nonmeaningful suffering works against flourishing and living well.[22] In response, Kinghorn argues for a Christian approach to healing from moral injury. Kinghorn's Christian perspective leads him to highlight the role of community and to learn from Christian approaches used in the past. Kinghorn regards moral injury as deeply social, occurring within a social context. As such, he sees healing as taking place both between veterans and God and between veterans and the community.

Kinghorn draws from Bernard Verkamp's research on ancient Christian practices of penance and fasting for soldiers returning from war.[23] Kinghorn points out that the medieval practices make way for opportunities to "lament" and "mourn"—important themes that come out of Christian reflection.[24] And Kinghorn suggests these practices may allow people to hold in tension the joy of soldiers returning from war and the reality that war may call on soldiers to do unseemly things. Kinghorn emphasizes the role of the community to support veterans to become "reconciled to God and to the Christian community."[25]

As Verkamp's work shows, from roughly the fourth to eleventh centuries, Christians returning from war were supposed to participate in some kind of penance. Views varied from Basil the Great in the fourth century claiming that soldiers who killed in war should not take communion for three years, to Theodore of Tarsus in the seventh century asserting that "one who slays a man by command of his lord shall keep away from the church for forty days" and "one who slays a man in public war shall do penance for forty days," to about the twelfth century when penances were no longer commonly invoked.[26] Later texts, such as Bonaventure's *Confessionale* and Thomas Aquinas's *Summa*, make no references to penance after war, according to Verkamp.

While the specifics varied, Verkamp argues that some of the reasoning for penance comes out of Augustine's concern that participation with *libido dominandi* (lust for domination) is predominate in war. In Augustine's view, individual acts within a just war could and would be sinful when done out of concupiscence with *libido dominandi*, and even if soldiers were not guilty, they were likely to feel shame for their actions.[27] Verkamp contends that the idea of penance was also supported by ancient ideas about the impurity of killing (*horror sanguinis*).[28]

Verkamp explains that the penitential requirements ranged from time away from the church, to abstaining from the eucharist, to fasting. Interestingly, he notes that penance occurred through communal ceremonies. These public confessions and "the absolution they conferred, therefore, w[ere] understood to be in the name of all the members of the *corpus Christianum*, both living and dead, including those who had been wronged," leading to "a process of reconciliation."[29] Verkamp points out that these were not ceremonies of punishment but rather displays of Jesus's love and attempts to right wrongs.

The implication for contemporary times is clear to Verkamp, who regards Christian medieval penances as a strategy for inviting veterans back in a society, a task that is still vital today, in his view. Verkamp regards current-day "liturgies of reconciliation" as one of a few, sparse attempts to do that.[30] The popularity of ancient penances suggests to Verkamp that contemporary attempts should be amplified. He looks to William Mahedy as providing a model for this.[31] Mahedy was a Catholic-priest-turned-Episcopal-priest and former army chaplain who served in Vietnam and who later worked with many veterans. Mahedy provides a program for a "Liturgy of Reconciliation" that veterans found moving when used to mark a decade after Vietnam.[32] In this liturgy, a communal opening prayer includes these lines: "Lord, you have delivered us from the scourge of war. May we who have been scarred by war be reconciled to each other, to our enemies, and to you. May we become peacemakers in all that we do."[33] This is followed by biblical readings and reflections, a communal confession and absolution, and then Holy Communion. The communal confession occurs after "personal reflection" and contains both general components and parts specific to war—"we confess that we have sinned against you [God] in thought, word, and deed, by what we have done, and by what we have left undone" and "We are sorry especially for our sins of violence and hatred."[34] The absolution then offers forgiveness and peace.

This liturgy channels the messages of ancient penances that Verkamp and Kinghorn recognize as relevant today, and these insights are instructive for healing from tragic dilemmas. As a communal liturgy, this serves the important task of giving veterans an on-ramp back into society after participating in war. Importantly, it acknowledges wrongdoing within the context of forgiveness. This is also a step toward holding together various and disparate responses to war, which Kinghorn rightly recognizes as important. As it relates to tragic dilemmas, moral agents in tragic dilemmas might also need a route for reconstituting oneself in the community in a way that holds together the tension of acting in the best way possible while still transgressing a non-negotiable obligation. The ancient penances and the modern Liturgy of Reconciliation underscore how the focus should be reconciling in Jesus's love and not judgment, an emphasis that is critical to healing from tragic dilemmas.

Lessons from Suffering

There is much wisdom to be gained from experiences of strength amid struggle and suffering. Emmanuel Katongole advances lessons from the African context in order to craft a political theology centered on the insights of heroic Christian witnesses. While his aims are distinct from mine, the powerful stories he learns from are enlightening for healing from tragic dilemmas. In the US context, Bryan Massingale and Emilie M. Townes give voice to the struggle for racial justice, demonstrating the strength inherent in admitting the depths of suffering and resistance.

Katongole deals with themes of trauma and healing after the atrocities of war and genocide, and he is concerned with how the church can productively engage with politics in Africa with the insight that the church has the power to inform "social imagination" and thus shape what is possible.[35] Katongole's investigation is prompted by the observation that despite the church's persistent presence in Africa, and its often-well-meant interventions, the church has essentially been ineffective at combating Africa's violent cycle of exploitation. As a result, "the church's role in Africa's social history helplessly swings between the postures of reticence, frantic activism, and total cooption."[36] To escape from its abusive colonial history and to reinvent its future, Katongole argues Africa needs a new "imagination" that the church is perfectly suited to inform because "all the realities of the Christian tradition—the Scriptures, prayer, doctrine, worship, Baptism, the Eucharist, the sacraments—point to and reenact a compelling story that should claim the whole of our lives."[37] Katongole asserts that the church must see itself as integral to the political order, rather than as an entity acting alongside politics. Essentially, Katongole's project is about healing and rebirth. In this sense, there is much to learn from the community-based, Christian approaches Katongole presents.

Katongole chronicles the story of Angelina Atyam, who embodies what is possible when one is open to new imaginative possibilities.[38] In 1996 Atyam's daughter, Charlotte, was one of 139 girls kidnapped by the Lord's Resistance Army, a rebel group in northern Uganda. The rebels released 109 girls, but 30 were not released, including Charlotte. Charlotte suffered greatly and "was regularly raped and used as a sex slave."[39] Atyam met regularly with the other parents of the girls who were captured. After a while Atyam observed that the parent group was hindered by their anger, so she suggested that they let go of their anger and forgive the kidnappers, even before the children were returned. Following Atyam's lead, the parents found themselves freed by "the strange gift of forgiveness."[40] They shared their new perspective with other parents who faced similar struggles. The possibility of forgiveness seemed so outrageous that a mother whose son had been horrifically kidnapped in another abduction remarked, "Angelina, are you from a different planet?"[41] Atyam went so far as to meet with the mother of Charlotte's kidnapper to embrace her and to let the mother know that Atyam had forgiven her son.[42] When Atyam's public work to call attention to the kidnapping led the rebel forces to offer to return her daughter in exchange for her silence, Atyam refused. She wanted all the girls to return. Eventually Charlotte escaped seven years and seven months after being abducted.

Atyam's example is filled with lessons on healing. Two components are particularly striking: the role of imaginative possibilities and the power of lament. People around Atyam thought she was "from a different planet." Her vision of the possibility of forgiveness, rooted in her relationship with God, allowed her to live in a different way. Katongole recognizes this as a strength of Christianity and what it can offer in the face of struggle. Katongole's vision for a political theology for Africa is rooted in the power of seeing oneself within the Christian story and the ways in which participation in this story can transform societal ideas and what people believe is possible. For Katongole, this takes root in a Christian imagination that prompts new, creative, and nonviolent visions for life. This showcases the power of the Christian story to reimagine what is possible in a variety of spheres, including the political. Atyam embodied this alternative way of viewing herself and in turn invited others into this radical view.

Additionally, Atyam lived out the power of lament. During the time that her daughter was gone, Katongole writes that Atyam lamented and hoped. Atyam says she had "trust" that her daughter would return, she mourned, prayed, and "wrestled with God."[43] Katongole makes the following observation about Atyam and others who triumphed in hardship: "Their agency and activism was born in and through the experience of suffering and social dislocation."[44] Katongole shows how the event of suffering incited Atyam's activism, and her hope sprouted from admitting the enormity of her suffering. Thus Atyam's hope is not a naive belief that all would be well but rather a commitment to remain steadfast in her faith. Atyam had an honest relationship with God—a relationship where she questioned and "wrestled" with God frequently and honestly. She cried to God about her situation. She continued to argue with God . . . and to pray.

This view of lament is not limited to Atyam's story. Massingale and Townes write about the power of lament when suffering racial injustices in the United States. Massingale is attentive to the US Catholic Church's disturbing inattention to racism.[45] He underscores the pernicious nature of racism and how it functions, arguing that "racial injustice, on its deepest levels, [is] impervious to rational appeals and cognitive strategies."[46] He regards lament as a fitting and powerful response. He explains that "laments are cries of anguish."[47] Massingale emphasizes that lament calls attention to difficult experiences, thus challenging the status quo.[48] In the context of racism, Massingale explains that the marginalized lament their situation, prompting the privileged to recognize and lament the harm they have caused.[49] Lament on the part of the privileged involves, according to Massingale, "acknowledging their individual and communal complicity in past and present racial injustices," which should lead to admitting responsibility for harm along with hope in the new world that is possible when there is a commitment to change.[50] Thus, Massingale shows how lament allows society and institutions to move forward in new ways. Townes proposes "communal lament" that centers Black lives and that involves everyone.[51] Townes explains that healing, justice, and authentic faith come about through this process. She draws out the connection between lament, faith, and hope and the ways in which honest lament calls forth God.[52]

In chapter 2 I discuss Augustinian lament. The lessons from Atyam, Massingale, and Townes highlight the critical function of lament. As such, hope and lament are further discussed as a specific consideration later in the chapter.

Healing in Terms of Restorative Justice

Geoff Broughton explains that while there is no agreed-upon definition of restorative justice, and no agreed-upon role for moral responsibility and forgiveness within restorative justice models, most scholars agree that restorative justice centers on healing and justice for perpetrators, victims, and communities.[53] Broughton invokes a restorative justice vision rooted in God's healing power where the whole community takes responsibility. He explains that this is beautifully embodied by South Africa's Truth and Reconciliation Commission (TRC). While the TRC is an expansive topic far outside the scope of this book, relevant to this book's understanding of restorative justice is that South Africa's TRC was founded, in part, on the Bantu notion of *ubuntu*, which acknowledges the profound relationship between the individual and the community.[54] The TRC's chairperson, Archbishop Desmond Tutu, explains what *ubuntu* means: "My humanity is caught up, is inextricably bound up, in yours."[55] Broughton argues that restorative justice thought of in this view focuses on the whole community.

At its core, restorative justice seeks to restore relationships justly. Karen Guth enhances this view and lays out the benefits of restorative justice:

> Among its numerous virtues, advocates emphasize its ability to uncover, acknowledge, and repair harms; to empower victims and address their needs; to further justice, responsibility, and accountability for individuals and institutions; to ascertain and recommend needed reforms or reparations; to maximize reintegration and reduce revictimization and recidivism; and to enable the possibility of apology, forgiveness, healing, and reconciliation.[56]

Guth acknowledges critiques of restorative justice and the way it sometimes ignores theology, among other things. Despite its shortcomings, she says that restorative justice is useful and able to identify the "stakeholders" in wrongdoing.[57]

The aspects of restorative justice that are crucial to my project are the recognition that wrongdoing can implicate the whole community due to the social aspect of injustice and the harm that reverberates throughout a community. Justice, then, involves accountability along with restoring relationships. Importantly, restorative justice is not about retribution. Invoking restorative justice when thinking about healing from tragic dilemmas is meant to emphasize the community context in which many tragic dilemmas occur because tragic dilemmas are often created by social conditions (as I discuss in chapter 4) and because tragic dilemmas can cause harm felt by the whole community.

The mitigated culpability of moral agents in tragic dilemmas (marked by lament and repugnance of the will, as I discuss in chapter 4) complicates the traditional categories within restorative justice. While in cases of tragic dilemmas the moral agents act in the best way possible, this is not necessarily the presumption of how perpetrators act in the restorative justice model. Furthermore, the social conditions that force otherwise innocent moral agents into tragic dilemmas blur who should be considered a victim and who should be considered a perpetrator.

Nevertheless, restorative justice is applicable to tragic dilemmas because it calls attention to healing the whole community. This emphasis is important for tragic dilemmas where many people may experience harm from a tragic dilemma. For instance, in the third case in the introduction, some mothers in the Holocaust were forced to decide between saving themselves or dying in the gas chambers with their children. The scenario is described by Holocaust survivor Clara L., who seems haunted by this memory. The bystanders she describes who call out to the mothers are likely haunted by this memory as well. All of this points to the mental anguish felt by those involved in the situation or witnessing it. This trauma was most likely induced by design of the Nazis. And in the case of the mother in the Philippines who must decide what to do about her son who needs the costly ventilator, it is also likely this has reverberating effects for the whole family. For instance, this will likely affect the siblings, who the mother had to balance care for and who have to live with the knowledge that their needs greatly informed the decision. The case does not mention people outside the close family, but it is easy to imagine a host of other family members and friends who are affected by the loss of the boy. In both of these cases, other people may not understand the mothers' decisions, and yet they presumably must interact within the same social spaces. This demonstrates the various social dynamics present after tragic dilemmas and the need for insights from restorative justice when healing from tragic dilemmas.

Healing after Trauma

Healing after trauma is a growing, interdisciplinary, interreligious field.[58] Scholar Deborah van Deusen Hunsinger crafts a theological approach to aid trauma survivors. She recognizes that trauma can arise from war, sexual assault, other types of violence, and a range of other harmful events. She points out that trauma can have psychological and physiological effects, and it can manifest itself in a variety of ways, from anger to silence and everything in between.[59] Trauma-informed approaches require meeting survivors where they are psychologically and working carefully to avoid retraumatizing the survivors.[60] A trauma-based approach is sensitive to survivors' past experiences and the ways that their coping mechanisms were adaptive and useful in and around the situations of trauma, and it is attentive to the reality that new coping adaptations are fitting when the person is removed from the situation/event of trauma.[61]

Hunsinger proposes a Christian theological response where trauma survivors find healing in a trusting community or with a companion. Hunsinger explains that the survivor should be invited into the Christian story and encouraged to feel God's redemption and all-encompassing love. She teaches that when approaching emotional pain, it is important to avoid any form of victim-blaming but rather to focus on how individuals acted in the best way possible.[62] This informs the considerations below. Also crucial here is that to the extent tragic dilemmas are traumatic events, these situations may evoke complex emotional responses that require thoughtful interventions guided by trauma-informed mental health experts.

Also pertinent to my investigation are practical applications of this field. Susan Nienaber details how Alban at Duke Divinity School performed a Resilient Congregations Study where researchers analyzed twelve congregations that successfully overcame various kinds of trauma, ranging from sexual misconduct to natural disasters to deaths to leadership crisis. "Success," according to the study, means that the churches remained open and were able to retain or even grow in membership size. From this study, Nienaber identifies various traits that the successful churches possess.[63] Nienaber's work informs some of the specific considerations in this chapter, and the study's insights are helpful here because of the congregational context. The study provides helpful ideas for what works in a church setting given various community and leadership dynamics.

CONSIDERATIONS FOR CHRISTIAN HEALING AFTER TRAGIC DILEMMAS

Working with lessons from those various approaches to healing, here I identify ten considerations for how communities can foster healing after tragic dilemmas. Taken together and embodied within a church community, these considerations build a Christian practice of healing that cultivates goods specific to healing from tragic dilemmas and that ushers in God's grace. Agents are reconstituted into the community and, at the same time, the community acknowledges its role in tragic dilemmas. Importantly, the specific actions a community chooses to engage in are highly dependent on the community's location and the needs of its members. Geographic location, culture, and socioeconomic realities will inform to what extent the considerations are fitting and how to embody them. For instance, a woman in the Philippines coping with having removed her son's ventilator confronts different needs than a veteran returning to his home in the United States. These differences can range from different material and practical needs to different emotional and spiritual needs. In light of this, the considerations are meant to be clear enough to offer guidance, yet general enough to account for the specific community and the particular needs of the moral agents. I offer the following considerations: (1) storytelling, truth-telling, and the Christian story; (2) attention to emotional and physical response; (3) attention to basic needs; (4) acknowledgment of God's presence; (5) particularity; (6) endurance and patience; (7) companionship; (8) moral discernment; (9) forgiveness; and (10) lament and hope.

Storytelling, Truth-Telling, and the Christian Story

In defending what it means to reimagine the social order in various parts of Africa and why it should be done, Katongole highlights the power of stories, something that must also be reckoned with after tragic dilemmas. Katongole writes: "Stories not only shape our values, aims, and goals; they define the range of what is desirable and what is possible."[64] The stories we tell ourselves can have both good and bad consequences, as stories can empower or disempower and expand or contract our worldviews. Stories engage the imagination, stretching or limiting how we see ourselves and what we can accomplish. Because of this, the stories we tell ourselves and each other and the biases and assumptions embedded in them must be made explicit. In the situations Katongole addresses, he believes the African political order can transform once people live within a new story. Through the Christian story and Christian resources, people can conceive new possibilities for African politics and for their place in the world, as Katongole shows through the life of Atyam.

Those who experience tragic dilemmas must have space to identify the story or stories they have told themselves or have been told about the event and the conditions surrounding it. Social context and cultural ideas can greatly influence how we think about ourselves, as I describe in chapter 4. For example, some veterans who may have experienced tragic dilemmas are met with a narrative about their heroic actions when they return home. Many find this narrative frustrating as it does not give them space to acknowledge the bad parts of war.[65] Others may return to families or social situations that look down on their involvement, automatically shrouding veterans' experience in guilt and shame. In the case of Mr. C., who asks to be removed from a ventilator, his mother's hesitancy about her action is met with confidence in the bioethics text that she did the right thing. These stories limit the agents, especially when they tell narratives that do not match the moral agents' experiences. Often the assumptions within the stories are not made explicit, so actors are left feeling guilty or misunderstood without knowing why.

Stories must be made explicit for transparency and accountability. Once the stories are out in the open, agents can reflect on them and choose to accept or reject the stories and the worldviews they offer. This is what Guth identifies as "truth-telling."[66] Guth explains that truth-telling is when one puts forward one's narratives, and in doing so, truth-telling calls out biases, injustices, and wrongdoing. She explains that truth-telling requires accurately naming wrongs and identifying all those involved in and affected by the event. Guth recognizes that it is not always possible to reveal the whole truth, but we must do the best we can.

Truth-telling is also a key to success for churches in the Alban at Duke study that have successfully dealt with trauma. Nienaber observes that the communities who overcame traumas were explicit in identifying and acknowledging the pain and problems they were facing.[67]

Christian healing is not only about revealing stories but also about interacting with the Christian story. In truth-telling, Christians affirm their beliefs.[68] The Christian story, at its core, is about God's love, about being loved by God and loving God, oneself, and one's neighbor, even (especially) the enemy. Believers further enter this story when they engage in various facets of the life of the church.

The importance of creating a new narrative imbued by the Christian story is made clear in work on healing after trauma. Those who suffer from trauma are struggling to integrate their traumatic event into a coherent narrative of the world. The Christian story offers a theological way for trauma survivors to reimagine themselves, for, as Hunsinger explains, "Healing, whether physical, emotional or spiritual, is always set within this larger context of the unimaginable reaches of God's salvation."[69] As such, Hunsinger explains that trauma survivors can reimagine their story within the Christian story where Jesus is savior: It is Jesus who suffers but also, more importantly, Jesus who redeems. And as Katongole argues, it is only through the vision of the Christian story that a new political order can be reimagined, just as the Christian story inspired Atyam's view when her daughter and the other girls were kidnapped.

Healing after tragic dilemmas requires entering the Christian story though engaging the church community and church events. Reconstituting moral agents into the Christian community after tragic dilemmas requires intentionally inviting these agents to be part of the church community and the Christian story. The goal is to help agents know themselves as loved by God.

Attention to Emotional and Physical Responses

Trauma studies highlight the principle of paying attention to agents' emotional and physiological responses. Stories and truth-telling are important, but they must be performed in responsible ways. As Hunsinger warns, "Talking about it [the traumatic experience] can, in actual fact, make matters worse."[70] This is why storytelling needs to be done responsibly, and likely under the guidance of a mental health professional trained in a trauma-informed approach. Truth-telling can only be done when agents feel safe. When truth-telling is performed in the context of a church community, this means ensuring that the group is a space where trust has been established. When agents are in safe spaces, they are more likely to feel as if they can talk freely to people who will listen generously and with their best interests at heart. This means listening without judgment while also making space for accountability.

Attention to Basic Needs

The realities that may impede a focus on personal growth—no free time, no childcare, work commitments, and so on—inform this consideration because healing will be thwarted if agents' basic needs are not met. For instance, if agents are concerned about their safety and well-being, if they don't know how they will get their next meal, if they are not sure where their children will sleep, and so on, they will be unable to worry about moral discernment or reflect on what story they are living. Communities must also recognize the importance of psychological healing and the importance of supporting professional therapeutic interventions when needed. Taking on all these needs will be hard, if not impossible, for most communities. This consideration, then, is about communities acknowledging what basic needs are preventing agents from healing and reflecting on how best to support agents in light of these urgent needs. It is about being realistic and attentive to what is possible.

Katongole describes people who did this in grand ways. For instance, to combat tribalism, Bishop Paride Taban started the Kuron Holy Trinity Peace Village.[71] To cultivate peace, he first made sure that basic needs were met. To combat fighting over food, he created a plot where people could learn about farming techniques and diet. He started schools for girls, boys, and adults, and he opened a clinic that offered not only medical aid but health care education. Katonogle points out that once competition for these basic needs was eliminated, people from various religions and tribes in the village were free to interact with one another in peaceful and friendly ways and embrace a new way of living.

Katongole also tells of Maggy Barankitse, who, during the civil war in Burundi, started Maison Shalom in Burundi, a village for children.[72] As Katongole explains, the civil war was in part due to the false narratives pitting Hutus and Tutsis against each other. Barankitse created a place apart from these narratives where Hutus and Tutsis could live together. She could confront these false stories because she was immersed in the Christian story where God's love is universal. She built four villages that served as refuges for orphans and child soldiers. Using her parents' land, she built houses where children could live in family units. She created businesses for the children to run, such as a salon, tailor, and mechanic shop. She provided various types of education, including computer education. She built a swimming pool and a cinema. Barankitse satisfied people's basic needs, and in doing so she offered them an alternative to the story of war and hate.

Most communities will find it impossible to meet basic needs in the way Barankitse and Taban did. However, these examples can serve as inspirations for imagining what is possible for a community to offer, and they underscore the necessity of providing practical support.

Acknowledgment of God's Presence

As Katongole points out, Atyam, Barankitse, and Taban recognize God working in their lives. Katongole observes, "Thus, Angelina, Taban, and Maggy constantly draw attention to God's story as foundational to their lives and work."[73] Katongole shows that they are persistently aware of God's presence, and this awareness sustains them. The charge of this consideration, then, is to be persistently mindful of God, to call God into the healing process, and to see God dwelling in oneself and others. It is crucial to seek God even, and especially, in difficult situations where God may seem hidden—for it is at those times that God sustains in unexpected and powerful ways. Who better than the Christian community to help one recognize God's presence?

This is powerfully seen in Atyam's story. Even during her suffering, she took note of God even—and especially—when that meant "wrestling with God." As Katongole shows, she was aware of God's presence within her sadness and frustration. She did not shy away from God during that difficult time but invited God into those hard feelings. Acknowledging God's presence does not mean that everything is going well or that God is only found in good times. This is also the challenge of acknowledging God's presence— finding it and accepting it in difficulty. Like Atyam, this might not be easy and may involve hurt toward God. But it is this commitment to seeing God in those times that makes this powerful and profound.

Particularity

Guth highlights restorative justice's commitment to particularity, a dimension that should be constitutive of healing from tragic dilemmas.[74] As such, she illuminates that what works in one context may not necessarily work in another context. Particularity accounts for how social location informs stories, needs, resources, and so on. An appreciation of particularity motivates these considerations, for I am using suggestions rather than prescriptions because I believe communities ought to implement these ideas in the ways they see fit. However, this is such an important point that it warrants specific attention.

Furthermore, particularity demands that moral agents' voices are central and that they are partners in the healing process. As such, healing after tragic dilemmas should be done in dialogue with the moral agents who acted in the dilemmas and in response to their needs and the needs of the community.

Endurance and Patience

Healing is a process, and it takes time. Healing requires endurance and patience. Growth happens in small increments. Patience is a trait of the survivor churches Nienaber discusses where the average time of recovery from the event of trauma was 4.75 years.[75] The extended timeframe gives a sense of how long a community could be committed to the healing process. This does not necessarily mean that a church community should put together a five-year healing plan for tragic dilemmas, but it does highlight that healing is a long-term process. Well after the community-based healing events have been performed, agents may still be in recovery. The community should not forget the agents and move on; rather, the community must remain sensitive and alert to the fact that healing is demanding and ongoing.

Atyam also embodies patience as she waited over seven years for her daughter to return. As her story shows, patience doesn't mean resignation. She advocated for the children to come back and worked with other parents during the long years of waiting for her daughter. She demonstrates patience as a process.

Healing from tragic dilemmas means remaining steadfast and committed, spurred on by incremental progresses and not giving up when healing and change occur slowly. This means not expecting quick healing. In our fast-paced, instant culture, patience can seem out of place. But embracing patience is important because healing doesn't always occur on our desired timeline.

Companionship

Beste's theological analysis of grace manifested in relationships highlights the importance of relationships insofar as she argues that God's grace works through our relationships.[76] In light of this, healing from tragic dilemmas honors the importance of connections.

Christians can learn from the Jewish grieving process, which ensures that mourners grieve in the presence of community.[77] The bereaved sit shiva for seven days. When sitting shiva, the grieving remain in their homes and mourn their losses for seven days in the company of family and community who are committed to supporting them through the difficult time. During this time, some community members offer company while others offer practical help such as providing food. Many people usually drop by the home to visit during this time. After seven days, the mourner walks around the block with a friend as a symbol of rejoining the society. Judaism honors the ongoing mourning process in many ways. For instance, the mourner says the Kaddish prayer—a prayer of praise and thanksgiving—for a year.

These Jewish rituals highlight the importance of companionship because they are not only about words but also about being present and available. Communities who offer healing after tragic dilemmas ought to prioritize offering companionship—to be present in caring ways.

This resonates with the idea of accompaniment used by the Jesuit Refugee Services (JRS), or Paul Farmer and Gustavo Gutiérrez.[78] Accompaniment includes many of the considerations already noted here, such as attention to needs and particularity. Accompaniment is a form of companionship that honors others; it is not about putting forward one's own agenda but about supporting others in their journeys. For instance, JRS's model of accompaniment means that they support refugees and their goals in various areas. Rather than a model focused on sending in international volunteers, JRS supports local projects and endeavors run by refugees in those areas. This demonstrates how accompaniment is not swooping in and taking over but, rather, being part of a support network.

Friendship is also an important component of companionship. Friendship is a topic with much theological currency and is outside the scope of this book, but it is fair to say that friendships are crucial relationships. Agents can find companionship and nurture friendships by participating in the work of the community, from outreach programs to social justice work to advocacy. These are ways that moral agents can contribute to the greater society.

Moral Discernment

Once agents know themselves as loved by God, they can engage in proper moral discernment. Without proper discernment, agents can become confused or overly reliant on authority figures to tell them whether their action was right or wrong. These are things to avoid. Ultimately, the goal is to empower moral agents with the needed resources for proper moral discernment and to accompany them in their process of discernment. The community responds by trusting the discernment of moral agents and supporting their discernment. Of course, discernment is done with the aid of the Holy Spirit, for moral discernment is ultimately about relationship with God.

I am proposing a model of moral discernment where agents engage in in-depth discussions and reflections on the topics of moral and causal responsibility, right, wrong, virtue, guilt, remorse, forgiveness, intention, object, and circumstances. These are complex issues. However, it is crucial that agents discern for themselves what their involvement in tragic dilemmas means using the proper ethical categories. I hope this book can be a resource for that. When a community respects each person's conscience and ability to make judgments about themselves, the community provides resources and space for intense moral discernment.

In his account of the historic development of moral discernment, theologian and ethicist James Keenan, SJ, describes a form of discernment that brings together the previous discussions on companionship and moral discernment. He brings to life the *Irish Penitentials*, which he describes as "a discernment marked by accompaniment."[79] Keenan explains that this Celtic practice of confession was common from around the sixth century until the thirteenth century, and it gave people (at first monks, but then it spread to include lay people) the opportunity to tell their sins to a spiritual director who helped them determine how to make up for the sins. Keenan emphasizes the phrase that theologian Hugh Connolly uses to translate into English the Gaelic term for spiritual advisor: "soul-friend."[80] Keenan explains that the soul-friend's role was "to accompany the individual through the trials of life."[81] Keenan points out that the soul-friend helped the seeker stay on the path to God by being in conversation about ways to reconnect to God.

This provides a helpful way of thinking about the role of the community in supporting moral discernment after tragic dilemmas. Church communities can be like soul-friends, offering an environment to think and pray with someone going through a difficult time. Like the role of the soul-friend, moral discernment in this view is not focused on judgment but on one's relationship with God. The community can be a kind of support network and springboard for thinking through a tragic dilemma. The categories of moral responsibility, repugnance of the will, and lament can help a moral agent and the community to more properly understand the tragic dilemma, which is necessary for moving forward in a way that heals relationships between individuals and between the moral agent and God. This should also support the community in finding ways to transform itself and thus prevent or mitigate similar, future tragic dilemmas.

Forgiveness

Margaret Farley draws our attention to the relationship between divine forgiveness and human forgiveness. She emphasizes that forgiveness is rooted in "God's creative love."[82] Farley explains that God freely creates and freely forgives, and we most clearly see God's forgiveness in Jesus Christ. She eloquently writes:

> But when we turn back now to experiences of human forgiving and being-forgiven, it helps to ponder something like a "dropping of the heart" that is active surrender, letting go of, whatever would bind us to past injuries inflicted on us by others, or whatever would prevent our acceptance of the new life held out to us in the forgiveness of those we have injured. In both there is a letting go of our very selves, a kenosis, that alone frees us to become ourselves; and there is an acceptance, an affective affirmation and *unio affectus*, of the one to be forgiven and the one who forgives. "Dropping our hearts," surrendering our selves, in forgiveness or in trust of being-forgiven, is the beginning choice that makes renewed relationships possible. It comes full circle in the mutuality that restored relationships promise.[83]

For Farley, forgiveness is a "letting go": for the wronged, it is letting go of hurt from the past, and for the wrongdoer, it is letting go of whatever is inhibiting

her from receiving forgiveness and moving into the future. Farley understands this in terms of kenosis, God's outpouring of love. In Farley's view,
when we forgive and accept forgiveness, we love like God loves.

Furthermore, since forgiveness is central to the Christian message, as
Farley points out, those who have accepted God's forgiveness can share with
others what this communicates about Christianity and God. This, then, is a
whole new and untapped way that those involved in tragic dilemmas can give
back or engage with the community—they can be regarded as embodying
wisdom and experience about God's love. In this view, they become teachers.

Christian forgiveness is inherently relational—that is, it always is done
in relationship—in relationship with God and with others. This emphasis
widens the scope of forgiveness offered by secular therapeutic approaches
that tend to focus on self-forgiveness, especially approaches in moral injury
studies that emphasize this.[84] Self-forgiveness is also critiqued as predicated
on a problematic splitting of the self where the good part of the self forgives
the bad part of the self.[85] Scholar Anthony Bash explains that self-forgiveness
can be necessary in some situations: when a wrongdoer must forgive herself
after the victim forgives her or when a victim cannot or does not forgive.[86]
But generally within the Christian view, self-forgiveness is only one component of forgiveness because forgiveness is between the wrongdoer, the victim, and God.

Given the social emphasis of tragic dilemmas, it is also necessary to recognize that communities are also in need of forgiveness for their participation in
structures that contribute to tragic dilemmas. As I discuss in chapter 4, sinful
social structures are the result of individual actions that, when taken together,
form systems where sin is supported. As a result, the community should reflect
on how it participates in the structures that cause tragic dilemmas—how they
benefit (or do not benefit) from unjust structures, at whose expense they experience these benefits, what choices they have within the system, what choices
they have that others do not have, and how they can make different decisions
that will change the system to benefit everyone. Community members should
commit to some kind of social justice action that works to undo the structure
that contributed to the tragic dilemma.

Lament and Hope

Lament and hope are particular ways of naming and responding to tragedy and calling for social changes. We must lament tragic dilemmas. For
Massingale, lament is the crucible of change because lament focuses on
the hard truths of a situation. Massingale asserts, "Lament is a profound

response to suffering, one that stems from acknowledging its harsh reality."[87] In Massingale's view, lament makes way for societies and institutions to move forward in new ways.[88] It is through lament that one finds strength, which is why, as Massingale explains, in the face of enormous suffering and hardship, the African American spiritual goes, "Nobody knows the trouble I've seen. Glory Hallelujah!"[89] The power of Massingale's description of lament is the way lament openly names grief but does not let pain have the final word. Massingale writes, "Lamenting holds together both sorrow and hope in ways that defy easy rational understanding. . . . Lament thus facilitates the emergence of something new. . . . It is indeed a paradox of protest and praise that leads to new life."[90] So when agents direct their suffering and grief to God with the hope that God will hear and answer them, this is properly called lament. This is different from venting stress to one's friend or releasing frustrations by hitting a punching bag. Those are fine expressions of emotions, but they are not lament because lament is suffering, arguing, grieving, and so on in the presence of God, trusting that healing will come about through God.

Offering insights from a womanist perspective, Townes reflects on how lament leads to healing.[91] In lyrical form, Townes meditates on Joel's lament, explaining that "the problem is the inhumanity and evil of others toward the people of Israel."[92] Townes focuses on turning to God. She explains how hope comes out of an "honest lament": "For it is only after the people enter honest lament / through a faith that leads them to hope / that God's answer is: grace."[93] Townes explains that through God and in lament, suffering can be transformed. And lament is powerful, according to Townes, because it acknowledges individual and communal shortcomings, and it admits the depths of mourning. On the communal levels, Townes writes, "Communal lament . . . names problems, seeks justice, and hopes for God's deliverance—so that we may not see that terrible Day of the Lord made real in our lives."[94] Townes's message is powerful because she argues that lament leads to a steadfast hope that demands change in the world.

Massingale and Townes teach that expressions of lament do not occur in isolation but are about mourning *in the presence of God*; lament is facing suffering *with God*. And in this view, lament sows the seeds of hope because the agent is committed to God, the God of hope.

Healing from tragic dilemmas requires lament and hope. Lament is how moral agents involved in tragic dilemmas and the communities that support them can confront tragic dilemmas. This includes naming the unjust structures that may have caused tragic dilemmas, acknowledging the complicity of society members, admitting the bad luck of finding oneself in such a situation, or sitting in the grief of losing a loved one. Lament can be expressed in a variety of ways—such as song, prayer, poetry, art, dance, plays, Scripture, crying, and so on. Healing, then, ought to create opportunities for authentic expressions of lament. By the grace of God, individuals and communities face suffering, and this is a movement of hope.

Taken together, these points are not meant to offer an exhaustive program for recovery; rather, these considerations give an outline of key theological tools for healing. Christian healing after tragic dilemmas will require a faith-based, community approach often paired with professional counseling therapy. An effective healing group will address tragic dilemmas by making space for individual reflections and group discussions. Agents will be invited into a new life in the Christian story. Healing will grow out of moral discernment, and then, when appropriate, taking personal responsibility will further deepen one's healing. Healing will address what forgiveness means and the obstacles to forgiveness. Within the healing process, the larger church community should acknowledge its role in causing tragic dilemmas and should accompany those who are suffering. Communities should responsibly account for particularity. Moral agents should be encouraged to be part of the community and should participate in community life, including acts of service. There should be space for lament and activities that strengthen hope. Through the embodiment of these considerations, healing from tragic dilemmas is a communal practice that cultivates the goods of openness and receptivity, creative embodiment, patience, hope, and lament. This process invites God's grace.

NOTES

1. See introduction of this book. The case is based on Brock and Lettini, *Soul Repair*, 86–89.
2. Brock and Lettini, 87.
3. Quoted in Brock and Lettini, 88.
4. Quoted in Brock and Lettini, 88.
5. MacIntyre, *After Virtue*, 187.
6. MacIntyre, 188.
7. MacIntyre, 188.
8. My details, expanding on MacIntyre's chess metaphor.
9. Dykstra and Bass, "A Theological Understanding of Christian Practices."
10. Dykstra and Bass, 21n8.
11. Dykstra and Bass, 22.
12. Dykstra and Bass, 25.

13. Beste, "Receiving and Responding to God's Grace."
14. Beste, 4–15. As previously noted, Beste is not discussing tragic dilemmas, nor would incest or sexual abuse be considered a tragic dilemma. I am homing in on her insights about God's grace and personal relationships.
15. Beste, "Receiving and Responding to God's Grace," 14.
16. Beste, 15.
17. Beste, 16–18.
18. Mahedy, *Out of Night*, 241–45. See Verkamp, *Moral Treatment of Returning Warriors*, 104, where Verkamp discusses Mahedy.
19. Litz et al., "Moral Injury and Moral Repair"; and Litz et al., *Adaptative Disclosure*.
20. Litz et al., "Moral Injury and Moral Repair," 704.
21. Litz et al., 704.
22. Kinghorn, "Combat Trauma and Moral Fragmentation," 67.
23. Kinghorn, 67–71; and Verkamp, *Moral Treatment of Returning Warriors*.
24. Kinghorn, "Combat Trauma and Moral Fragmentation," 69.
25. Kinghorn, 70.
26. Quotes are from Verkamp, *Moral Treatment of Returning Warriors*, 2.
27. Verkamp, 6–7, 22, 34.
28. Verkamp, 11–12.
29. Verkamp, 105, 107.
30. Verkamp, 104.
31. Verkamp, *Moral Treatment of Returning Warriors*, 104; and Mahedy, *Out of Night*.
32. Mahedy, *Out of Night*, 241–45.
33. Mahedy, 241.
34. Mahedy, 242.
35. Katongole, *The Sacrifice of Africa*.
36. Katongole, 50.
37. Katongole, 61, 61–62.
38. Katongole uses this story in both *The Sacrifice of Africa*, 148–65, and *Born from Lament*, xi–xiii. I use Katongole's accounts to describe the events relating to Atyam.
39. Katongole, *The Sacrifice of Africa*, 158.
40. Katongole, 156.
41. Quoted in Katongole, 156.
42. Katongole, 157.
43. Quoted in Katongole, *Born from Lament*, xi, xiii. See also Katongole, *The Sacrifice of Africa*, 159, where Katongole also discusses this.
44. Katongole, *Born from Lament*, xiii.
45. Massingale, "Has the Silence Been Broken?"; Massingale, *Racial Justice and the Catholic Church*; and Massingale, "Systemic Erasure of the Black/Dark-Skinned Body."
46. Massingale, *Racial Justice and the Catholic Church*, 104–5.
47. Massingale, 105.
48. Massingale, 110.
49. Massingale, 111–13.
50. Massingale, 111.
51. Townes, *Breaking the Fine Rain of Death*, 9–25.
52. Townes, 11, 24–26.

53. Broughton, "Restorative Justice," 304.
54. There are many good texts on South Africa's TRC. For an informative and influential text, see Tutu, *No Future without Forgiveness*.
55. Tutu, 31.
56. Guth, "Complex Legacy of Yoder," 122.
57. Guth, 121.
58. A full discussion of this topic is beyond the scope of this book. For some important texts, see Hunsinger, "Bearing the Unbearable"; Rambo, *Resurrecting Wounds*; Rambo, "Trauma and Faith"; and Walker and Aten, "Future Directions for the Study and Applications of Religion, Spirituality, and Trauma Research."
59. Hunsinger, "Bearing the Unbearable."
60. Substance Abuse and Mental Health Services Administration (SAMHSA), "Trauma-Informed Care," 12–14.
61. SAMHSA, "Trauma-Informed Care."
62. Hunsinger, "Bearing the Unbearable."
63. Nienaber, "Leading into the Promised Land."
64. Katongole, *The Sacrifice of Africa*, 2.
65. Wood, "Moral Injury."
66. Guth, "Complex Legacy of Yoder," 126–28.
67. Nienaber, "Leading into the Promised Land."
68. Guth, "Complex Legacy of Yoder," 127.
69. Hunsinger, "Bearing the Unbearable," 19.
70. Hunsinger, 17.
71. Katongole, *The Sacrifice of Africa*, 135–47. I rely on Katongole for my description of Taban's work.
72. Katongole, 166–92. I rely on Katongole for my description of Barankitse's work.
73. Katongole, 194.
74. Guth, "Complex Legacy of Yoder," 128–29.
75. Nienaber, "Leading into the Promised Land."
76. Beste, "Receiving and Responding to God's Grace."
77. Wolfson, "How to Make a Shiva Call"; and Winner, *Mudhouse Sabbath*, 27–39. These texts inform my understanding of the Jewish grieving process as described in this paragraph.
78. Farmer and Gutiérrez, *In the Company of the Poor*; and Jesuit Refugee Service, "40 Years of Accompaniment."
79. Keenan, "Moral Discernment in History," 671.
80. Quoted in Keenan, 671. "Soul-friend" derives from the Gaelic word for spiritual adviser at that time, "*anamchara*." On this, see also Connolly, *The Irish Penitentials*, 14.
81. Keenan, "Moral Discernment in History," 672.
82. Farley, "Forgiveness in the Service of Love," 160.
83. Farley, 166.
84. Litz et al., "Moral Injury and Moral Repair."
85. Vitz and Meade, "Self-Forgiveness in Psychology and Psychotherapy."
86. Bash, *Forgiveness and Christian Ethics*, 13–18. Note that forgiveness is not the same as reconciliation because reconciliation involves restoring the relationship in some way. On this, see Bash, 25.

87. Massingale, *Racial Justice and the Catholic Church*, 105.
88. Massingale, "Systemic Erasure of the Black/Dark-Skinned Body."
89. Quoted in Massingale, "Systemic Erasure of the Black/Dark-Skinned Body," 121.
90. Massingale, 121.
91. Townes, *Breaking the Fine Rain of Death*.
92. Townes, 10.
93. Townes, 11.
94. Townes, 25, 175–81.

CONCLUSION

The existence of moral and tragic dilemmas is highly debated, and discussions on the topic leave many questions open: Why do some moral requirements remain? What makes some moral dilemmas tragic? How might tragic dilemmas harm an agent? Are agents involved in tragic dilemmas blameworthy? And what does healing after a tragic dilemma look like? This book has set out to define tragic dilemmas in a Christian context and to answer these questions.

Although Augustine and the Augustinian tradition do not defend moral or tragic dilemmas, they do take up hard cases that are not always neatly solved. Augustine's famous judge is miserable yet guiltless. While Augustine does not go so far as to say that the judge is in a dilemma, I have argued that the judge's enduring misery and lament indicate that he faces nonnegotiable moral requirements. I have also argued that the different theological anthropologies Augustine uses to support his ethics of war and his sexual ethics reveal a weakness in his theological system. Without a category of moral or tragic dilemmas to apply to the problem of war, Augustine is unable to make consistent claims about the human person in relation to the ethics of both sex and war.

Paul Ramsey uses Augustinian ideas to tackle contemporary issues, arguing for the power of love to transform the demands of justice in hard cases. But even Ramsey seems to admit that a moral agent might be sullied by such events. This suggests that love does not always transform all of the demands of justice. Ramsey's references to uncleanliness suggest that some acts are, at the very least, morally ambiguous. Furthermore, Ramsey admits that on the way to achieving her admirable political goals, the shrewd Christian politician will likely have to agree to, and atone for, morally problematic acts. Ramsey does not call these moral or tragic dilemmas, but they share the features of dilemmas, for the agent deals with troubling consequences even while acting in the best way possible.

I have also shown how moral dilemmas and, by implication, tragic dilemmas have been dismissed by Aquinas and Thomists who argue that they are the result of personal sin or can be solved with creative thinking. Within the Thomistic tradition, the hierarchy of goods and the principle of double effect are sufficient for solving cases that may initially seem to be dilemmas. But I have argued that these are inadequate. I have also shown that while traditional Thomistic views focus on Aquinas's denial of moral dilemmas, his reflection on mixed actions is a fresh site for engaging with the dilemmas debate because there Aquinas deals with issues that are pressing for moral dilemma theorists, such as hard cases, constrained situations, and mitigating circumstances. I have argued that Aquinas's references to repugnance of the will indicate that he makes space for a view of intention that includes foreseeable consequences that repulse the will. This calls into question the way the principle of double effect has developed to claim that unwanted, foreseeable consequences are unintended. Repugnance of the will challenges this because it refers to an agent willing consequences that are foreseeable yet undesirable and therefore repugnant. Contrary to traditional views where the unwanted and forseeable consequences are deemed unintended, I have argued that Aquinas indicates these consequences are intended by the fact that the will is repulsed, thus his phrase "repugnance of the will." While this is not a Thomistic affirmation of the category of tragic dilemmas, this opens up spaces for Thomistic thought to connect to the notion of tragic dilemmas. Just as in a tragic dilemma, here Aquinas discusses how a moral agent intentionally performs an action she would rather not do in order to act in the best way possible. I have shown how this plays out in Aquinas's reflection on mixed actions, where different grades of actions share features with moral and tragic dilemmas.

Building from there, I have developed a robust definition and understanding of tragic dilemmas in a Christian context. I have argued that in a tragic dilemma an agent chooses, with sufficient knowledge, how to fulfill at least two nonnegotiable moral requirements that cannot both be satisfied. I use Lisa Tessman's distinction between negotiable and nonnegotiable moral requirements, but I argue for them in a Christian context. I argue that these requirements arise from Christian nonnegotiable commitments to protect the vulnerable and to protect human life. These commitments are supported by Catholic social teaching and scripture and are recognized by Augustinian lament. When one of these moral requirements goes unfulfilled, an agent commits a transgression (wrongdoing) and great harm is inevitably caused. Therefore, moral dilemmas in the Christian context are specifically tragic dilemmas. I have argued that when an agent chooses an action with sufficient knowledge, the agent is partially responsible for the unmet non-negotiable moral requirements. Using a relational autonomy, I have discussed how our relationships produce obligations to which we are beholden. Due to constrained circumstances, blame is mitigated when the agent acts reluctantly—that is, with repugnance of the will. Many tragic dilemmas are the result of unjust social structures, so the category of tragic dilemmas demands that society consider how unjust structures create situations where moral agents are placed in impossible moral situations. As such, there exists social responsibility for the events of tragic dilemmas. Evidence from moral injury studies shows the possibly detrimental effects of acting in a tragic dilemma and the vital role of healing. This harm is akin to the marring that Rosalind Hursthouse describes in relation to tragic dilemmas.

Christianity brings an urgency to healing as well as special resources for recovery. I have argued that community-based healing after tragic dilemmas is a practice that cultivates goods internal to the communal healing process and that brings forth God's grace. Furthermore, Christian notions of forgiveness emphasize the importance of relationships. Christian concepts of community draw out the ways in which individuals are accountable to the community and likewise, the community is responsible for how it shapes and forms individuals. To the extent that tragic dilemmas are the result of structural injustices, the Christian community must take responsibility for its participation in actions that perpetuate injustice. I have identified ten considerations for how Christian communities can support those moral agents who have acted in tragic dilemmas: (1) storytelling, truth-telling, and the Christian story; (2) attention to emotional and physical response; (3) attention to basic needs; (4) acknowledgment of God's presence; (5) particularity; (6) endurance and patience; (7) companionship; (8) moral discernment; (9) forgiveness; and (10) lament and hope. These are meant to be implemented as communities see fit in light of their contexts and the specific needs of their members.

In closing, I return to the cases from the introduction of this book and defend why they are tragic dilemmas in a Christian context according to the understanding I have argued for in this book. These cases are tragic dilemmas because in every situation the agents choose one nonnegotiable obligation over other nonnegotiable obligations. The obligations are nonnegotiable in the Christian view because at stake are human life or human needs that arise from human vulnerabilities, and these are central Christian commitments. The inability to fulfill these obligations sparks lament in moral agents. Moral agents perform transgressions when these obligations are not met and tragedy ensues. These are tragic dilemmas. Moral responsibility is mitigated in these cases so long as the agents act with repugnance of the will, but the agents must accept some responsibility for the lingering, unmet, nonnegotiable moral obligation. The events ought to spur society to recognize the moral harm of structural injustices and the ways in which individuals sustain unjust structures. The moral agents may experience personal harm—marring—from acting in a tragic dilemma. In the Christian context, agents involved in these cases would benefit from healing where they can admit wrongdoing, atone and accept forgiveness from God and others, and become reconstituted into the Christian community.

The case of resource allocation during the COVID-19 pandemic highlights the damaging effects of structural injustice and how the pandemic exacerbated inequalities already present in the US health system. The power of applying the category of tragic dilemmas to critical resource allocation cases, such as ventilator allocation, is that it demonstrates the gravity of such situations. The category of tragic dilemmas underscores that society is implicated in these deaths insofar as unjust structures and personal choices led to many of the hard cases. For instance, the coronavirus pandemic exacerbated health care inequalities in the United States. And sometimes reckless personal decisions contributed to unnecessary infections, leading to overwhelmed hospital systems. Not following social distancing practices or refusing to wear masks are not merely personal choices with individual effects; rather, these actions lead to consequences that others bear, especially the most vulnerable in society.

Furthermore, identifying these cases as tragic dilemmas stresses the moral implications for deciding who receives a critical ventilator and, thus, the importance of not afflicting individual health care professionals with these types of decisions. It is crucial that these decisions are made at high levels and interpreted and implemented by hospital ethics committees or other management groups. Expecting individual health care professionals to make these decisions, especially in the midst of navigating caretaking when hospitals are overwhelmed, is not only inappropriate but also unfair because it is morally taxing on those essential workers. Yet real life shows that decision-making protocols and ethics committees will not necessarily alleviate the harm of making these decisions. The intensity and effects of such decisions on health care professionals are expressed by Dr. Sayeed who, recall from the introduction, laments that "our humanity will be chipped away."[1] The category of tragic dilemmas widens the scope for analyzing resource allocation during the coronavirus pandemic to ensure that the broader social structures are accounted for while being attentive to both the moral stress of individuals involved in the cases and the tragedy of the loss of so many lives.

The cases from Celia K. and Clara L. share similar features as tragic dilemmas. The woman that Celia K. describes is faced with the nonnegotiable requirements to protect her daughter, her son, and the other vulnerable Jews she encounters in the woods. Those are nonnegotiable moral requirements because life is sacred, and everyone hiding is vulnerable. Protecting the life of her son remains an unfulfilled obligation. She is morally responsible for ending his life. However, her moral responsibility is mitigated as, we presume, she acted with repugnance of the will, evidenced by the description of her acting "wild" at the proposition of killing him.[2] Healing will require acknowledging the role that society played in such a horrific event.

Clara L. describes mothers choosing to give their children to elderly relatives because keeping the children ensures the mothers' death. Regardless of whether the children stay with their mothers, the children will die. The question here is whether the mothers should accept their own death sentences in order to stay with their children. This dilemma highlights the nature of obligations borne from vulnerability, for it is children's special dependence on their mothers that creates the obligation that the children should face a horrifying death sentence with their mothers, even if the mothers' lives can be saved by rejecting the obligation. Loss of life results no matter what. These are tragic dilemmas. The category of tragic dilemmas draws out the evil of the Nazi regime by identifying not only physical and mental pain and destruction but also the moral anguish that decisions like these caused. The mothers, children, and even those who witnessed these events were all likely affected by the moral choices at stake, and thus lamented the tragedies at hand.

The cases of the mother in Ethiopia and Sophie both involve choosing between symmetrical goods where children are inherently and equally worthy of dignity and life. As such, there are no obvious, relevant, moral reasons to choose one child over the other, and even if there were, the cases still involve deliberating and choosing against the life of one child. These cases demonstrate how the hierarchy of goods is ineffective to solve cases of symmetry. As I have noted, for some theorists, the lack of moral reason to choose one child over another would suggest that the choices are not moral. However, such an assessment is contrary to experience, for certainly these agents perceive themselves to be in a moral quandary. And like the cases Hursthouse describes, there are many ways in which the agents can try to act well and responsibly while determining what to do, so virtuous action is still required. For instance, it is likely that the mother thinks carefully about her final words and actions when she leaves one child and goes off to find food.

For those who ascribe to "ought implies can," the cases of the mother in Ethiopia and Sophie are resolved after choosing one child, for that choice makes it impossible, and therefore not obligatory, to save the other child. Many moral dilemma theorists deny this approach because they deny ought implies can. For theorists such as Tessman (and myself, following Tessman), ought does not necessarily imply can when dealing with nonnegotiable moral requirements, but it does apply to negotiable requirements. Christianity supports the idea that the vulnerability of the children and the commitment to protect the sanctity of life are nonnegotiable requirements. This means that the requirements remain even if they are impossible to uphold.

In these cases the mothers are responsible for the unmet obligations to the children they could not save because the moral requirements involved are nonnegotiable and because they make decisions with sufficient knowledge of what will happen. However, the constrained circumstances mitigate moral responsibility for these transgressions, as we can assume that the parents act with repugnance of the will, for they reluctantly and lamentfully make the best choice they can. The stakes are very high, and the losses are so great. In these ways these constitute tragic dilemmas.

It is also likely that being involved in these cases can mar the agents' lives. A problem with claiming that the cases are morally sorted out is that this obscures the emotional and moral effects on the moral agents. These mothers are suffering, and it is incumbent upon the Christian community to respond. The Christian community ought to offer healing possibilities for these agents where healing includes opportunities for discernment, taking responsibility, atonement, forgiveness, and reentry into the community. This might look different in different contexts, but it should involve drawing agents into the Christian story, guiding the agents in moral discernment, attending to basic needs, and offering patient companionship. When appropriate, such as in the cases of the mother in Ethiopia and Sophie, it will be necessary for the community to acknowledge its involvement in perpetuating unjust structures. In the case of the mother in Ethiopia, this means asking how a mother could be faced with such a terrible choice. Details in that specific case are sparse, but we can fill in the blanks. Such reflection prompts an evaluation of how society at large and the global community perpetuate unjust structures that support, for instance, corruption and violence that leaves villages ravaged so that mothers have to search for food.

In the case of the mother in the Philippines, the mother is forced into a hard decision due to unjust health care resource distribution that leads her family to incur exorbitant health care costs and consequent financial distress in an effort to care for the health needs of the son, Mr. C. The mother deliberates a decision with multiple obligations at stake: obligations to protect her son, to respect his autonomy, and to take care of her family. Her obligation to protect her son is not eliminated even when care for him is particularly onerous. And so her obligation to her vulnerable son remains. However, the mother's moral responsibility is mitigated if she acts with repugnance of the will—and her reluctance indicates that she does. The loss of her son's life renders this a tragic dilemma, and the Christian community ought to offer healing. It is also likely that other loved ones lament and feel the effects of this hard decision as well.

The case of drone warfare is a tragic dilemma according to my definition because it involves choosing between nonnegotiable moral requirements to protect the innocent girl and the innocent people who will be killed by the bomb the terrorists are making. As I have discussed at various points throughout the book, this is a classic example of how the principle of double effect is used. According to the principle of double effect, the girl's death is justified because her death is not the means for how the terrorists are killed, it is not desired by those involved, and it is considered a proportionately appropriate cost given what is at stake. However, the concept of tragic dilemmas asserts that the obligation to protect the girl is a nonnegotiable obligation that remains, even when the best decision is made. Thus, wrongdoing occurs and the decision-makers are morally responsible for the death of the girl.

After the strike, the sober silence of those involved in deploying the mission points to the lament of many decision-makers. However, their moral culpability is diminished when the agents act with repugnance of the will. The situation is tragic because great harm is caused—the loss of the life of an innocent girl. And this situation can have the power to mar those involved. Thus, healing is required. There is also the issue of whether killing the aggressors— the terrorists in the compound planning the attack—is a violation of the obligation to protect life. This is addressed in the cases of Camilo and Nick.

The cases of killing at war involving Camilo and Nick are different from the previous case because these cases focus on the morality of killing an active aggressor. These are tragic dilemmas because they involve the nonnegotiable moral requirement of protecting human life. Moral responsibility is mitigated, however, if Camilo and Nick act with repugnance of the will. The evidence from moral injury shows that these situations can cause emotional harm that mars the agents' lives.

The Christian community should aid in healing after tragic dilemmas. This is a practice that brings forth God's grace and thus enables the community and the moral agents to live in a new way. The specifics of healing should be appropriate for the context of the community as determined by the community.

To help imagine the healing process, I briefly sketch here how healing could play out in an urban, North American, Christian community. As I have discussed, the community can work to satisfy some basic needs that will give the agents freedom to pursue healing. This might take the form of offering childcare, providing meals during healing events, or offering healing opportunities at no cost.

This healing could occur through a faith-based group that specializes in healing after tragic dilemmas. Perhaps the group meets at the local Catholic church; maybe they meet weekly or over the course of a weekend retreat. The group would be composed of people who have experienced a variety of tragic dilemmas and led by people who are trained to address trauma, dilemmas, forgiveness, and Christian resources.

The Christian healing approach I propose takes seriously the agents' qualms. Instead of dismissing agents' feelings and telling them they acted rightly, the agents' concerns are acknowledged. Participants would be given space to reflect on the tragic dilemmas individually and with the group. The group leaders would explain to participants that they offer theological resources for healing and that this ought to be supplemented with therapy. Individual work with a trauma-informed mental health professional would help participants to access these memories in a safe and meaningful way.

The group would help the individuals to think about the tragic dilemma against the backdrop of God's love, God's unrelenting forgiveness, and moral responsibility. One way this could be done is by using the *Spiritual Exercises*, for St. Ignatius appreciates that we can only reflect on wrongdoing after we have internalized God's awesome love.[3] St. Ignatius's *Examen* could also be used, as it is a prayer that prompts personal reflection for it asks participants to sit in God's presence, show gratitude to God, reflect on one's emotions, and look for God in one's life.[4] The group would encourage a variety of methods for self-reflection such as journaling, listening to music, walking a labyrinth, walking through nature, and dance. Participants would alternate between time for personal reflection, time with a therapist, discussions with group leaders, and time to talk to the group. Agents would meet with a therapist and a spiritual adviser to help them process the event. When participants are ready, they could share their experiences with the group if they desired.

Moral discernment is crucial to healing. Agents should be given the tools and resources to think through important moral categories, such as moral responsibility, blame, agency, deliberation, and knowledge. This could be done with a trained professional who could help to elucidate these complex categories through conversation modeling the spirit of "soul-friends," as discussed in chapter 5.

Lament is a part of personal reflection. Space for lament gives the agents room to acknowledge suffering and move forward in hope. Lament may be performed in a variety of ways, including poetry, scripture, art, and song. Scripture can help to name lament, such as the Book of Job, Lamentations, and Rachel crying in Matthew's gospel.

Perhaps participants could reflect on imagery of the "Pensive Christ," such as that found on this book's cover. The image is associated with Lithuania, where it is seen throughout the country often in the form of woodcarvings, and it depicts a seated, sorrowful Jesus wearing a crown of thorns and anticipating the crucifixion.[5] Theologian Ligita Ryliškytė explains that the image and its name have a substantial history, appearing in Germany in the fourteenth century, then arriving in Lithuania from Poland in the early sixteenth century, and since the twentieth century being called "Rūpintojėlis."[6] She explains that the image is now connotated with the message that Jesus is "'one who sits with you in your sorrow.'"[7] The evocative image is filled with emotion, and when used during the healing process I describe, it invites meditation on how Jesus is present amid tragic dilemmas.

Importantly, as moral injury studies suggest, moral agents should be helped to integrate the tragic dilemma into their self-understanding so they can accept moral responsibility for the event without erroneously thinking that the event somehow makes them "bad" or irredeemable. God's loving forgiveness underscores the goodness of everyone, which is why the group should help participants think through what forgiveness looks like. They would frame forgiveness in a relational way as to stress that forgiveness comes from God. The group would discuss God's unrelenting forgiveness and the difficulty, at times, of accepting God's forgiveness. Again, the *Spiritual Exercises* could be a helpful way to pray through and reflect on God's love. Within the Catholic tradition, confession is a practice where one receives God's forgiveness. A communal Liturgy of Reconciliation adapted to tragic dilemmas could be a way for the community to support God's healing grace.

Once participants have felt God's loving presence, they could engage in activities that help them to move forward. This could include stories, songs, or poems. Because familial and social relationships are important, the group could include family members and friends in the recovery process. Perhaps families attend some group meetings where they can listen to their loved one discuss the tragic dilemma and the effect it had on them.

The healing group would also be engaged with the greater church community. The larger church community could put together a service that acknowledges those who experienced tragic dilemmas. At this service, the church community should also lament. They should acknowledge and apologize for their contribution to tragic dilemmas. This is vital because change begins when we recognize and name the extent of harm—physical, emotional, and moral—caused by unjust structures.

The group would help participants and the Christian community turn to God in hope. Hope is lived out in efforts to make change in the world. The moral agent who experienced the tragic dilemma and the church community should give back to society. It might be helpful to perform actions that specifically relate to the good lost as the result of the tragic dilemma. For example, participants could tutor the imprisoned, visit retirement homes, plan a baby shower for a mother in need, provide meals for the homeless, volunteer in local politics, and so on. The community can discern what policies and actions contributed to the creation of tragic dilemmas and then work to dismantle those structures in concrete ways, such as through advocacy, divestment, and service-related projects. These activities are not only ways to enact Jesus's request in Matthew 25 in the parable about the sheep and goats; they are also ways to make change. This work is also important because it shows agents that their lives are meaningful, and it draws out the good in themselves and others. In these ways, it is my hope that a church community could offer tools for healing to those who experience tragic dilemmas, as well as admit and atone for their participation in unjust structures that contribute to these situations.

Those involved will feel God's healing grace in various ways as participants or facilitators. The movement toward healing, enacted in the community through the proposed ten considerations and embodied in particular ways, will mold those involved to live in a new way. This is how healing from tragic dilemmas is a practice. Ultimately—hopefully—God's grace will be manifested through this communal process.

Tragic dilemmas are tragic for many reasons. They involve situations where nonnegotiable obligations cannot be met, so tragedy ensues because life is lost or people are left vulnerable. They require that otherwise good agents perform moral transgressions in an attempt to act in the best way possible. They are often the result of unjust social structures where harm is systemic and thus tragic. And they often produce wounds that moral agents must carry. The value of a category of tragic dilemmas is that it reveals these harms in all of their various forms. Without this category, hurt and destruction goes—and has gone—unnamed, unnoticed, and even covered-up by moral strategies that claim to solve hard cases. It is only after this harm is brought to light that healing can begin. It is incumbent on the Christian community to support restoration and recovery. This involves healing those involved in tragic dilemmas, as well as transforming the social structures that often cause these tragedies.

NOTES

1. Sayeed, "The Psychological Toll."
2. Greene and Kumar, *Witness*, 85.
3. Ignatius of Loyola, *Spiritual Exercises*.
4. Fleming, *What Is Ignatian Spirituality?*
5. Ryliškytė, "Post-Gulag Christology," 472–73. Note that the image is also found elsewhere.
6. Ryliškytė, 473.
7. Ryliškytė, 473.

BIBLIOGRAPHY

Aeschylus. *Agamemnon*. Translated by David D. Mulroy. Wisconsin Studies in Classics. Madison: University of Wisconsin Press, 2016.

Antonelli, Mildred. "Moral Injury." *American Journal of Psychoanalysis* 77, no. 4 (2017): 406–16.

Aquinas, Thomas. *Commentary on the Book of Job*. Edited by The Aquinas Institute. Translated by Brian Thomas Becket Mullady, OP. Lander, WY: Emmaus Academic, 2016.

———. *Commentary on the Nicomachean Ethics*. Translated by C. I. Litzinger. 2 Vols. Chicago: Henry Regnery, 1964. https://isidore.co/aquinas/english/Ethics.htm.

———. *On Kingship to the King of Cyprus*. Translated by Gerald B. Phelan. Revised by I. Th. Eschmann, OP. Toronto: Pontifical Institute of Medieval Studies, 1949. https://isidore.co/aquinas/english/DeRegno.htm.

———. *Questiones Disputatae de Veritate*, Questions 10–20. Translated by James V. McGlynn, SJ. Chicago: Henry Regnery, 1953, St. Isidore. https://isidore.co/aquinas/QDdeVer.htm.

———. "S Thomae de Aquino Opera Omnia." Fundación Tomás de Aquino, 2016, Corpus Thomisticum. http://www.corpusthomisticum.org/iopera.html.

———. *Summa Theologiae*. 2nd ed. Translated by Fathers of the English Dominican Province. New Advent, 2017. http://www.newadvent.org/summa/.

Aristotle. *The Nicomachean Ethics*. Edited by Lesley Brown. Translated by David Ross. New York: Oxford University Press, 2009.

Augustine. *City of God*. Edited by Philip Schaff. Translated by Marcus Dods. From *Nicene and Post-Nicene Fathers, First Series*, Vol. 2. Buffalo, NY: Christian Literature Publishing Co., 1887. Revised and edited for New Advent by Kevin Knight. https://www.newadvent.org/fathers/1201.htm.

———. *Concerning the Nature of Good, Against the Manichaens*. Edited by Philip Schaff. Translated by Albert H. Newman. From Nicene and Post-Nicene Fathers, First Series, Vol. 4. Buffalo, NY: Christian Literature Publishing Co., 1887. Revised and edited for New Advent by Kevin Knight. https://www.newadvent.org/fathers/1407.htm.

———. *The Confessions of St. Augustine*. Edited and translated by Albert Cook Outler. Mineola, NY: Dover, 2002.

———. *Contra Faustum*. Edited by Philip Schaff. Translated by Richard Stothert. From *Nicene and Post-Nicene Fathers, First Series*, Vol. 4. Buffalo, NY: Christian Literature Publishing, 1887. Revised and edited for New Advent by Kevin Knight. https://www.newadvent.org/fathers/1406.htm.

———. *The Excellence of Marriage*. In *Marriage and Virginity*. Edited by David G. Hunter. Translated by Ray Kearney. Hyde Park, NY: New City Press, 1999.

———. *On Free Choice of the Will*. Translated by Anna S. Benjamin and L. H. Hackstaff. Upper Saddle River, NJ: Prentice-Hall, 1964.

——. *On Grace and Free Will.* Edited by Philip Schaff. Translated by Peter Holmes and Robert Ernest Walls. From *Nicene and Post-Nicene Fathers, First Series,* Vol. 5. Buffalo, NY: Christian Literature Publishing, 1887. Revised and edited for New Advent by Kevin Knight. https://www.newadvent.org/fathers/1510.htm.

——. "Letter 138: Augustine to Marcellinus." Edited by Boniface Ramsey. Translated by Roland Teske, SJ. In *The Works of Saint Augustine: A Translation for the 21st Century,* vol. 2, 225–37. New York: New City Press, 2003.

——. "On the Sermon on the Mount." Edited by Philip Schaff. Translated by William Findlay. From *Nicene and Post-Nicene Fathers, First Series,* Vol. 6. Buffalo, NY: Christian Literature Publishing, 1888. Revised and edited for New Advent by Kevin Knight. http://www.newadvent.org/fathers/16011.htm.

——. "Sixth Book—Questions on Joshua Son of Nun." In *Questions on the Heptateuch,* ed. Boniface Ramsey, trans. Joseph T. Lienhard and Sean Doyle. In *The Works of Saint Augustine: A Translation for the 21st Century,* vol. 14, 355–80. New York: New City Press, 2016.

Baker, Deane-Peter. "*Eye in the Sky* and the Moral Dilemmas of Modern Warfare." *The Conversation,* March 31, 2016. http://theconversation.com/eye-in-the-sky-and-the-moral -dilemmas-of-modern-warfare-56989.

Bash, Anthony. *Forgiveness and Christian Ethics.* New York: Cambridge University Press, 2007.

Benedict XVI. *Caritas in veritate.* Encyclical letter. Vatican website. June 29, 2009. https://www .vatican.va/content/benedict-xvi/en/encyclicals/documents/hf_ben-xvi_enc_20090629 _caritas-in-veritate.html.

Bentham, Jeremy. *The Collected Works of Jeremy Bentham: An Introduction to the Principles of Morals and Legislation.* Edited by J. H. Burns and H. L. A. Hart. Oxford: Clarendon, 1970.

Beste, Jennifer. "Receiving and Responding to God's Grace." *Journal of the Society of Christian Ethics* 23, no. 1 (2003): 3–20.

Bonhoeffer, Dietrich. *The Cost of Discipleship.* New York: Touchstone, 1995.

——. *Ethics.* New York: Touchstone, 1995.

Bowlin, John R. *Contingency and Fortune in Aquinas's Ethics.* New York: Cambridge University Press, 1999.

Bradley, F. H. "Collision of Duties." In *Moral Dilemmas,* edited by Christopher Gowans, 62–82. New York: Oxford University Press, 1987.

Brock, Rita Nakashima, and Gabriella Lettini. *Soul Repair: Recovering from Moral Injury after War.* Boston: Beacon, 2013.

Broughton, Geoff. "Restorative Justice: Opportunities for Christian Engagement." *International Journal of Public Theology* 3, no. 3 (May 2009): 299–318.

Brown, Neil. "Experience and Development in Catholic Moral Theology." *Pacifica* 14, no. 3 (2001): 295–312.

Brown, Peter. *Augustine of Hippo: A Biography.* Berkeley: University of California Press, 2000.

——. *The Body and Society: Men, Women, and Sexual Renunciation in Early Christianity.* 20th ann. ed. Columbia Classics in Religion. New York: Columbia University Press, 2008.

Burns, J. Patout. "Augustine on the Origin and Progress of Evil." *Journal of Religious Ethics* 16, no. 1 (1988): 9–27.

Cahill, Lisa Sowle. *Blessed Are the Peacemakers: Pacifism, Just War, and Peacebuilding.* Minneapolis: Fortress, 2019.

——. *Global Justice, Christology and Christian Ethics.* New York: Cambridge University Press, 2013.

———. *Theological Bioethics: Participation, Justice, and Change*. Moral Traditions. Washington, DC: Georgetown University Press, 2005.

———. "Using Augustine in Contemporary Sexual Ethics: A Response to Gilbert Meilaender." *Journal of Religious Ethics* 29, no. 1 (Spring 2001): 25–33.

Callahan, Sidney. "Abortion and the Sexual Agenda." *Commonweal*, April 25, 1986.

Card, Claudia. *The Unnatural Lottery: Character and Moral Luck*. Philadelphia: Temple University Press, 2010.

Carnahan, Kevin. *Reinhold Niebuhr and Paul Ramsey: Idealist and Pragmatic Christians on Politics, Philosophy, Religion, and War*. Lanham, MD: Lexington, 2010.

Catechism of the Catholic Church. 2nd ed. Vatican City: Libreria Editrice Vatican, 2000.

Cates, Diana Fritz. *Aquinas on the Emotions: A Religious-Ethical Inquiry*. Moral Traditions. Washington, DC: Georgetown University Press, 2009.

Cavadini, John C. "Feeling Right: Augustine on the Passions and Sexual Desire." *Augustinian Studies* 36, no. 1 (2005): 195–217.

Cavanaugh, T. A. *Double-Effect Reasoning: Doing Good and Avoiding Evil*. Oxford: Oxford University Press, 2006.

Cieslak, Paul. "FAQs from the 2011 CMA Annual Conference." *Linacre Quarterly* 81, no. 1 (2014): 71–91.

Cloutier, David. "Critical Realism and Climate Change." In *Moral Agency within Social Structures and Culture: A Primer on Critical Realism for Christian Ethics*, edited by Daniel Finn, 59–72. Washington, DC: Georgetown University Press, 2020.

Coady, C. A. J. "The Problem of Dirty Hands." In *Stanford Encyclopedia of Philosophy Archive*, edited by Edward N. Zalta. Stanford, CA: Metaphysics Research Lab, Stanford University, Spring 2014. https://plato.stanford.edu/archives/spr2014/entries/dirty-hands/.

Conee, Earl. "Against Moral Dilemmas." *Philosophical Review* 91, no. 1 (1982): 87–97.

———. "Why Moral Dilemmas Are Impossible." *American Philosophical Quarterly* 26, no. 2 (April 1, 1989): 133–41.

Connell, Francis Jeremiah, and Christopher Kaczor. "Principle of Double Effect." In *New Catholic Encyclopedia Supplement 2012–2013: Ethics and Philosophy*, edited by Robert L. Fastiggi, 395–97. Detroit: Gale, 2013.

Connolly, Hugh. *The Irish Penitentials*. Dublin: Four Courts, 1995.

Couenhoven, Jesse. "The Indicative in the Imperative: On Augustinian Oughts and Cans." In *Free Will and Classical Theism: The Significance of Freedom in Perfect Being Theology*, edited by Hugh J. McCann, 71–92. New York: Oxford University Press, 2017.

Curran, Charles E. *The Catholic Moral Tradition Today: A Synthesis*. Moral Traditions. Washington, DC: Georgetown University Press, 1999.

———. "Paul Ramsey and Traditional Roman Catholic Natural Law Theory." In *Love and Society: Essays in the Ethics of Paul Ramsey*, edited by James Turner Johnson and David H. Smith, 47–65. JRE Studies in Religious Ethics 1. Missoula, MT: Scholars Press, 1974.

Daly, Daniel J. "Guidelines for Rationing Treatment During the COVID-19 Crisis." *Health Progress*, Summer 2020, 50–56.

———. *The Structures of Virtue and Vice*. Moral Traditions. Washington, DC: Georgetown University Press, 2021.

———. "Structures of Virtue and Vice." *New Blackfriars* 92, no. 1039 (May 1, 2011): 341–57.

Davies, Brian, and Eleonore Stump, eds. *The Oxford Handbook of Aquinas*. New York: Oxford University Press, 2012.

Davis, Scott. "'Et Quod Vis Fac': Paul Ramsey and Augustinian Ethics." *Journal of Religious Ethics* 19, no. 2 (1991): 31–69.

Decosimo, David. *Ethics as a Work of Charity: Thomas Aquinas and Pagan Virtue.* Encountering Traditions. Stanford, CA: Stanford University Press, 2016.

de Sousa, Ronald. "Emotion." In *Stanford Encyclopedia of Philosophy Archive*, edited by Edward N. Zalta. Stanford, CA: Metaphysics Research Lab, Stanford University, Winter 2017. https://plato.stanford.edu/archives/win2017/entries/emotion/.

De Wijze, Stephen. "Tragic Remorse—The Anguish of Dirty Hands." *Ethical Theory and Moral Practice* 7, no. 5 (2005): 453–71.

DeYoung, Rebecca Konyndyk, Colleen McCluskey, and Christina van Dyke. *Aquinas's Ethics: Metaphysical Foundations, Moral Theory, and Theological Context.* Notre Dame, IN: University of Notre Dame Press, 2009.

Donagan, Alan. "Consistency in Rationalist Moral Systems." *Journal of Philosophy* 81, no. 6 (1984): 291–309.

———. *The Theory of Morality.* Chicago: University of Chicago Press, 1977.

Dougherty, M. V. *Moral Dilemmas in Medieval Thought: From Gratian to Aquinas.* New York: Cambridge University Press, 2011.

Dramm, Sabine. *Dietrich Bonhoeffer and the Resistance.* Minneapolis: Fortress, 2009.

Drescher, Kent D., David W. Foy, Caroline Kelly, Anna Leshner, Kerrie Schutz, and Brett Litz. "An Exploration of the Viability and Usefulness of the Construct of Moral Injury in War Veterans." *Traumatology* 17, no. 1 (2011): 8–13.

Dykstra, Craig, and Dorothy Bass. "A Theological Understanding of Christian Practices." In *Practicing Theology: Beliefs and Practices in Christian Life*, edited by Miroslav Volf and Dorothy C. Bass, 13–32. Grand Rapids, MI: Eerdmans, 2002.

Emanuel, Ezekiel J., Govind Persad, Ross Upshur, Beatriz Thome, Michael Parker, Aaron Glickman, Cathy Zhang, Connor Boyle, Maxwell Smith, and James P. Phillips. "Fair Allocation of Scarce Medical Resources in the Time of Covid-19," *New England Journal of Medicine* 328, no. 21 (May 21, 2020): 2049–55. https://www.nejm.org/doi/full/10.1056/nejmsb2005114.

Endō, Shūsaku. *Silence.* New York: Picador, 2016.

Eshleman, Andrew. "Moral Responsibility." In *Stanford Encyclopedia of Philosophy Archive*, edited by Edward N. Zalta. Stanford, CA: Metaphysics Research Lab, Stanford University, 2014. https://plato.stanford.edu/archives/win2016/entries/moral-responsibility/.

Farley, Margaret A. *Compassionate Respect: A Feminist Approach to Medical Ethics and Other Questions.* Madeleva Lecture in Spirituality. New York: Paulist, 2002.

———. "Forgiveness in the Service of Love." In *Love and Christian Ethics: Tradition, Theory, and Society*, edited by Frederick V. Simmons and Brian C. Sorrells, 155–70. Moral Traditions. Washington, DC: Georgetown University Press, 2016.

Farmer, Paul, and Gustavo Gutiérrez. *In the Company of the Poor: Conversations between Dr. Paul Farmer and Fr. Gustavo Gutiérrez.* Edited by Michael Griffin and Jennie Weiss Block. Maryknoll, NY: Orbis, 2013.

Finn, Daniel K. "What Is a Sinful Social Structure?" *Theological Studies* 77, no. 1 (March 1, 2016): 136–64.

Finnis, John, and Germain Grisez. "The Basic Principles of Natural Law: A Reply to McInerny." In *Natural Law and Theology*, edited by Charles E. Curran and Richard A. McCormick, 157–70. Vol. 7 of *Readings in Moral Theology.* New York: Paulist, 1991.

Fleming, David. *What Is Ignatian Spirituality?* Chicago: Loyola Press, 2008.

Foot, Philippa. "Moral Dilemmas Revisited." In *Moral Dilemmas and Other Topics in Moral Philosophy*, 175–88. New York: Oxford University Press, 2002.

———. "Moral Realism and Moral Dilemma." In *Moral Dilemmas and Other Topics in Moral Philosophy*, 37–58. New York: Oxford University Press, 2002.

Gallagher, David M. "The Will and Its Acts (Ia IIae, Qq. 6-17)." In *The Ethics of Aquinas*, edited by Stephen J. Pope, 69–89. Moral Traditions. Washington, DC: Georgetown University Press, 2002.

Głąb, Anna. "Moral Dilemmas, the Tragic and God's Hiddenness. Notes on Shusaku Endo's *Silence*." *Diametros* 58 (2018): 18–33.

Goldie, Peter. *The Oxford Handbook of Philosophy of Emotion*. Oxford: Oxford University Press, 2010.

Gowans, Christopher. "The Debate on Moral Dilemmas." In *Moral Dilemmas*, edited by Christopher W. Gowans, 3–33. New York: Oxford University Press, 1987.

———. *Innocence Lost: An Examination of Inescapable Moral Wrongdoing*. New York: Oxford University Press, 1994.

———. "Moral Theory, Moral Dilemmas, and Moral Responsibility." In *Moral Dilemmas and Moral Theory*, edited by H. E. Mason, 199–215. New York: Oxford University Press, 1996.

———. "Review of *Moral Failure: On the Impossible Demands of Morality* by Lisa Tessman." *Ethics* 126, no. 4 (June 22, 2016): 1124–29.

Green, Clifford. "Peace Ethic or 'Pacifism'? An Assessment of *Bonhoeffer the Assassin*?" *Modern Theology* 31, no. 1 (December 11, 2014): 201–8.

Greene, Joshua, and Jonathan Haidt. "How (and Where) Does Moral Judgment Work?" *Trends in Cognitive Sciences* 6, no. 12 (December 2002): 517–23.

Greene, Joshua, and Shiva Kumar, eds. *Witness: Voices from the Holocaust*. New York: Free Press, 2000.

Guth, Karen V. "Doing Justice to the Complex Legacy of John Howard Yoder: Restorative Justice Resources in Witness and Feminist Ethics." *Journal of the Society of Christian Ethics* 35, no. 2 (December 10, 2015): 119–39.

Gutiérrez, Gustavo. *A Theology of Liberation: History, Politics, and Salvation*. Maryknoll, NY: Orbis, 1988.

Haidt, Jonathan. *The Righteous Mind: Why Good People Are Divided by Politics and Religion*. New York: Pantheon, 2012.

Harris, J. Irene, Crystal L. Park, Joseph M. Currier, Timothy J. Usset, and Cory D. Voecks. "Moral Injury and Psycho-Spiritual Development: Considering the Developmental Context." *Spirituality in Clinical Practice* 2, no. 4 (2015): 256–66.

Hegel, G. W. F. *Aesthetics: Lectures on Fine Art*. 2 vols. Translated by T. M. Knox. Oxford: Oxford University Press, 1975.

Hernández, Prisco R. "Killing in War as a Persisting Problem of Conscience in the Context of Christian Eschatology." *Journal of Catholic Social Thought* 11, no. 1 (2014): 203–27.

Herper, Matthew. "The Coronavirus Outbreak Exposes Our Health Care System's Weaknesses." *STAT* (blog). March 2, 2020. https://www.statnews.com/2020/03/02/the-coronavirus-exposes-our-health-care-systems-weaknesses-we-can-be-stronger/.

Hill, Thomas E. "Kant on Imperfect Duty and Supererogation." *Kant-Studien* 62, no. 1–4 (1971): 55–76.

Himes, Kenneth, ed. *Modern Catholic Social Teaching: Commentaries and Interpretations*. Washington, DC: Georgetown University Press, 2005.

Honnefelder, Ludger. "The Evaluation of Goods and the Estimation of Consequences: Aquinas on the Determination of the Morally Good." In *The Ethics of Aquinas*, edited by Stephen J. Pope, 426–36. Moral Traditions. Washington, DC: Georgetown University Press, 2002.

Hood, Gavin, dir. *Eye in the Sky*. Entertainment One Ltd., 2015. Film.

Hsieh, Nien-hê. "Incommensurable Values." In *Stanford Encyclopedia of Philosophy Archive*, edited by Edward N. Zalta. Stanford, CA: Metaphysics Research Lab, Stanford University, Spring 2016. https://plato.stanford.edu/archives/spr2016/entries/value-incommensurable/.

Hume, David. *A Treatise of Human Nature*. Philosophical Classics. Rev. ed. Mineola, NY: Dover, 2003.

Hunsinger, Deborah van Deusen. "Bearing the Unbearable: Trauma, Gospel and Pastoral Care." *Theology Today* 68, no. 1 (April 1, 2011): 8–25.

Hursthouse, Rosalind. "Acting and Feeling in Character: 'Nicomachean Ethics' 3.I." *Phronesis* 29, no. 3 (January 1, 1984): 252–66.

———. *On Virtue Ethics*. New York: Oxford University Press, 1999.

Ignatius, of Loyola. *The Spiritual Exercises of Saint Ignatius: Saint Ignatius' Profound Precepts of Mystical Theology*. Translated by Anthony Mottola. New York: Doubleday, 1964.

Jackson-Meyer, Kate. "Moral Distress in Health Care Professionals." *Health Progress*, Summer 2020, 23–29.

———. "Just War, Peace, and Peacemaking: Moral Dilemmas." In *Reimagining the Moral Life: On Lisa Sowle Cahill's Contribution to Christian Ethics*, edited by Ki Joo Choi, Sarah M. Moses, and Andrea Vicini, SJ, 83–95. Maryknoll, NY: Orbis, 2020.

Jaycox, Michael P. "The Civic Virtues of Social Anger: A Critically Reconstructed Normative Ethic for Public Life." *Journal of the Society of Christian Ethics* 36, no. 1 (2016): 123–43.

Jesuit Refugee Service. "40 Years of Accompaniment: Fr. Jim Martin, SJ," February 21, 2020. https://www.jrsusa.org/story/40-years-of-accompaniment-fr-jim-martin-sj/.

John Paul II. *Reconciliatio et paenitentia*. Apostolic exhortation. Vatican website. December 2, 1984. https://www.vatican.va/content/john-paul-ii/en/apost_exhortations/documents/hf_jp-ii_exh_02121984_reconciliatio-et-paenitentia.html.

———. *Sollicitudo rei socialis*. Encyclical letter. Vatican website. December 30, 1987. https://www.vatican.va/content/john-paul-ii/en/encyclicals/documents/hf_jp-ii_enc_30121987_sollicitudo-rei-socialis.html.

———. *Veritatis splendor*. Encyclical letter. Vatican website. August 6, 1993. https://www.vatican.va/content/john-paul-ii/en/encyclicals/documents/hf_jp-ii_enc_06081993_veritatis-splendor.html.

Johnson, James T. "Just War in the Thought of Paul Ramsey." *Journal of Religious Ethics* 19, no. 2 (1991): 183–207.

Kamm, F. M. *Creation and Abortion: A Study in Moral and Legal Philosophy*. New York: Oxford University Press, 1992.

Kant, Immanuel. *Critique of Practical Reason*. Translated by Mary J. Gregor. Cambridge Texts in the History of Philosophy Critique of Practical Reason. Rev. ed. Cambridge: Cambridge University Press, 1997.

———. *Groundwork for the Metaphysics of Morals*. Edited and translated by Allen W. Wood. New Haven, CT: Yale University Press, 2002.

———. *The Metaphysics of Morals*. Edited and translated by Mary Gregor. New York: Cambridge University Press, 1996.

———. "Moral Duties." In *Moral Dilemmas*, edited by Christopher W. Gowans, 34–51. New York: Oxford University Press, 1987.

————. "On a Supposed Right to Tell Lies from Benevolent Motives." In *Kant's Critique of Practical Reason and Other Works on the Theory of Ethics*. Translated by Thomas Kingsmill Abbott. 6th ed., 361–65. London: Longmans, Green, 1948.

Katongole, Emmanuel. *Born from Lament: The Theology and Politics of Hope in Africa*. Grand Rapids, MI: Eerdmans, 2017.

————. *The Sacrifice of Africa: A Political Theology for Africa*. Grand Rapids, MI: Eerdmans, 2010.

Kauppinen, Antti. "Moral Sentimentalism." In *Stanford Encyclopedia of Philosophy Archive*, edited by Edward N. Zalta. Stanford, CA: Metaphysics Research Lab, Stanford University, Spring 2017. https://plato.stanford.edu/archives/spr2017/entries/moral-sentimentalism/.

Kaveny, M. Cathleen. *Ethics at the Edges of Law: Christian Moralists and American Legal Thought*. New York: Oxford University Press, 2017.

————. "Intrinsic Evil and Political Responsibility: Is the Concept of Intrinsic Evil Helpful to the Catholic Voter?" *America Magazine*, October 27, 2008. https://www.americamagazine.org/issue/673/article/intrinsic-evil-and-political-responsibility.

Keenan, James F. *A History of Catholic Moral Theology in the Twentieth Century: From Confessing Sins to Liberating Consciences*. New York: Continuum, 2010.

————. "Moral Discernment in History." *Theological Studies* 79, no. 3 (2018): 668–79.

————. "University Ethics and Contingent Faculty." *Journal of Moral Theology* 8, no. 1 (2019): 8–26.

————. "Vulnerable to Contingency." *Journal of the Society of Christian Ethics* 40, no. 2 (2020): 221–36.

Kellison, Rosemary B. "Impure Agency and the Just War." *Journal of Religious Ethics* 43, no. 2 (2015): 317–41.

Kelly, Gerald. "The Duty to Preserve Life." *Theological Studies* 12, no. 4 (1951): 550–56.

Kierkegaard, Søren. *Fear and Trembling/Repetition: Kierkegaard's Writings*, vol. 6. Edited and translated by Howard V. Hong and Edna H. Hong. Princeton, NJ: Princeton University Press, 1983.

Kinghorn, Warren. "Combat Trauma and Moral Fragmentation: A Theological Account of Moral Injury." *Journal of the Society of Christian Ethics* 32, no. 2 (Winter 2012): 57–74.

Kirk, Kenneth E. *Conscience and Its Problems: An Introduction to Casuistry*. New York: Longmans, Green, 1948.

Koenig, Harold, Donna Ames, Nagy Youssef, John Oliver, Fred Volk, Ellen Teng, Kerry Haynes, et al. "The Moral Injury Symptom Scale-Military Version." *Journal of Religion and Health* 57, no. 1 (2018): 249–65.

Kotva, Joseph J. *The Christian Case for Virtue Ethics*. Moral Traditions. Washington, DC: Georgetown University Press, 1996.

Langer, Lawrence L. *Holocaust Testimonies: The Ruins of Memory*. New Haven, CT: Yale University Press, 1991.

Lawler, Michael G., and Todd A. Salzman. "Human Experience and Catholic Moral Theology." *Irish Theological Quarterly* 76, no. 1 (2011): 35–56.

Lawrence-Lightfoot, Sara, and Jessica Hoffmann Davis. *The Art and Science of Portraiture*. San Francisco: Jossey-Bass, 1997.

Leonard, Ellen. "Experience as a Source for Theology." *Proceedings of the Catholic Theological Society of America* 43 (1988): 44–61.

Litz, Brett T., Leslie Lebowitz, Matt J. Gray, and William P. Nash. *Adaptive Disclosure: A New Treatment for Military Trauma, Loss, and Moral Injury*. New York: Guilford, 2015.

Litz, Brett T., Nathan Stein, Eileen Delaney, Leslie Lebowitz, William P. Nash, Caroline Silva, and Shira Maguen. "Moral Injury and Moral Repair in War Veterans: A Preliminary Model and Intervention Strategy." *Clinical Psychology Review* 29, no. 8 (2009): 695–706.

Lumitao, Josephine M. "Death and Dying." In *Beyond a Western Bioethics: Voices from the Developing World*, edited by Angeles Tan Alora and Josephine M. Lumitao, 94–99. Washington, DC: Georgetown University Press, 2001.

MacIntyre, Alasdair. *After Virtue: A Study in Moral Theory*. 3rd ed. Notre Dame, IN: University of Notre Dame Press, 2007.

Mahedy, William. *Out of the Night: The Spiritual Journey of Vietnam Vets*. Knoxville, TN: Radix, 2004.

Mann, William E. "Jephthah's Plight: Moral Dilemmas and Theism." *Philosophical Perspectives* 5 (1991): 617–47.

Marcus, Ruth Barcan. "Moral Dilemmas and Consistency." *Journal of Philosophy* 77, no. 3 (1980): 121–36.

Massingale, Bryan. "Has the Silence Been Broken? Catholic Theological Ethics and Racial Justice." *Theological Studies* 75, no. 1 (March 2014): 133–55.

———. *Racial Justice and the Catholic Church*. Maryknoll, NY: Orbis, 2010.

———. "The Systemic Erasure of the Black/Dark-Skinned Body in Catholic Ethics." In *Catholic Theological Ethics, Past, Present, and Future: The Trento Conference*, edited by James F. Keenan, 116–24. Maryknoll, NY: Orbis, 2011.

Matthews, Gareth. "Saint Thomas and the Principle of Double Effect." In *Aquinas's Moral Theory: Essays in Honor of Norman Kretzmann*, edited by Scott MacDonald and Eleonore Stump, 63–78. Ithaca, NY: Cornell University Press, 1999.

McCluskey, Colleen. *Thomas Aquinas on Moral Wrongdoing*. Cambridge: Cambridge University Press, 2016.

McConnell, Terrance. "Moral Dilemmas." In *Stanford Encyclopedia of Philosophy Archive*, edited by Edward N. Zalta. Stanford, CA: Metaphysics Research Lab, Stanford University, Fall 2014. https://plato.stanford.edu/archives/fall2014/entries/moral-dilemmas/.

McInerny, Daniel J. *The Difficult Good: A Thomistic Approach to Moral Conflict and Human Happiness*. New York: Fordham University Press, 2006.

McInerny, Ralph. "The Principles of Natural Law." In *Natural Law and Theology*. Edited by Charles E. Curran and Richard A. McCormick. Readings in Moral Theology, vol. 7, 139–156. New York: Paulist Press, 1991.

McIntyre, Alison. "Doctrine of Double Effect." In *Stanford Encyclopedia of Philosophy Archive*, edited by Edward N. Zalta. Stanford, CA: Metaphysics Research Lab, Stanford University, Winter 2014. https://plato.stanford.edu/archives/win2014/entries/double-effect/.

Mejía, Camilo. *Road from Ar Ramadi: The Private Rebellion of Sergeant Camilo Mejía*. New York: New Press, 2007.

Metaxas, Eric. Forward to *The Cost of Discipleship*, by Dietrich Bonhoeffer, 5–13. New York: Touchstone, 2018.

Mill, John Stuart. *Utilitarianism*. Orchard Park: Broadview, 2000.

———. "Utilitarianism and Moral Conflicts." In *Moral Dilemmas*, edited by Christopher Gowans, 52–61. New York: Oxford University Press, 1987.

Nagel, Thomas. "The Fragmentation of Value." In *Moral Dilemmas*, edited by Christopher W. Gowans, 174–87. New York: Oxford University Press, 1987.

Niebuhr, Reinhold. "The Bombing of Germany." In *Love and Justice: Selections from the Shorter Writings of Reinhold Niebuhr*, edited by D. B. Robertson, 222–23. Louisville, KY: Westminster John Knox Press, 1957.

Nienaber, Susan. "Leading into the Promised Land: Lessons Learned from Resilient Congregations." *Alban at Duke Divinity School* (blog), July 13, 2006. https://alban.org/archive/leading-into-the-promised-land-lessons-learned-from-resilient-congregations/.

Nussbaum, Martha C. "The Costs of Tragedy: Some Moral Limits of Cost-Benefit Analysis." *Journal of Legal Studies* 29, no. S2 (2000): 1005–36.

———. *Creating Capabilities: The Human Development Approach.* Cambridge: Belknap Press of Harvard University Press, 2011.

———. *The Fragility of Goodness: Luck and Ethics in Greek Tragedy and Philosophy.* 2nd ed. New York: Cambridge University Press, 2001.

———. *Upheavals of Thought: The Intelligence of Emotions.* Cambridge: Cambridge University Press, 2003.

O'Brien, William Vincent. *The Conduct of Just and Limited War.* New York: Praeger, 1981.

O'Donnell, James J. "Augustine: His Time and Lives." In *The Cambridge Companion to Augustine*, edited by Eleonore Stump and Norman Kretzmann, 8–25. New York: Cambridge University Press, 2001.

O'Meara, Thomas F. "Virtues in the Theology of Thomas Aquinas." *Theological Studies* 58, no. 2 (1997): 254–85.

"Opinion: Gratuitous Cruelty by Homeland Security: Separating a 7-Year-Old from Her Mother," editorial. *Washington Post*, March 4, 2018. https://www.washingtonpost.com/opinions/gratuitous-cruelty-by-homeland-security-separating-a-7-year-old-from-her-mother/2018/03/04/98fae4f0-1bff-11e8-ae5a-16e60e4605f3_story.html.

Patel, Bhakti, John Kress, Jesse Hall. "Alternatives to Invasive Ventilation in the COIVD-19 Pandemic." *Journal of the American Medical Association* 324, no. 1 (2020): 43–44.

Plato. *Republic.* Translated by G. M. A. Grube. Revised by C. D. C. Reeve. Indianapolis: Hackett, 1992.

Pope, Stephen J. "Overview of the Ethics of Thomas Aquinas." In *The Ethics of Aquinas*, edited by Stephen J. Pope, 30–53. Moral Traditions. Washington, DC: Georgetown University Press, 2002.

Porter, Jean. "Choice, Causality, and Relation: Aquinas's Analysis of the Moral Act and the Doctrine of Double Effect." *American Catholic Philosophical Quarterly* 89, no. 3 (2015): 479–504.

Prinz, Jesse. *The Emotional Construction of Morals.* Oxford: Oxford University Press, 2007.

Quinn, Philip. "Agamemnon and Abraham: The Tragic Dilemma of Kierkegaard's Knight of Faith." *Literature & Theology* 4, no. 2 (1990): 181–93.

———. "*Moral Dilemmas* by Walter Sinnott-Armstrong." *Philosophy and Phenomenological Research* 51, no. 3 (1991): 693–97.

———. "Tragic Dilemmas, Suffering Love, and Christian Life." *Journal of Religious Ethics* 17, no. 1 (1989): 151–83.

Rahner, Karl. *Foundations of Christian Faith: An Introduction to the Idea of Christianity.* Translated by William V. Dych. New York: Crossroad, 1982.

Rambo, Shelly. *Resurrecting Wounds: Living in the Afterlife of Trauma.* Waco, TX: Baylor University Press, 2017.

———. "Trauma and Faith: Reading the Narrative of the Hemorrhaging Woman." *International Journal of Practical Theology* 13, no. 2 (2010): 233–57.

Ramsey, Paul. *Basic Christian Ethics.* New York: Westminster John Knox Press, 1950.

———. *Nine Modern Moralists.* Englewood Cliffs, NJ: Prentice-Hall Inc., 1962.

———. *The Patient as Person: Explorations in Medical Ethics.* New Haven, CT: Yale University Press, 1970.

———. *Speak Up for Just War or Pacifism: A Critique of the United Methodist Bishops' Pastoral Letter "In Defense of Creation."* University Park: Pennsylvania State University Press, 1988.

———. *War and the Christian Conscience: How Shall Modern War Be Conducted Justly?* Durham, NC: Duke University Press, 1961.

Rawls, John A. *Theory of Justice.* Cambridge, MA: Harvard University Press, 1971.

Reichberg, Gregory M. *Thomas Aquinas on War and Peace.* Cambridge: Cambridge University Press, 2017.

Ross, W. D. "Prima Facie Duties." In *Moral Dilemmas*, edited by Christopher Gowans, 83–100. New York: Oxford University Press, 1987.

———. *The Right and the Good.* Indianapolis: Hackett, 1988.

Ryliškytė, Ligita. "Post-Gulag Christology: Contextual Considerations from a Lithuanian Perspective." *Theological Studies* 76, no. 3 (2015): 468–84.

Santurri, Edmund N. *Perplexity in the Moral Life: Philosophical and Theological Considerations.* Charlottesville: University of Virginia Press, 1987.

Sartre, Jean Paul. *Existentialism Is a Humanism.* Edited by John Kulka. Translated by Carol Macomber. New Haven, CT: Yale University Press, 2007.

Sayeed, Sadath A. "The Psychological Toll of Health Care Rationing Should Not Be Underestimated." *Newsweek*, April 6, 2020. https://www.newsweek.com/2020/04/24/psychological-toll-health-care-rationing-should-not-underestimated-opinion-1496321.html.

Scola, Angelo. "You Shall Not Kill." In *Thou Shalt Not Kill: A Political and Theological Dialogue*, by Adriana Cavarero and Angelo Scola. Translated by Margaret Adams Groesbeck and Adam Sitze, 23–36. New York: Fordham University Press, 2015.

Second General Conference of Latin American Bishops. *The Church in the Present Day Transformation of Latin America in Light of the Council.* Bogata, Colombia: Latin American Episcopal Council, 1970.

Second Vatican Council. *Gaudium et spes.* Vatican website. December 7, 1965, https://www.vatican.va/archive/hist_councils/ii_vatican_council/documents/vat-ii_const_19651207_gaudium-et-spes_en.html.

Selling, Joseph A. "Proportionate Reasoning and the Concept of Ontic Evil." *Louvain Studies* 27, no. 1 (2002): 3–28.

Shadle, Matthew. "Culture." In *Moral Agency within Social Structures and Culture: A Primer on Critical Realism for Christian Ethics*, edited by Daniel Finn, 43–57. Washington, DC: Georgetown University Press, 2020.

———. "Where Is Structural Sin in *Laudato si'*?" *Catholic Moral Theology* (blog). November 2, 2015. https://catholicmoraltheology.com/where-is-structural-sin-in-laudato-si/.

Shanley, Brian J. *The Thomist Tradition.* Boston: Kluwer Academic, 2002.

Shay, Jonathan. *Achilles in Vietnam: Combat Trauma and the Undoing of Character.* New York: Scribner, 1994.

———. "Moral Injury." *Intertexts* 16, no. 1 (December 19, 2012): 57–66.

Singer, Peter. "Ethics and Intuitions." *Journal of Ethics* 9, no. 3/4 (2005): 331–52.

———. *Practical Ethics.* 3rd ed. New York: Cambridge University Press, 2011.

Sinnott-Armstrong, Walter. *Moral Dilemmas.* New York: Basil Blackwell, 1988.

Smith, David H. "Paul Ramsey, Love and Killing." In *Love and Society: Essays in the Ethics of Paul Ramsey*, edited by James T. Johnson and David H. Smith, 3–17. JRE Studies in Religious Ethics 1. Missoula, MT: Scholars Press, 1974.

Smith, Michael. "The Humean Theory of Motivation." *Mind* 96, no. 381 (1987): 36–61.

Sophocles. *Antigone*. Translated by Paul Woodruff. Indianapolis: Hackett, 2001.

Spohn, William C. *Go and Do Likewise: Jesus and Ethics*. New York: Continuum, 1999.

Statman, Daniel. "The Debate over the So-Called Reality of Moral Dilemmas." *Philosophical Papers* 19, no. 3 (1990): 191–211.

———. *Moral Dilemmas*. Atlanta: Rodopi, 1995.

Stoljar, Natalie. "Feminist Perspectives on Autonomy." In *Stanford Encyclopedia of Philosophy Archive*, edited by Edward N. Zalta. Stanford, CA: Metaphysics Research Lab, Stanford University, Fall 2015. https://plato.stanford.edu/archives/fall2015/entries/feminism-autonomy/.

Stramondo, Joseph A. "COVID-19 Triage and Disability: What NOT to Do." *Bioethics*, March 30, 2020. http://www.bioethics.net/2020/03/covid-19-triage-and-disability-what-not-to-do/.

Stratton-Lake, Philip. "Intuitionism in Ethics." In *Stanford Encyclopedia of Philosophy Archive*, edited by Edward N. Zalta. Stanford, CA: Metaphysics Research Lab, Stanford University, Winter 2016. https://plato.stanford.edu/archives/win2016/entries/intuitionism-ethics/.

Stump, Eleonore. "Aquinas on the Sufferings of Job." In *Reasoned Faith: Essays in Philosophical Theology in Honor of Norman Kretzmann*, edited by Eleonore Stump, 328–57. Ithaca, NY: Cornell University Press, 1993.

———. "Providence and the Problem of Evil." In *Christian Philosophy*, edited by Thomas Flint, 51–91. Notre Dame, IN: University of Notre Dame Press, 1990.

Styron, William. *Sophie's Choice*. New York: Vintage, 1992.

Substance Abuse and Mental Health Services Administration (SAMHSA). *Quick Guide for Clinicians Based on TIP 57: Trauma-Informed Care in Behavioral Health Services*. HHS Publication No. (SMA) 15-4912: 2015. https://store.samhsa.gov/sites/default/files/d7/priv/sma15-4912.pdf.

Tessman, Lisa. "Against the Whiteness of Ethics: Dilemmatizing as a Critical Approach." In *The Center Must Not Hold: White Women Philosophers on the Whiteness of Philosophy*, edited by George Yancy, 193–211. Lanham, MD: Lexington, 2011.

———. *Burdened Virtues: Virtue Ethics for Liberatory Struggles*. New York: Oxford University Press, 2005.

———. *Moral Failure: On the Impossible Demands of Morality*. New York: Oxford University Press, 2015.

Thomson, Judith Jarvis. "A Defense of Abortion." *Philosophy & Public Affairs* 1, no. 1 (1971): 47–66.

Townes, Emilie M. *Breaking the Fine Rain of Death: African American Health Issues and a Womanist Ethic of Care*. Eugene, OR: Wipf & Stock, 2006.

Tutu, Desmond. *No Future without Forgiveness*. New York: Image, 2000.

United States Conference of Catholic Bishops. *Ethical and Religious Directives for Catholic Health Care Services*. 6th ed. Washington, DC: United States Conference of Catholic Bishops, 2018. https://www.usccb.org/about/doctrine/ethical-and-religious-directives/upload/ethical-religious-directives-catholic-health-service-sixth-edition-2016-06.pdf.

van Wormer, Katherine. "Restorative Justice as Social Justice for Victims of Gendered Violence: A Standpoint Feminist Perspective." *Social Work* 54, no. 2 (April 1, 2009): 107–16.

Verkamp, Bernard. *The Moral Treatment of Returning Warriors in Medieval and Modern Times*. Scranton, PA: University of Scranton Press, 2006.

Vitz, Paul C., and Jennifer M. Meade. "Self-Forgiveness in Psychology and Psychotherapy: A Critique." *Journal of Religion and Health* 50, no. 2 (2011): 248–63.

Walker, Donald F., and Jamie D. Aten. "Future Directions for the Study and Applications of Religion, Spirituality, and Trauma Research." *Journal of Psychology and Theology* 40, no. 4 (2012): 349–53.

Walzer, Michael. "Emergency Ethics." In *Arguing about War*, 33–50. New Haven, CT: Yale University Press, 2004.

———. *Just and Unjust Wars: A Moral Argument with Historical Illustrations.* New York: Basic Books, 1977.

———. "Political Action: The Problem of Dirty Hands." *Philosophy & Public Affairs* 2, no. 2 (1973): 160–80.

Wieland, Georg. "Happiness (Ia IIae, qq. 1–5)." In *The Ethics of Aquinas*, edited by Stephen J. Pope. Translated by Grant Kaplan, 57–68. Moral Traditions. Washington, DC: Georgetown University Press, 2002.

Wiinikka-Lydon, Joseph. *Moral Injury and the Promise of Virtue.* London: Palgrave-Macmillan, 2019.

———. "Moral Injury as Inherent Political Critique: The Prophetic Possibilities of a New Term." *Political Theology* 18, no. 3 (2017): 219–32.

Williams, Bernard. "Conflicts of Values." In *Moral Luck: Philosophical Papers, 1973–1980*, 71–82. New York: Cambridge University Press, 1981.

———. "Ethical Consistency." In *Problems of the Self: Philosophical Papers 1956–1972*, 166–86. New York: Cambridge University Press, 1973.

———. "Moral Luck." In *Moral Luck: Philosophical Papers, 1973–1980*, 20–39. New York: Cambridge University Press, 1981.

———. "Politics and Moral Character." In *Moral Luck: Philosophical Papers, 1973–1980*, 54–70. New York: Cambridge University Press, 1981.

Winner, Lauren F. *Mudhouse Sabbath: An Invitation to a Life of Spiritual Discipline.* Brewster, MA: Paraclete, 2007.

Wolfson, Ron. "How to Make a Shiva Call." My Jewish Learning. Accessed January 15, 2018. https://www.myjewishlearning.com/article/how-to-make-a-shiva-call/.

Wood, David. "Moral Injury: The Grunts." *Huffington Post*, March 18, 2014. http://projects.huffingtonpost.com/projects/moral-injury/the-grunts.

World Health Organization, "Shortage of Personal Protective Equipment Endangering Health Workers Worldwide." News Release. March 3, 2020. https://www.who.int/news/item/03-03-2020-shortage-of-personal-protective-equipment-endangering-health-workers-worldwide.

Wright, Vinita Hampton. "Two Differences between Forgiveness and Reconciliation." Ignatian Spirituality. N.d. Accessed August 25, 2021. https://www.ignatianspirituality.com/22748/two-differences-between-forgiveness-and-reconciliation.

INDEX

Abraham P., 44–45, 56n223
abortion, 55n212, 70–71, 91
accidental homicide, 96
adultery, 40, 66, 84
Afghanistan, 12
Africa, 58, 141–42, 147
agape, 69
agency, 137, 168; absent morality, 44; and
  activism, 143; atomistic ideas of, 115–
  16; of culture, 121; guilt, 6; as impure,
  116; lack of, 45; moral, 117, 120; moral
  dilemmas, 44–45; personal, 119–20;
  power, 45; as relational, 115–16; tragic
  dilemmas, 45
agglomeration principle, 33, 52n118,
  52n120, 52n122
Ambrose, 58
Antigone (Sophocles), 18, 76n33
Aquinas, Thomas, 1, 4, 7, 14n24, 24, 68,
  75n11, 98, 104n51, 104n53, 105n80,
  105n98; on accidental homicide (*see*
  accidental homicide); Alcmaeon,
  example of, 101; on Aristotle's cargo
  scenario, 93, 99; on cardinal virtues,
  80; on *caritas*, as highest virtue, 80; on
  common good, 85–86; on discernment,
  101; on double effect, 97, 106n123; on
  ethics, God as center of, 80; on ethics
  of war, 58; on faith, 80; foreseen and
  unforeseen consequences, distinction
  between, 97; on friendship, 80; on God,
  as highest good, 80; on grace, 80–81; on
  hard cases, 82, 84, 98; hierarchy of goods
  of, 29, 84–85, 94; on ignorance, 118;
  on intended effect, 95–96; on intention,
  81, 91, 95, 97; on involuntary action,
  92–93; on killing, defense of, 24; on

lesser evil, 87; on mixed actions, 92–94;
  on moral dilemmas, 7, 14n24, 79, 82, 88,
  92, 102, 162; on *perplexus*, 82–83, 88,
  122; on repugnance of the will, 93, 95,
  98, 119, 162; on right action, 80, 85; on
  right choice, 5; on right emotion, 87; on
  self-defense, 86; and sin, 99–100; and
  structural sin, 92; on tragic dilemmas,
  7, 79, 82, 92, 100–102, 122, 162; on
  unintended effect ("beside the intention"), 95–96; on voluntariness, 45; on
  voluntary action, 92–93
Aristotelian thought, 27, 80
Aristotle, 40, 56n234, 80, 92; Alcmaeon,
  example of, 101; on discernment,
  101–2; on grades of action, 98, 101; on
  mixed actions, 93; on repugnance of the
  will, 98; throwing cargo example of, 93
Atyam, Angelina, 142–43, 147, 150–52
Atyam, Charlotte, 142
Augustine, 1, 7, 24, 58, 61, 76n33, 130n19;
  on celibacy, 66; on chastity, 62–63; on
  ethics of war, 58, 65, 67–68, 161; Fall,
  error of, 65–66; on just war ethic, 64,
  75n11; killing, defense of, 24, 68, 74;
  marriage, defense of, 59; on "miseries"
  of this life, 1, 5; on moral dilemmas,
  7, 57, 59, 64–65, 74, 161; and "ought
  implies can" (OIC), 59, 62–64, 75n16;
  on Sermon on the Mount, 64–65; on
  sexual ethics, 65–68, 161; on torture,
  59, 63; on tragic dilemmas, 7, 57, 59, 65,
  74, 161; on wise judge, 7, 57, 59–60, 62,
  113, 161
Augustinian lament, 1–2, 59, 63–64, 74,
  109, 113–14, 128, 143, 162
Augustinian thought, 73

ABOUT THE AUTHOR

KATE JACKSON-MEYER is a part-time faculty member at Boston College, where she teaches in the Theology Department and for the Faith, Peace, and Justice minor. Her scholarship and teaching are focused on theological ethics, fundamental moral theology, bioethics, and the ethics of war and peacemaking. She earned her PhD from Boston College in 2018. She lives in Acton, Massachusetts, with her husband and two daughters.